Quantitative Trading with R

This page intentionally left blank

Quantitative Trading with R

**Understanding Mathematical and
Computational Tools from a
Quant's Perspective**

Harry Georgakopoulos

palgrave
macmillan

QUANTITATIVE TRADING WITH R

Copyright © Folk Creations, Inc., 2015.

First published in 2015 by
PALGRAVE MACMILLAN®
in the United States—a division of St. Martins Press LLC,
175 Fifth Avenue, New York, NY 10010.

Where this book is distributed in the UK, Europe and the rest of the world,
his is by Palgrave Macmillan, a division of Macmillan Publishers Limited,
registered in England, company number 785998, of Houndmills,
Basingstoke, Hampshire RG21 6XS.

Palgrave Macmillan is the global academic imprint of the above companies
and has companies and representatives throughout the world.

Palgrave® and Macmillan® are registered trademarks in the United States,
the United Kingdom, Europe and other countries.

ISBN: 978–1–137–35407–5

Library of Congress Cataloging-in-Publication Data

Georgakopoulos, Harry.
    Quantitative trading with R : understanding mathematical and
computational tools from a quant's perspective / Harry Georgakopoulos.
      pages cm
    ISBN 978–1–137–35407–5 (hardback)—

    1. Stocks—Mathematical models.   2. Investment
analysis—Mathematical models.   3. Corporations—Finance—Computer
programs.   4. Commodity exchanges. I. Title.

HG4661.G46 2015
332.640285'5133–dc23   2014028408

A catalogue record of the book is available from the British Library.

Design by Newgen Knowledge Works (P) Ltd., Chennai, India.

First edition: January 2015

10 9 8 7 6 5 4 3 2 1

To Pinelopi, Maria, and Anastasia

This page intentionally left blank

Contents

This page intentionally left blank

Figures

This page intentionally left blank

Tables

This page intentionally left blank

Acknowledgments

You know that saying about standing on the shoulders of giants? Well, this book is dedicated to all those giants who, in one way or another, inspired and guided my work throughout the years. This book would not have been possible without the contribution of people like Jeff Ryan, Dirk Eddelbuettel, Ilya Kipnis, Hadley Wickham, Joshua Ulrich, Romain Francois, Guy Yollin, Bernhard Pfaff, Eric Zivot, Paul Teetor, Yihui Xie, Peter Carl, Jan Humme, Brian G. Peterson, Thomas Hutchinson, Steven Todd, Dimitrios Liakakos, Ed Zarek, and many others.

First and foremost, I would like to thank Ilya Kipnis for contributing excellent content on the backtesting of trading strategies via the use of the **quantstrat** package. Ilya maintains an insightful blog here: http://quantstrattrader.wordpress.com/. He is also a prolific R developer, and his projects can be found on GitHub here: www.github.com/IlyaKipnis.

My gratitude and appreciation also go out to Tick Data, Inc. for graciously providing historical intraday data for use throughout this book. Tick Data, Inc. provides research-quality historical market data solutions to practitioners and academics. Their website is www.TickData.com. Readers of this book get a special 20 percent discount on all data purchases from Tick Data's online store by using promo-code: 13FC20.

Dirk Eddelbuettel (of **Rcpp**, **RProtoBuf** and **RQuantLib** fame) was gracious enough to provide guidance and insight during the beginning stages of this publication. I would like to thank him for this contribution of his, among those of many others within the R community.

A big thank you goes out to the graduate students of FINC 621 (Financial Mathematics and Modeling II) at Loyola University in Chicago for inspiring a lot of the content in this book.

Last, but not least, I am grateful to the R-core team, as well as the numerous third-party contributors for maintaining and improving the R language, which has become such an integral part of my daily work routine.

This page intentionally left blank

1 | An Overview

My primary intent in writing this book is to provide the reader with basic programming, financial, and mathematical tools that can be successfully leveraged both in industry and academia. I cover the use of the R programming language, as well as the R environment as a means for manipulating financial market data and for solving a subset of problems that quants and traders typically encounter in their day-to-day activities. The chapters that follow should be treated as a tutorial on a recommended set of tools that I have personally found useful and that have served me well during the last few years of my career as a quant trader/developer. I am writing this book from the vantage point of a quant practitioner and not that of an academic. A significant portion of the content is based on my lecture notes from a graduate level class in quantitative finance that I teach on a part-time basis at Loyola University in Chicago.

This is an introductory-level book. No prior programming experience or advanced mathematical knowledge is assumed. Having said this, some chapters will tend to flow easier if you have had some prior exposure to the following topics. On the math side, I recommend a review of basic calculus, linear algebra, statistics, and probability.[1] On the programming side, familiarity with VBA, Python, and SQL[2] is helpful.

This book is also aimed at practitioners and seasoned traders who want to learn more about how to conduct data analysis on financial data and how to write useful R scripts to automate some of their workflow.

Trading and programming are vast topics in their own right, and by no means will I attempt to give a thorough explanation of each concept. You will not become an expert programmer by reading this book, nor will you make a ton of money in the markets by following my advice. This book will, however, provide tools and ideas that can assist in the analysis, implementation, and presentation of trading strategies and other related quantitative topics. Figure 1.1 provides an illustration of the items I will address in subsequent chapters.

The mission statement

I will attempt to take a somewhat fuzzy concept—that of creating a trading strategy—and provide plausible answers to some questions that will naturally arise.

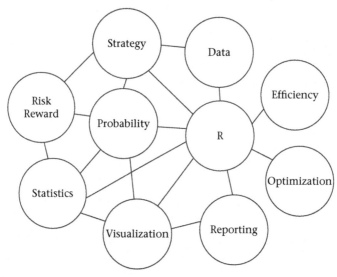

Figure 1.1 Topic graph.

Questions like the following: How can I automate some of my trading ideas? What programming language should I use and why? What are the mathematical, financial, and programming tools needed to evaluate my strategy? Where do I get the data to test a trading strategy? How do I know that my strategy is any good? How do I present my results to others?

Most books on programming can be used as references. You go to the index and find the topic that interests you, and then you simply go to that particular page for further information. To get the most out of this book, I recommend that you do not follow this approach. Rather, start from the beginning and read all the chapters in a linear fashion. There is a method behind this madness. I intend to expose you to a methodology of thinking about quantitative finance and to give you the confidence to tackle some of the real-world problems that naturally arise in this context. And you will accomplish all this, while utilizing R to automate the required tasks.

It is prudent to form a mental map of where we are headed and what obstacles lie in our path. One of our end goals will be to obtain the necessary programming skills so as to tackle some very specific problems that quants and traders typically care about. The other end goal will be to manipulate financial data and to use mathematical techniques to evaluate trading strategies.

For the purpose of making these goals more concrete, I will bake them directly into a mission statement. Here is a first attempt at such a statement:

We will come up with an automated trading strategy that will trade a portfolio of liquid instruments in the market. The strategy will be efficient, robust, and scalable. Furthermore, the strategy will be profitable and have low risk.

Here are some questions that might arise after reading the mission statement:

1. What is a **market**?
2. What is meant by **instruments**, and furthermore, what is meant by **liquid instruments**?
3. What is a **trading strategy**, and how does one go about formulating such a thing?
4. How is **profitability** of a trading strategy defined?
5. What is **risk**? Specifically, how can one quantify risk in the context of a trading strategy?
6. How can a trading strategy be **automated**?
7. What is meant by **efficiency**?

Financial markets and instruments

A market is either a physical or a virtual place where transactions occur between participants. In ancient Greece, the Athenian citizens would gather in the agora[3] and trade honey, olive oil, other agricultural products, and works of art in exchange for similar items. Transactions would be carried out with in-kind merchandise and currency. Similar marketplaces existed all over the ancient world. In those physical markets, as in today's physical markets, participants would have to physically meet and agree both on the price and the terms of delivery before a transaction was confirmed.

Today, many of the physical marketplaces of the world are giving way to virtual ones. Take amazon.com, ebay.com, and alibaba.com as examples of this trend. These are vast online marketplaces where buyers and sellers interact and transact entirely via computer. Similar trends have been occurring in the financial markets over the last few years. The old floor pits of the futures, stocks, and options exchanges are giving way to electronic platforms. Table 1.1 lists approximate electronic versus floor trading volume percentages on the CME exchange. Globex refers to the Chicago Mercantile Exchange (CME) electronic platform.

An organized market's primary objective is to bring together participants who are willing to trade their goods and services at an agreed-upon price. A secondary objective of a successful marketplace is to facilitate the orderly conduct of such transactions. Electronic financial markets certainly fit this description.

Over the years, literally hundreds of financial exchanges and alternate electronic venues have popped up all over the globe. Some of the more notable stock trading venues are outlined in Table 1.2.

Some of the more notable futures exchanges are listed in Table 1.3.

Such exchanges enable the efficient and orderly transaction of standardized financial contracts. Financial instruments are stocks, futures, bonds, currencies, vanilla options, exotic options, swaps, swaptions, and so forth. Some of these instruments have become more popular than others [35]. The E-mini financial futures and eurodollar contracts traded on the CME, for example, are some of the most

Table 1.1 Globex volume estimates by year

Year	CME volume profile	
	Globex (%)	Other (%)
1992	0.2	99.8
1993	0.4	99.6
1994	0.5	99.5
...	...	...
2007	78	22
2008	82	18
2009	86	14
...	...	...
2014	93	7

Table 1.2 Popular stock exchanges

Country	Name	Website
USA	NYSE	www.nyse.nyx.com
USA	NASDAQ	www.nasdaqomx.com
USA	BATS	www.batstrading.com
USA	Direct Edge	www.directedge.com
Japan	TSE	www.tse.or.jp/english
UK	LSE	www.nasdaqomx.com
UK	NYSE Euronext	www.euronext.com

Table 1.3 Popular futures exchanges

Country	Name	Website
USA	CME	www.cmegroup.com
USA	ICE	www.theice.com
UK	Euronext	www.euronext.com
Germany	Eurex	www.eurexchange.com

liquid contracts in the world. Investors and traders rely on these to manage their market and interest rate risks on a daily basis. The following table lists the average daily volumes of a few of these CME futures contracts [36].

Liquidity is really a measure of how easy it is to buy or sell a certain quantity of an instrument at a favorable price. Liquidity can be loosely thought of as a proxy for transacted volume. Investors and traders love liquid products because they can potentially trade a lot of size in those products without adversely affecting the price.

Table 1.4 Active contract volumes

Most active contracts		
Contract	Ticker	Volume
Eurodollar	GE	2,482,899
E-mini S&P 500	ES	1,804,469
10-Year treasury note	ZN	1,322,388
5-Year treasury note	ZF	773,183

Trading strategies

Financial institutions are some of the most heavily regulated entities on the planet.[4] This is both a good and a bad thing. It is bad, because this tends to stifle competition and innovation. It is good, because this enables market participants to have more confidence in the validity, and fairness of their transactions. Having confidence in the validity of ones trades is a very important concept. This is what enables investors and traders to invest large amounts of time and money in the development of electronic trading platforms that actively participate in these electronic marketplaces. Trading strategies arise when an investor or a trader spots an opportunity that can be legally exploited by placing buy or sell orders for certain financial instruments. These transactions have to be offset at a later point in time in order for the trader to realize a profit on the trades. Trading strategies have holding periods that can range anywhere from microseconds to years. Various flavors of trading strategies exist: long term, short term, opportunistic, high-frequency, low latency, and so forth. Whatever the nomenclature used, a trading strategy is just a set of well-defined rules that traders apply with the end goal of making a profit in the financial markets. These strategies exploit either structural effects in the marketplace, statistical relationships between financial instruments, or some kind of external information flow.

High-frequency trading

To most people, the term **high-frequecy trading** refers to trading strategies in which trades execute within a very small amount of time. In reality, high-frequency trading is actually a broader encompassing term than that. The holding periods of trades do not necessarily have to be in the subsecond range. It is often the case that trades are entered into the market within a small time span, but kept on for a much longer amount of time. The term also refers to algorithms that continuously scour the market for opportunities, but only place a limited number of trades when that opportunity arises. These algorithms still process market data at a high-frequency, but they do not execute trades at such frequencies. To make matters even more confusing, high-frequency trading is also sometimes referred to as low-latency trading. Since these trading approaches always involve the use of fast computers and

	12	150, 5
	11	230, 1
	10	202, 3
	9	100, 4
125, 1	10	
200, 4	7	
300, 5	6	
210, 8	5	

Figure 1.2 An orderbook.

network connections, it is natural that such naming conflicts exist. Most of these strategies can, furthermore, be broken down into market-making, market-taking, and opportunistic strategies.

A high-frequency, market-making strategy is one in which the trading algorithm constantly provides liquidity to other market participants. There is inherent risk that the active investor (taking the other side of the trade) has more information than the passive (making) algorithm. Some exchanges offer monetary compensation to market-making traders due to this information asymmetry. The profit that market-making strategies capture is relatively small compared to that of their taking counterparts. What they lack in profitability per trade, though, they make up in volume. Such a market-making strategy might be willing to capture only 1-tick of edge for every trade. A tick refers to the minimum price increment allowed by the exchange for any instrument. In actuality, due to adverse price moves, such strategies might only end up capturing a small fraction of a tick when everything is said and done.

Market-taking strategies will, on average, cross the bid-ask spread whenever a trading opportunity manifests. Such a trading opportunity might be the result of a buy or sell signal from an algorithm that is analyzing market data, or from a bullish/bearish news event. Immediacy of execution is usually favored over price in these types of strategies. Market-taking strategies require more edge per trade than their making counterparts.

About the orderbook

An orderbook can be conceptualized as the aggregation of buy and sell limit orders[5] from all market participants. The orderbook is a convenient data structure employed by traders and exchanges for the purposes of click-trading and/or matching orders between buyers and sellers. An orderbook can be depicted as having all the resting bids on the left vertical side and all the offers on the right vertical side. Figure 1.2 lists the prices, volume and trade-count per level in such a vertical arrangement [29].[6]

The best-bid price is the highest price at which a passive trader would be willing to buy. The best-ask, or best-offer price is the lowest price at which a passive trader would be willing to sell. In our example, the best-bid price is 8, and the best-offer price is 9. The quantities associated with the best-bid and best-ask prices are 125 and 100 respectively. We also observe that there is 1 distinct order on the best-bid and 4 distinct orders on the best-offer. Anytime there is a change in any one of these numbers, we say a market data event has occurred. A market data event might be the cancellation of a 1-lot on the 7 price level or even the arrival of a new order on the second best-ask price. In this case, the new quantity reflected at the second best-bid would become 199, and the second best-ask quantity would also increase. Given that multiple products trade on any one exchange, it is easy to see that the amount of information transmitted and stored by the exchanges is enormous. If we couple this with the fact that exchanges also have to relay order-status information to traders on a real-time basis, then one really starts to appreciate the complexity of the infrastructure involved in processing and storing all of this data.

Trading automation

Not too long ago, the vast majority of trades occurred in the pits. The typical order flow went as follows: investors would inform their brokers of their trading intentions over the phone or even in person. The brokers would then relay that information to their guys in the pits. If a counterparty wanted to take the other side of the trade, a transaction would occur and a confirmation would be sent back to the broker. In turn, the broker would convey the fill price and quantity to the customer.

Today, technology allows us to enter and exit trades at a much faster pace. Automated trading platforms such as those offered by Interactive Brokers, Etrade, and Ameritrade, just to mention a few, can be used to enter orders into the market at a rapid pace and at low cost. The matching between a buyer and a seller happens almost instantaneously within centralized matching engines that are hosted by the exchanges themselves. Matching engines are computer systems that keep track of all the order flow and make sure the correct number of contracts is allocated to the buyers and sellers in a timely fashion. Once a transaction is established by the matching engine, an order acknowledgment report is sent back to the trader who initiated the trades. The exchanges also disseminate other types of information other than the order reports. These include market data, as well as, exchange-related status messages.

Many proprietary trading firms, banks, and hedge funds interact with the exchanges via direct connections to their matching engines and market data feeds. The exchanges take advantage of the "need for speed" that these institutions have and offer collocation facilities to these traders at a hefty premium. Collocation simply means that the traders can store their servers as close to the exchange as physically possible. If a particular trading strategy is very sensitive to latency, then this collocation service is worth paying for.

The automated trading industry has evolved to one in which coding, math, and critical thinking skills are valued just as much as financial skills, sometimes even more so. Swarms of coders from fields such as engineering, computer science, physics and applied mathematics can be found working at various hedge funds and trading firms worldwide. For the most part, these technologists deal with issues in network infrastructure, data storage, system integration, data processing, visualization, and algorithm development.

In today's electronic markets, the roles between trader, technologist, and quant are indeed becoming blurred. The acumen to process, analyze, and present information from disparate sources, as well as the ability to develop trading strategies based on the results, are widely sought after skill sets in the industry. It is my prediction that in the not too distant future, the word trader will mean something entirely different from what it means today. A trader will likely be a savvy technologist with a keen sense of market dynamics who also utilizes a data-driven approach to build, monitor, and exploit profitable trading strategies.

To get a comprehensive discussion on market connectivity, execution, algorithmic trading and automation in general, Barry Johnson's book titled *Algorithmic Trading and DMA: An Introduction to Direct Access Trading Strategies* is highly recommended. The website for the book is located here: http://www.algo-dma.com.

Where to get data from

Financial data is the the lifeblood of any successful trading business. Prior to trading, it is important to get a feel for how a strategy can behave in production. We accomplish this by analyzing historical data and by monitoring real-time data of proposed strategies, market events, and economic announcements. But where can we find such data? Specifically, where can we find time series data for stock prices, option prices, futures prices, and other economic indicator series? For daily granularity, a few of the popular and free choices are

- **Yahoo Finance:**
  http://finance.yahoo.com/
- **Quandl:**
  http://www.quandl.com/
- **Google Finance:**
  http://www.google.com/finance
- **Federal Reserve Bank Of St. Louis:**
  http://research.stlouisfed.org/fred2/

We will utilize the first option heavily in this book. Most of the data will be daily open, high, low, and close prices for single stock names and Exchange Traded Funds

(ETF's). This data is available for free, and thus comes with the usual caveats. One needs to be vigilant of the quality of such data and put processes in place to clean, filter, and potentially delete erroneous values.

The best alternative is to actually capture the data on your own. This requires a lot of infrastructure and can be a costly and time-consuming endeavor. This is the approach that a lot of institutional traders, banks, and proprietary trading firms take. They accomplish this by being directly connected to the various exchanges around the world. Typically, servers are co-located right at the exchanges, and these machines record the data locally onto disks. The raw data is subsequently processed, cleaned, and stored in a database for future retrieval.

The intermediate solution is to obtain the data from a third-party vendor. Many such vendors exist, and the quality of the data can range from poor to excellent. A few recommended data vendors are

- **Tick Data, Inc:**
  http://www.tickdata.com/
- **Bloomberg:**
  http://www.bloomberg.com/enterprise/data/
- **Thomson Reuters:**
  http://thomsonreuters.com/financial/market-data/
- **CME Group:**
  http://www.cmegroup.com/market-data/datamine-historical-data/
- **NYSE Market Data:**
  http://www.nyxdata.com/Data-Products/NYSE
- **Hanweck Associates:**
  http://www.hanweckassoc.com/
- **Activ Financial:**
  http://www.activfinancial.com/
- **Markit:**
  http://www.markit.com/

Summary

The first few sections of this chapter elaborate on the purpose and potential audience of this book. Some math and programming resources are recommended as useful guides for understanding the technical discussions that will be presented in upcoming chapters. For the purpose of motivating the subsequent analysis, a mission statement is presented that outlines the end goals of a desirable trading strategy. A brief explanation of financial markets, financial instruments and trading strategies is provided. The chapter ends with a discussion of high-frequency trading, the automation of such strategies, and on the issue of obtaining daily and intra-day financial data.

This page intentionally left blank

2 | Tools of the Trade

The primary tools that quants and traders rely on to perform their daily activities include intuition, data, computer hardware, computer software, mathematics, and finance. They utilize these tools in ingenious ways as a means to an end. The end, of course, is the generation of consistent profits in the financial markets. Many traders have done well for themselves by relying on intuition alone. But intuition alone, on average, will not yield superior results. A tool chest of sorts is required in order to maximize the quant/trader's chances of producing consistent and favorable outcomes. A programming language is one such tool. In this book, we will learn how to wield the R programming language for the purposes of manipulating data, performing math operations, automating workflows, displaying informative visualizations, creating reproducible results, and doing lots of other cool stuff.

The R language

R [88] is an open-source scripting language that has become very popular among statisticians, data science practitioners, and academics over the years. It is a functional programming language by nature, but it also supports the object oriented and imperative programming paradigms.[1] In some sense, R is both a programming language as well as a development framework. The framework has support for some advanced graphing capabilities and provides access to multiple state-of-the-art statistical packages. The language itself supports conditional statements, loops, functions, classes, and most of the other constructs with which VBA and C++ users are familiar. The plethora of contributed packages by third parties, a solid user-base, and a strong open-source community are some other key strengths of **R**.

The R system can be divided into two conceptual parts:

1. the `base` installation downloadable from CRAN
2. everything else

The base R installation contains, among other things, the necessary code to run R. Many useful functions and libraries are also part of this base package. Some of these include: `utils`, `stats`, `datasets`, `graphics`, `grDevices`, and `methods`.

R is a dialect of the S language. The S language was developed by John Chambers, Rick Becker, and Allan Wilks at Bell Laboratories in the late 1970s. It started off as a collection of Fortran libraries. The language was used internally at Bell Labs for statistical analysis. In 1988, the bulk of the system was rewritten in C, and in 1998, version 4 of the language was released [93]. Insightful Corporation was granted an exclusive license in 1993 to commercially develop and market software products related to the S language. R was created by Ross Ihaka and Robert Gentleman in 1991 at the University of Auckland, New Zealand. Legend has it that the name R is a play on the name S, as well as the fact that the names Ross and Robert both start with an R. R became public in 1993, and in 1995 the General Public License (GNU) was used to effectively make R free software [96]. The R Core Group was formed in 1997. This group currently controls the R source code and is responsible for all the major software releases. The first version of R (R 1.0.0) was released in 2000. R version 3.0 was released in April 2013 and included support for long vectors, among other major improvements.

R is free, has thousands of add-on statistical and analytical libraries available for download, is very popular in the quantitative finance and academic fields, allows for the rapid prototyping of ideas and is the programming language with which the author has the most experience. Theoretically speaking, we can use any Turning Complete[2] programming language to accomplish our goals. Some, of course, are easier than others to learn and apply.

The following examples illustrate how the same "Hello World!" output can be obtained in different programming languages. These examples are referenced from Wikipedia [124]:

In Assembly x86-64 Linux:

```
    .section    .rodata
string:
    .ascii "Hello, world!\n"
length:
    .quad . -string
    .section    .text
    .globl _start
_start:
    movq $4, %rax
    movq $1, %rbx
    movq $string, %rcx
    movq length, %rdx
    int $0x80
    movq %rax, %rbx
    movq $1, %rax
    int $0x80
```

In Brainfuck:

```
++++++++++[>+++++++>
++++++++++>+++>+>+++
+<<<<<-]> ++.>+.+++++++
..+++.>>>++++.<<++.<+++
+++++.--------.+++.------.-----
---.>+.>.
```

In C++:

```
#include <iostream>

int main()
{
  std::cout << "Hello, world!" << std::endl;
  return 0;
}
```

In Julia:

```
println("Hello, world!")
```

In Swift:

```
println("Hello, world!")
```

In Python 2:

```
print "Hello, world!"
```

In R:

```
cat("Hello, world!\n")
```

Ideally, we need a programming language that allows for the rapid prototyping of an idea, provides instant feedback to the programmer (interpreted versus compiled execution),[3] enables the creation of charts and more complex graphics in an efficient manner, exposes additional functionality through the inclusion of third-party libraries, is platform independent (can be used on Windows, Mac, and Linux), has methods for easily accessing and manipulating data, allows for extensibility (being able to write custom functions not only in R itself, but also C, Fortran, or even C++), is fast, and is free.

Quite a few computational frameworks satisfy most of the above requirements. No programming languages exist, however, that satisfy all of these requirements. The most commonly used languages in the quantitative-finance realm include

Figure 2.1 R console.

(in no particular order): Python, R, Matlab, Julia,[4] C++, C#, Java, and VBA. As a general rule, Python, Julia, Matlab, VBA and R are used as prototyping/research languages, whereas C++, C#, and Java tend to be used for more application/infrastructure development.

Getting started with R

Here are the instructions for installing R on either a Windows or a Mac machine.

1. Navigate to the following website: http://www.r-project.org/. Click on the download R link in the "Getting Started" section, or alternatively, click on the "CRAN" link in the left-hand menu.
2. Select the appropriate mirror site that is closest to where the target machine resides.
3. Select the appropriate base package for Linux, Mac, or Windows.
4. Select all the default options for the installation of choice. After the installation is complete, click on the resulting R-icon to bring up the console.

   Figure 2.1 illustrates what the R console looks like on a Mac computer. There are at least three ways to enter commands into R:

1. by typing expressions directly into the console
2. by copying code from an open text file and by pasting that code into the R console
3. by sourcing (via the source() command) the code from an external file

The next few examples demonstrate some of this basic R functionality. The recommended workflow for following along is to enter the commands in a text file and then copy them into the R console. This will make it easier to repeat or amend statements. The history() function will assist with the recollection of previously entered commands. Typing the following into R will return the last four commands entered: history(4). To get the entire history of a session, we can use the history(Inf) statement.

First and foremost, R can be used as a scientific calculator. All the usual mathematical operations can directly be entered and evaluated in the console. Operations such as addition, subtraction, multiplication, division, and exponentiation are referenced by the known symbols (+, -, *, /, ^). The basic building blocks in R are numbers, strings, and booleans.

Numbers are the familiar symbols 1, 2, 3, 1e+06, 3.1415, and so forth. Strings are character sequences of 0 or more symbols encapsulated by either single or double quotes. Examples are

- "1"
- " "
- ""
- "this is a string"
- 'Hello'
- '2 + 4'

Boolean variables evaluate to either a TRUE or a FALSE statement. In R, the following evaluates to TRUE: 1 + 2 == 3. Notice the use of the double equal sign. The single equal sign is reserved for assignment operations. The following R expression would yield an error: 1 + 2 = 3. A few other symbols that show up often in R programs are the open and closed parentheses (), the open and close curly braces {}, the open and closed square brackets [], and the assignment operator <-.

Here are some example expressions that will return numerical answers:

```
1 + 1
sqrt(2)
20 + (26.8 * 23.4) / 2 + exp(1.34) * cos(1)
sin(1)
5^4
sqrt(-1 + 0i)
```

Advanced math operations are also possible in R. The following code-snippet creates a function called integrand() and then calls the R-defined function integrate(). Writing custom functions in R will be covered in detail in a subsequent section. The purpose of this example is to show that advanced numerical algorithms are readily accessible by calling pre-canned functionality:

```
integrand <- function(x) 1 / ((x + 1) * sqrt(x))
integrate(integrand, lower = 0, upper = Inf)
```

The above code evaluates the integral:

$$\int_0^\infty \frac{1}{(x+1)\sqrt{x}} dx \qquad (2.1)$$

The assignment of a value to a variable is accomplished via the <- operator:

```
x <- 3
x <- x + 1
z <- x ^ 2
z <- "hello quants"
y <- "a"
Z <- sqrt(2)
new.X <- 2.3
```

A few things to notice from the previous example are the following:

- In R, expressions are case sensitive. The variable z is not the same as Z. Spaces or special characters are not allowed within variable names. The dot . operator is an exception. It is perfectly valid to have a variable name start with a dot (i.e., .myVar). Variable names are not allowed to start with numeric characters.
- Variables in R do not have to be declared as int, double, or string as in other languages. R, dynamically figures out what the type of the variable is during run-time.
- Contents of variables can be copied into other variables.
- The example z <- x ^ 2 does not actually modify the value of x. Rather, x is squared, and the result is assigned to the new variable z.
- Other languages use the = operator in place of the <- operator to denote assignment. R is capable of supporting both conventions. The <- operator will be used throughout the rest of this book for consistency purposes.

Entering 5+4 should return the value 9. The [1] before the 9 means that this is the first element of a vector. We will use two number signs in a row (##) to denote the output of a piece of code. The single number sign will be used for comments within the code. This is simply a convention we will adopt for this book. They are both equally valid comment initiators.

```
5 + 4
## [1] 9
```

White spaces between the numbers and the + sign do not affect the output. Neither do they produce any warnings. The expression 5   + 4 still yields 9. Warnings and errors usually occur when R cannot successfully parse a command into meaningful code. For example, if one forgets to type in the + sign, 5   4, will issue the following error: Error: unexpected numeric constant in "5 4".

Before any meaningful work with data can be conducted, that data has to be stored inside a suitable container. The important data containers in R are

- vector
- matrix

- data frame
- list
- environment

Once the data is placed inside such a data structure, it can be manipulated in various ways.

The c() object

A vector can be thought of as a 1-dimensional array. Vectors only hold data of a similar type. That is to say, only numbers, only characters or only booleans can be placed inside a vector. The following example creates three vectors of type numeric and character:

```
first_vector  <- c(1, 2, 3, 4, 5, 6)
second_vector <- c("a", "b", "hello")
third_vector  <- c("a", 2, 23)
```

The concatenation operator c() is used to create a vector of numbers, characters, or booleans. The third example mixes numbers with characters. R will convert the type of any numeric value into characters. Typing the variable name into the R console reveals the contents of our newly created vectors:

```
first_vector
## [1] 1 2 3 4 5 6

third_vector
## [1] "a" "2" "23"
```

The concatenation operator c() can also be used to combine existing vectors into larger ones:

```
new_vector <- c(first_vector, 7, 8, 9)

new_vector
## [1] 1 2 3 4 5 6 7 8 9
```

The extraction of elements from within a vector can be accomplished via a call to the [] operator.

The following examples illustrate various operations that can be performed on vectors. The idea of an index becomes important when we start talking about extracting elements from containers. R uses a 1-based indexing scheme (i.e., the first element of a vector has an index of 1.) This is in contrast to other languages (i.e., C++, Java, Python) in which the first element has an index of 0.

The first example specifies a single index to use for extracting the data. The second example specifies two indexes. Notice the c() operator that is used to create a vector of indexes. These indexes are subsequently used to extract the elements from the initial vector. This method of extracting data elements from containers is very important, and we will use it over and over again:

```
# Extract the 4th element
example_1 <- new_vector[4]

# Extract the 5th and the 8th elements
example_2 <- new_vector[c(5, 8)]

example_2
## [1] 5 8
```

The following examples address another important concept, that of vectorization. Instead of performing operations on one element at a time, vectorization allows us to perform the same operation on all the elements at the same time. Conceptually, we can treat a vector of numbers as a single number. Here are some rudimentary examples:

```
x   <- c(1, 5, 10, 15, 20)
## [1] 1 5 10 15 20

x2 <- 2 * x
## [1] 2 10 20 30 40

x3 <- x ^ 2
## [1] 1 25 100 225 400

x4 <- x / x2
## [1] 0.5 0.5 0.5 0.5 0.5

x5 <- round(x * (x / x2) ^ 3.5 + sqrt(x4), 3)
## [1] 0.795 1.149 1.591 2.033 2.475

x6 <- round(c(c(x2[2:4], x3[1:2]), x5[4]), 2)
## [1] 10.00 20.00 30.00 1.00 25.00 2.03
```

- Vectorization allows us to avoid looping through all the elements of the vector. Rather, the operation of interest is performed on all the elements at once.
- If we only wanted to perform an operation on the fourth and sixth elements of our vector, we would have to "index" into the vector and extract the elements of interest (y <- x[4] + x[6]). The last example, x6, combines some of the

operations discussed earlier in this tutorial. We are extracting specific elements from vectors x2, x3, and x5, and then concatenating them into a single vector. The result of the operation is then truncated to 2 decimal places.

The `matrix()` object

A matrix can be thought of as a two-dimensional vector. Matrices also hold data of a similar type. The following code defines a matrix with two rows and three columns. In R, matrices are stored in columnar format.

```
my_matrix <- matrix(c(1, 2, 3, 4, 5, 6),
  nrow = 2, ncol = 3)

my_matrix
##         [,1] [,2] [,3]
## [1,]    1    3    5
## [2,]    2    4    6
```

The default `matrix()` command assumes that the input data will be arranged in columnar format. In order to arrange the data in row format, we need to modify our previous example slightly:

```
my_matrix <- matrix(c(1, 2, 3, 4, 5, 6),
  nrow = 2, ncol = 3, byrow = TRUE)

my_matrix
##         [,1] [,2] [,3]
## [1,]    1    2    3
## [2,]    4    5    6
```

A `matrix` is an object. Objects have `attributes`. Attributes are extra pieces of information that adorn objects. For matrices, a useful attribute is a character vector of names for the rows and another character vector of names for the columns. These can both be entered into a `list` object and passed as an argument to the `dimnames()` function:

```
dimnames(my_matrix) <- list(c("one", "hello"),
  c("column1", "column2", "c3"))

my_matrix
##         column1 column2 c3
## one         1       2   3
## hello       4       5   6
```

We can query the object for its attributes:

```
attributes(my_matrix)
## $dim
## [1] 2 3

## $dimnames
## $dimnames[[1]]
## [1] "one"    "hello"

## $dimnames[[2]]
## [1] "column1" "column2" "c3"
```

This output tells us that the matrix has two rows and three columns. It also tells us what the row and column names are.

The extraction of elements from a matrix can be accomplished via the use of the [,] operator. To extract the element located in row 1 and column 3, we need to issue the following command:

```
ans <- my_matrix[1, 3]

ans
## [1] 3
```

Operations on matrices can also be vectorized:

```
new_matrix_1 <- my_matrix * my_matrix

new_matrix_1
##          [,1] [,2] [,3]
## [1,]    1    4    9
## [2,]   16   25   36

new_matrix_2 <- sqrt(my_matrix)

new_matrix_2
##          [,1]      [,2]      [,3]
## [1,]    1  1.414214 1.732051
## [2,]    2  2.236068 2.449490
```

Here are some examples that utilize vectorization and single element operations:

```
mat1 <- matrix(rnorm(1000), nrow = 100)
round(mat1[1:5, 2:6], 3)
##          [,1]    [,2]    [,3]    [,4]    [,5]
## [1,] -1.544  1.281  1.397  0.407 -0.459
## [2,]  0.483  0.046 -1.817 -0.289  0.597
```

```
## [3,]   0.405   1.045 -0.726 -0.163   0.258
## [4,]   0.141 -0.294 -1.225 -0.217 -0.771
## [5,]  -0.537   0.226   0.126 -1.584 -1.237
```

```
mat2 <- mat1[1:25, ] ^ 2
head(round(mat2, 0), 9)[,1:7]
##      [,1] [,2] [,3] [,4] [,5] [,6] [,7]
## [1,]    1    2    2    2    0    0    7
## [2,]    0    0    0    3    0    0    0
## [3,]    0    0    1    1    0    0    1
## [4,]    0    0    0    2    0    1    4
## [5,]    1    0    0    0    3    2    1
## [6,]    2    1    3    1    1    1    1
## [7,]    0    0    0    0    0    1    0
## [8,]    1    2    0    0    1    2    0
## [9,]    0    0    3    0    2    2    0
```

The data.frame() object

It often helps to think of a data.frame() object as a single spreadsheet. A data frame is a hybrid, two-dimensional container that can include numeric, character, boolean, and factor types. Whenever data is read into R from an external environment, it is likely that the resulting object will end up being a data frame. The following code creates such a structure:

```
df <- data.frame(price  = c(89.2, 23.2, 21.2),
   symbol = c("MOT", "AAPL", "IBM"),
   action = c("Buy", "Sell", "Buy"))
```

```
df
##   price symbol action
## 1  89.2    MOT    Buy
## 2  23.2   AAPL   Sell
## 3  21.2    IBM    Buy
```

A data frame accepts columns of data as input. Different names can be assigned to each column of data. In a data frame, as in a matrix, it is important to ensure that the number of rows is the same for all columns. The data need to be in rectangular format. If this is not the case, R will issue an error message.

Factors are a convenient data type that can assist in the categorization and analysis of data. For our subsequent analysis we will not be needing these constructs. In order to disable the conversion of any character vector into a factor, we can use the stringsAsFactors = FALSE argument within the data.frame() call:

```
df3 <-data.frame(price  = c(89.2, 23.2, 21.2),
   symbol = c("MOT", "AAPL", "IBM"),
   action = c("Buy", "Sell", "Buy"),
   stringsAsFactors = FALSE)

class(df3$symbol)
## [1] "character"
```

Some takeaways from the previous examples are the following:

- Functions can take multiple input arguments. To figure out what arguments are available for standard R functions, use the ? operator in front of the function name. i.e. ?data.frame.
- Objects can be passed directly into other functions. Functions are objects. In fact, everything in R is an object!

Data frames can also be indexed via the [,] operator:

```
price <- df[1, 1]

price
## [1] 89.2

df2 <- data.frame(col1 = c(1, 2, 3),
   col2 = c(1, 2, 3, 4))

## Error in data.frame(col1 = c(1,2,3),
## col2 = c(1,2,3,4)) : arguments imply
## differing number of rows: 3, 4
```

The $ operator extracts data columns by name:

```
symbols <- df$symbol

symbols
## [1] MOT  AAPL IBM
## Levels: AAPL IBM MOT
```

The "Levels" descriptor for the symbols column implies that the type of variable is a "factor":

```
class(symbols)
## [1] "factor"
```

The symbols column from the df3 data frame, however, yields a character vector instead:

```
symbols <- df3$symbol

symbols
## [1] "MOT"  "AAPL" "IBM"
```

The list() object

A list object is one of those data structures that is very useful to R programmers. It is one of the most general containers in the sense that it can store objects of different types and sizes. The following code creates a list and populates it with three separate objects:

```
my_list <- list(a = c(1, 2, 3, 4, 5),
   b = matrix(1:10, nrow = 2, ncol = 5),
   c = data.frame(price = c(89.3, 98.2, 21.2),
   stock = c("MOT", "IBM", "CSCO")))

my_list
## $a
## [1] 1 2 3 4 5

## $b
##      [,1] [,2] [,3] [,4] [,5]
## [1,]    1    3    5    7    9
## [2,]    2    4    6    8   10

## $c
##   price stock
## 1  89.3   MOT
## 2  98.2   IBM
## 3  21.2  CSCO
```

The first element of the list my_list is named a, and it holds a numeric vector of length 5. The second component is a matrix, and the third one, a data frame. Many functions in R use this list structure as a general container to hold the results of computations.

Lists can be indexed by passing a number (the index of the list element) or by passing the element name into the double bracket operator [[]]:

```
first_element <- my_list[[1]]
```

```
first_element
## [1] 1 2 3 4 5
```

```
class(first_element)
## [1] "numeric"
```

An alternate extraction method is the following:

```
second_element <- my_list[["b"]]
```

```
second_element
##       [,1] [,2] [,3] [,4] [,5]
## [1,]    1    3    5    7    9
## [2,]    2    4    6    8   10
```

```
class(second_element)
## [1] "matrix"
```

The single bracket operator [] is used to extract a section of a list. This is a source of confusion for many novice R programmers. As a reminder, double brackets [[]] return list elements, whereas single brackets return lists. Here's an example:

```
part_of_list <- my_list[c(1, 3)]
```

```
part_of_list
## $a
## [1] 1 2 3 4 5
```

```
## $c
##    price   stock
## 1  89.3    MOT
## 2  98.2    IBM
## 3  21.2    CSCO
```

```
class(part_of_list)
## [1] "list"
```

The size of the list can be determined by calling the length() function.

```
size_of_list <- length(my_list)
```

```
size_of_list
## [1] 3
```

The new.env() object

An environment is a powerful data structure that R leverages quite a bit under the hood for performance reasons. It differs from the other structures in that it has reference semantics.[5] It is most similar to the list object, with an added reference to a parent environment. Environments are often used to emulate hash maps with O(1) lookup performance.[6] The link http://adv-r.had.co.nz/Environments.html contains more in-depth information on the semantics and use of this construct.

A new environment can be created with the new.env() command:

```
env <- new.env()
env[["first"]] <- 5
env[["second"]] <- 6
env$third <- 7
```

Just as in a list object, the assignment of name-value pairs can be accomplished via the $ or [[]] operators. Here is where the differences begin. Typing the name env into the console does not reveal the names nor the associated data we are accustomed to seeing:

```
env
## <environment: 0x101ef2f18>
```

Instead, we get back a cryptic hexadecimal code. To obtain the names, we have to use the ls command:

```
ls(env)
## [1] "first"  "second" "third"
```

To obtain the values associated with those names, we can use the get() command:

```
get("first", envir = env)
## 5
```

Removing elements from an environment is accomplished via the rm() command:

```
rm("second", envir = env)
ls(env)
## [1] "first" "third"
```

The copy and modify rules we have covered thus far for lists, data frames, matrices, and vectors do not apply to environments. Due to the reference semantics, when we create a copy of an environment and then proceed to modify one of

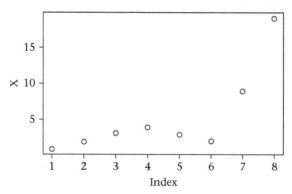

Figure 2.2 Default plot of a vector.

its elements, the elements of the original object will also be modified. Here is an example:

```
env_2 <- env
env_2$third <- 42

get("third", envir = env)
## [1] 42
```

Using the plot() function

One of the highlights of the R programming framework is the rich graphing functionality that even the base installation exposes to end users. Most of the advanced graphing functionality, however, is provided by external packages such as ggplot2, ggvis, rCharts, and rgl. The graphics CRAN[7] task view has a nice list of relevant packages. For the bulk of our subsequent work, we will stick to the basic plot() command, which is more than adequate in satisfying our graphical needs. Here is what a default plot() output produces:

```
# Create a vector of numbers x and plot them
x <- c(1, 2, 3.2, 4, 3, 2.1, 9, 19)
plot(x)
```

The type argument can be used to modify the graph from a points-plot to a line-plot:

```
# Convert the graph into a line plot
plot(x, type = "l")
```

A call to ?plot reveals a few more useful plot types:

- "p" for points
- "l" for lines

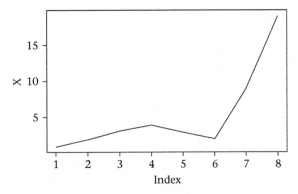

Figure 2.3 Vector line plot.

- "b" for both
- "c" for the lines part alone of "b"
- "o" for both overplotted
- "h" for histogram like (or high-density) vertical lines
- "s" for stair steps
- "S" for other steps
- "n" for no plotting

It helps to think of a plot as a painting canvas. A blank canvas is created by calling the plot() command with some default data and arguments. Lines and text are then drawn on the canvas by issuing calls to the respective functions. The following example demonstrates the creation of a plot with a main title, axis-labels, and a basic grid. A vertical and a horizontal line are also placed on the graph after the initial points have been rendered by plot():

```
# Set up the canvas
plot(rnorm(1000), main = "Some returns", cex.main = 0.9,
   xlab = "Time", ylab = "Returns")

# Superimpose a basic grid
grid()

# Create a few vertical and horizontal lines
abline(v = 400, lwd = 2, lty = 1)
abline(h = 2, lwd = 3, lty = 3)
```

Further information on v, h, lwd, lty, and other arguments of abline() can be found by calling ?abline. The lwd argument defines the line-width, and the lty argument defines the line-type.

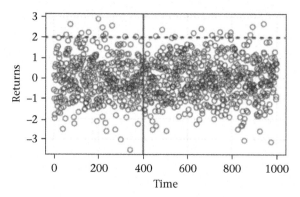

Figure 2.4 A plot with extra attributes.

The `par()` command is used to query or set up global graphical parameters that can be used by all subsequent calls to `plot()`. The following code splits the viewing window into a rectangular format with two rows and two columns. A `plot()` command can then be issued for each one of the child windows. Lines and text can subsequently be added to each unique child plot:

```
# Create a 2-row, 2-column format
par(mfrow = c(2, 2))

# First plot (points).
plot(rnorm(100), main = "Graph 1")

# Second plot (lines).
plot(rnorm(100), main = "Graph 2", type = "l")

# Third plot (steps) with a vertical line
plot(rnorm(100), main = "Graph 3", type = "s")
abline(v = 50, lwd = 4)

# Fourth plot
plot(rnorm(100), type = "h", main = "Graph 4")

# Reset the plot window
par(mfrow = c(1, 1))
```

It becomes evident that the order in which arguments are passed into functions does not matter, as long as they are given proper names. Behind the scenes, R uses either named matching or positional matching[8] to figure out the correct assignment. The call to `plot(x, main = "Hello", type = "h")` is identical to `plot(x, type = "h", main = "Hello")`.

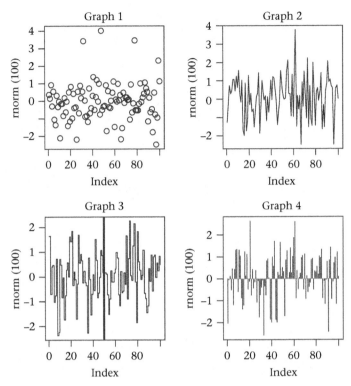

Figure 2.5 Four plots on a canvas.

Here's how to add some text and a legend to the plot:

```
plot(rnorm(100), main = "A line plot",
  cex.main = 0.8,
  xlab = "x-axis",
  ylab = "y-axis",
  type = "l")

# Extra text
mtext("Some text at the top", side = 3)

# At x = 40 and y = -1 coordinates
legend(40, -1, "A legend")
```

There are many settings that can be enabled within plot(). Entering ?plot.default in the console will list what these are. Alternatively, the formals() function can be used to extract the arguments of the function:

```
formals(plot.default)
## $x
```

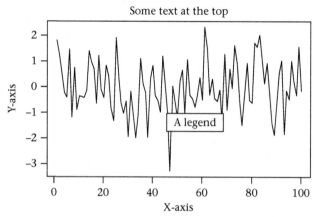

Figure 2.6 Graph with legend and text.

```
##   $y
## NULL

## $type
## [1] "p"
## ...
```

Functional programming

Functional programming is a programming style that is often used by R programmers. The main actor in the functional programming arena is the `function` itself.
The idea that differentiates this type of programming from others (i.e., imperative programming) is the the concept of nonmutability of state [85]. The resulting
answer is solely a function of the input data. Nothing outside of the function is
affected. The answers obtained from a program are exactly the same given the same
input data. There exists a solid mathematical theory underlying the ideas inherent
in functional programming. R, per se, does not impose a strict functional programming framework. Imperative, object-oriented, and functional concepts can,
and often are, combined to yield R programs.

How do we add up all the numbers between 1 and 100? Here is a vectorized,
functional approach:

```
ans <- sum(1:100)

ans
## [1] 5050
```

Functional programming helps abstract away many unnecessary details. For example, if all we want to do is sum a vector of numbers, then sum(x), where x is a vector, seems like the most intuitive thing to do. There is no need to loop through the vector, assign the value of each element to a temporary variable, keep track of the sum, and manage the mechanics of the branching logic, for or while loops. Internally, of course, there are for loops and imperative programming concepts at work. This is how the abstraction is accomplished in the first place. In R, this is typically implemented in a low-level language such as C, C++ or Fortran.

The following is an imperative example in R:

```
answer <- 0
for(i in 1:100) {
  answer <- answer + i
}
answer
## [1] 5050
```

Almost all operations in R can be vectorized and implemented using a functional programming paradigm. Not only will the resulting code be faster (in most cases), it will also be more succinct and less error prone.

Writing functions in R

Programming is like baking a cake. Given the raw ingredients (data and parameters), the application of a specific recipe will yield a cake as the end product. The data typically reaches the program either in real time, through a network connection in almost realtime, or through a database query of some kind. The recipe (program) provides the necessary instructions that transform and combine the data into the desired end result. At a basic level, a program can be thought of as one long sequence of instructions. Using the cake analogy, the high-level pseudocode of the program might look something like this:

1. Take all the eggs out of the refrigerator and put them on the counter.
2. Consciously make an effort to move your right hand over the eggs.
3. Zero-in on one of the eggs and spread your fingers apart.
4. Lower your hand and clamp your fingers.
5. Lift your arm and rotate your body clockwise by 60 degrees.
6. Move your right arm up and down in short bursts over the edge of the bowl. Etc.

And we have only cracked one egg at this point! One can imagine how tedious this becomes when the same instructions have to be repeated over and over again for all the eggs, let alone all the other ingredients. One way to alleviate this pain is to abstract away or to encapsulate some of the repetitive tasks. This is what functions do. Functions can be thought of as little black boxes that take some, or no inputs, and return one, many, or no outputs. We can conceptually create a function that takes as an input parameter the number of eggs at our disposal and simply returns a true or false response when all the eggs are either successfully cracked or unsuccessfully cracked.

A function declaration helps define the interface between the user and the underlying function logic. An example of such a declaration in C++ would be: `bool CrackEggs(int)`. This means that the function `CrackEggs()` takes as an input an integer and returns a boolean. R does not force us to declare what the type of the inputs or the output needs to be up front. R can infer what the inputs are at run time. The statement `CrackEggs(4)` and `CrackEggs("wow")` will both work in R. In the first case, R realizes that the input to the function is a number, whereas in the second case, the input to the function is a character vector. Depending on the internal implementation of the function, this might issue an error message. We need to tell R that `CrackEggs()` is a function that takes in one input and returns a boolean. The `function()` argument is used for this purpose:

```
crack_eggs <- function(number_of_eggs) {

    # Code that determines whether eggs have been cracked.
    # If they have, set have_all_eggs_been_cracked <- TRUE,
    # otherwise, set to FALSE

    return(have_all_eggs_been_cracked)
}
```

Now, our recipe can look something like this:

1. `gather_ingredients()`
2. `crack_eggs()`
3. `add_ingredients()`
4. `bake_cake()`

And this, in a nutshell, is how abstraction[9] works. Throughout this book, we will attempt to write small functions with the aim of accomplishing a certain task and then group these functions into larger programs to get our end result.

The base R installation includes many predefined functions. Unfortunately, it is difficult for newcomers to find detailed information on how to use these functions. This is also one of the few reasons why R is deemed to have a steep learning curve at first. The documentation included with the base version of R lacks rigor, and is short on examples and recommended use cases. Having said this, there are many great tutorials on most aspects of the R language available online and in print. Some of the references[10] included at the end of this book should steer the reader in the right direction. The following examples contain a few functions that are worth memorizing:

```r
# Greate 100 standard normals
x <- rnorm(100, mean = 0, sd = 1)

# Find the length of the vector x.
length(x)

# Compute the mean of x
mean(x)

# Compute the standard deviation of x
sd(x)

# Compute the median value of the vector x
median(x)

# Compute the range (min, max) of a variable
range(x)

# Find the sum of all the numbers in x
sum(x)

# Do a cumulative sum of the values in x
cumsum(x)

# Display the first 3 elements of x
head(x, 3)

# Display summary statistics on x
summary(x)

# Sort x from largest to smallest.
sort(x, decreasing = TRUE)

# Compute the successive difference in x
diff(x)

# Create an integer sequence from 1 to 10
1:10

# A sequence from 1 to 10 in steps of 0.1
seq(1, 10, 0.1)
```

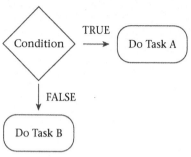

Figure 2.7 If statement flow chart.

```
# Print the string hello to the screen
print("hello")
```

Branching and looping

Before we move on to the fun stuff, here is a cursory look at the `if()` and `for()` commands. These constructs work in the same way as they do in most of the other programming languages.

The `if()` command acts as a branching mechanism that redirects the flow of the program based on the evaluation of the boolean expression that is passed in as an argument.

The following example will always print "XYZ" to the screen since the number 1 is most certainly not equal to 2:

```
# Define a boolean variable
my_boolean <- 1 == 2

if (my_boolean) {
  print("not correct")
} else {
  print("XYZ")
}
```

The commands `ifelse()` and `switch()` are also used for controlling the flow of execution. For the repetitive execution of code, the `for()`, `while()`, and `repeat()` commands should be used. The `for()` loop is used to execute certain functionality multiple times in a row. According to the `help("for")` documentation, the syntax of the for loop is of the form: `for(var in seq) expr`, where var is a variable, in is a reserved keyword, and seq is an expression evaluating to a vector. Here are two examples:

```
for(i in 1:5) {
  cat(i, "\n")
```

```
}
## 1
## 2
## 3
## 4
## 5

some_list <- list()
for(z in c("hello", "goodbye")) {
  some_list[[z]] <- z
}

some_list
## $hello
## [1] "hello"

## $goodbye
## [1] "goodbye"
```

At this point, we have sufficient information to start combining some of these commands into useful programs. As a motivating example, we will write a function to compute the pairwise correlations between 6 different stocks passed in by the user. Functionality already exists in R, which facilitates such computations in a straightforward manner. For pedagogical reasons, we will do it the hard way. This problem can be loosely decomposed into the following tasks:

1. Obtain the names of the six stocks.
2. Make sure they are valid stock names.
3. Connect to a database that has the prices for these stocks and pull that information into memory.
4. Clean up the data by identifying missing values.
5. Place all the filtered data into a suitable container like a matrix or a data frame.
6. Compute the pairwise correlations and return the result to the user.
7. Create a visualization of these correlations.

But before we write our first custom function, we need to talk about style.

A recommended style guide

Different people have different ways of writing code. This is good from a creative standpoint, but bad from a stylistic viewpoint. Various coding style guides have been proposed for almost all of the programming languages out there. A style guide is a set of rules on the visual appearance and layout of code. These guidelines specify the number of spaces to use, the naming convention of variable and function names, the proper use of comments, and so forth. Why is it important to adhere to a style guide? It is important because it allows for better readability of code, as well as portability of code between developers. Consider the following two examples. Functionally, they both produce the same output. One, however, is better than the other:

```
#sum numbers
x<-0;for(i in 1:10){x=x+1};x
```

or

```
# Sum numbers
x <- 0
for(i in 1:10) {
  x <- x + 1
}
x
```

The second variant is visually more appealing as it does a better job of separating out the functionality. Notice that the assignment in the first case is x = x + 1, whereas in the second case, x <- x + 1. In the cleaner version, a consistent assignment operator was used for both the initialization (x <- 0) and the incrementing (x <- x + 1) stages. Again, the functionality does not change, the quality of the code, however, feels better in the second variant.

Hadley Wickham has drafted a style guide that will be adopted throughout this book. The rules can be found here: http://r-pkgs.had.co.nz/style.html. The following list contains a subset of these rules:

- File names should be meaningful and end in .r. For example, file-name.r is recommended, whereas, file-name.R is not.
- Variable and function names should be lowercase, and the underscore _ should be used to separate out the words. The camel case variable name firstFunction should be written as first_function instead.
- For code indentation, use two spaces. Don't mix tabs and spaces.
- Use <- rather than =, for assignment.

A pairwise correlation example

Now, back to writing our pairwise correlation function. In an attempt to break down the task, we will write a few helper functions. The first helper function will validate whether a vector of stock symbols contains valid names, and will return only the valid ones for further processing. For simplicity, we will assume that a valid symbol is any sequence of 2 to 4 letters of the English alphabet. Numbers will not be allowed as part of the symbol identifier. We will make use of regular expressions[11] to accomplish this initial filtering task.

```
filter_and_sort_symbols <- function(symbols) {
  # Name: filter_symbols
  # Purpose: Convert to upper case if not
  # and remove any non valid symbols
  # Input: symbols = vector of stock tickers
  # Output: filtered_symbols = filtered symbols

  # Convert symbols to uppercase
  symbols <- toupper(symbols)

  # Validate the symbol names
  valid <- regexpr("^[A-Z]{2,4}$", symbols)

  # Return only the valid ones
  return(sort(symbols[valid == 1]))
}
```

Regular expressions are a powerful string filtering mechanism. Even though their syntax can appear quite daunting at first, it is worth spending the time to learn how to apply them. They provide a very concise and efficient way to perform text manipulations. The regular expression pattern used in the previous example (`^[A-Z]{2,4}$`) specifies that the string to be matched should start with an uppercase letter and end with an uppercase letter. It also requires that there be exactly two, three, or four letters present. Anything else will not be considered as a valid stock symbol. The `regexpr()` function returns a vector of equal length to that of the `symbols` vector. An entry of 1 is used to denote the valid names, and an entry of -1, the invalid ones. The `topper()` function is used to convert all the letters into uppercase prior to applying the regular expression. Here is a test of the function we just wrote:

```
filter_symbols(c("MOT", "cvx", "123", "Gog2", "XLe"))
## "MOT" "CVX" "XLE"
```

The next step requires us to pass the filtered vector of symbols into a function that will read in a .csv file and extract only the relevant data for those symbols. This function can later be augmented to read in price data from multiple sources, including external databases.

For the purposes of this exercise, we will use a .csv file that contains 1856 trading days of prices for the following nine stocks: AAPL, CVX, IBM, XOM, GS, BA, MON, TEVA and CME. The time range of the data is from January 3, 2007 to May 16, 2014. We can consider this file as our database. These prices were obtained from Yahoo and the format looks as follows:

	AAPL	CVX	IBM	XOM	GS	BA	MON	TEVA	CME
2014-05-09	585.54	123.97	190.08	101.95	157.20	131.10	115.66	48.91	69.59
2014-05-12	592.83	124.18	192.57	102.23	159.55	132.60	115.97	49.64	70.91
2014-05-13	593.76	124.78	192.19	102.36	160.28	133.45	116.91	50.85	70.59
2014-05-14	593.87	125.35	188.72	102.29	159.45	132.99	117.00	50.18	69.81
2014-05-15	588.82	123.81	186.46	100.78	156.64	131.21	115.40	49.72	69.48
2014-05-16	597.51	123.18	187.06	100.74	156.43	130.81	116.04	49.81	68.68

Figure 2.8 Sample stock price file.

```
extract_prices <- function(filtered_symbols, file_path) {
  # Name: extract_prices
  # Purpose: Read price data from specified file
  # Inputs: filtered_symbols = vector of symbols,
  #                 file_path = location of price data
  # Output: prices = data.frame of prices per symbol

  # Read in the .csv price file
  all_prices <- read.csv(file = file_path, header = TRUE,
    stringsAsFactors = FALSE)

  # Make the dates row names
  rownames(all_prices) <- all_prices$Date

  # Remove the original Date column
  all_prices$Date <- NULL

  # Extract only the relevant data columns
  valid_columns <- colnames(all_prices) %in% filtered_symbols

  return(all_prices[, valid_columns])
}
```

A few new concepts were introduced in the extract_prices() function that need further clarification: The use of NULL and the use of the %in% command. By assigning a column name of a data frame to NULL, we effectively remove that column from the data frame. This operation can also be used to remove elements from a list. The %in% command asks the following question: which elements of vector A are also in vector B?

```
A <- c(1, 2, 5, 6, 9)
B <- c(0, 3, 6, 9, 10)

A %in% B
## [1] FALSE FALSE FALSE  TRUE  TRUE
```

Now that we have the prices of the filtered stocks in a data frame, we can perform some basic filtering. For now, we will take a look at the data and identify the rows with missing values. At this stage, we will not use this information to filter the data. We just care about the mechanics of identifying bad entries.

```
filter_prices <- function(prices) {
    # Name: filter_prices
    # Purpose: Identify the rows with missing values
    # Inputs: prices = data.frame of prices
    # Output: missing_rows = vector of indexes where
    # data is missing in any of the columns

    # Returns a boolean vector of good or bad rows
    valid_rows <- complete.cases(prices)

    # Identify the index of the missing rows
    missing_rows <- which(valid_rows == FALSE)

    return(missing_rows)
}
```

The next step in our list requires us to compute pairwise correlations between all the stocks.[12] The mathematical formula for the **Pearson** sample correlation coefficient ρ between two vectors of numbers is

$$r_{xy} = \frac{\sum_{i=1}^{n}(x_i - \bar{x})(y_i - \bar{y})}{\sqrt{\sum_{i=1}^{n}(x_i - \bar{x})^2 \sum_{i=1}^{n}(y_i - \bar{y})^2}} \tag{2.2}$$

There is no need to delve into the details of the above formulation. We will implement it directly by calling the cor() function.

```
compute_pairwise_correlations <- function(prices) {
    # Name: compute_pairwise_correlations
    # Purpose: Calculates pairwise correlations of returns
    # and plots the pairwise relationships

    # Inputs: prices = data.frame of prices
    # Output: correlation_matrix = A correlation matrix

    # Convert prices to returns
    returns <- apply(prices, 2, function(x) diff(log(x)))

    # Plot all the pairwise relationships
    pairs(returns, main = "Pairwise return scatter plot")
```

	AAPL	CVX	IBM	XOM	BA	TEVA
AAPL	1.0000000	0.4555762	0.4974812	0.4152326	0.4221255	0.2793489
CVX	0.4555762	1.0000000	0.5789544	0.8912227	0.6004590	0.4228898
IBM	0.4974812	0.5789544	1.0000000	0.5668389	0.5214248	0.3214548
XOM	0.4152326	0.8912227	0.5668389	1.0000000	0.5955963	0.4112595
BA	0.4221255	0.6004590	0.5214248	0.5955963	1.0000000	0.3479621
TEVA	0.2793489	0.4228898	0.3214548	0.4112595	0.3479621	1.0000000

Figure 2.9 Correlation matrix output.

```
# Compute the pairwise correlations
correlation_matrix <- cor(returns, use = "complete.obs")

return(correlation_matrix)
}
```

Now that our helper functions have been defined, it is time to tie everything together:

```
# Stock tickers entered by user
symbols <- c("IBM", "XOM", "2SG", "TEva",
  "GOog", "CVX", "AAPL", "BA")

# Location of our database of prices
file_path <- "path/prices.csv"

# Filter and sort the symbols
filtered_symbols <- filter_and_sort_symbols(symbols)
filtered_symbols
## [1] "AAPL" "BA"   "CVX"  "IBM"  "TEVA" "XOM"

# Extract prices
prices <- extract_prices(filtered_symbols, file_path)

# Filter prices
missing_rows <- filter_prices(prices)
missing_rows
## integer(0)

# Compute correlations
correlation_matrix <- compute_pairwise_correlations(prices)
correlation_matrix
```

Here is the correlation matrix:

As a side effect, the same function also generates a scatter plot of all the returns in a nice rectangular layout. This is courtesy of the pairs() function.

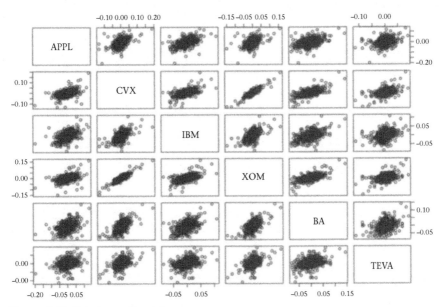

Figure 2.10 Pairwise scatter plot.

Summary

This chapter addresses the basics of the R programming language. A brief history of the language is outlined, and the main reasons to use the R programming language are presented. Some of these include the ease of data manipulation and processing, the open-source nature of the framework, the plethora of add-on packages, and a vibrant online community. The important data containers (c(), matrix(), data.frame(), list()), as well as the most frequently used operations on these containers are showcased, and examples are provided. Some of the base graphical capabilities of the R language are also explored. The chapter ends with an introduction to creating customized functions within R. After briefly discussing the use of code-styling conventions, a practical use-case on calculating pairwise correlations between stocks is provided.

This page intentionally left blank

3 | Working with Data

Financial data comes in many forms and sizes. In this book, we will mostly concern ourselves with a particular class of financial data, namely, time series data. Time series data contain a time component that is primarily used as an index (key) to identify other meaningful values. Another way to think about time series data is as key-value pairs in which the key is the time, and the value is either a single entry or a vector of entries. The following table gives an idea of what a typical daily time series for the stock AAPL might look like. This data was downloaded from Yahoo[1] in the form of a .csv file.

The first column contains the date, and the other columns contain price and volume information. Now that we have the downloaded file available on our computer, it is time to load the data into R for further manipulation.

Getting data into R

As a first step, we might want to take a look at what the closing price for AAPL looks like on a daily basis. There is a quick way to get data from a spreadsheet directly into the R environment. Simply copy the closing price column from the .csv file and then issue the following command inside the R console:

```
# In Windows
aapl <- read.table("clipboard")

# On Mac/Linux
aapl <- read.table(pipe("pbpaste"))
```

This will, in effect, read the contents of the clipboard into a variable named aapl. We can look at the first few entries of this object by using the head() command.

```
head(aapl)
##      V1
## 1 523.48
## 2 530.32
## 3 523.44
```

Prices						
Date	Open	High	Low	Close	Volume	Adj Close*
Apr 10, 2014	530.68	532.24	523.17	523.48	8,530,600	523.48
Apr 9, 2014	522.64	530.49	522.02	530.32	7,337,800	530.32
Apr 8, 2014	525.19	526.12	518.70	523.44	8,697,800	523.44
Apr 7, 2014	528.02	530.90	521.89	523.47	10,309,400	523.47
Apr 4, 2014	539.81	540.00	530.58	531.82	9,830,400	531.82
Apr 3, 2014	541.39	542.50	537.64	538.79	5,798,000	538.79
Apr 2, 2014	542.38	543.48	540.26	542.55	6,443,600	542.55
Apr 1, 2014	537.76	541.87	536.77	541.65	7,170,000	541.65
Mar 31, 2014	539.23	540.81	535.93	536.74	6,023,900	536.74

Figure 3.1 Time series data of AAPL price.

```
## 4 523.47
## 5 531.82
## 6 538.79
```

What kind of object is aapl anyway? Is it a matrix? A list? A data.frame?

```
class(aapl)
## [1] "data.frame"
```

It seems that the aapl object is indeed a data frame. We also notice that R has provided its own name for the extracted column of data (V1). Upon closer inspection, it appears that the data is printed out in reverse chronological order onto the screen. This can be remedied by either sorting the original spreadsheet in chronological order or by reversing the contents of the aapl object we just created. Here is the latter approach:

```
aapl <- aapl[rev(rownames(aapl)), , drop = FALSE]
```

The rev() command reverses the entries as expected. This syntax is somewhat confusing. We are effectively telling R to reverse the row entries of the data frame aapl, and to keep the original structure of the object. The drop = FALSE argument prevents the data frame from degrading into a vector.

In order to extract and visualize the raw vector of prices, we can do the following:

```
prices <- aapl$V1
plot(prices, main = "AAPL plot", type = 'l')
```

The functions read.table() and read.csv() have many options that make reading input data into R a breeze. Instead of copying the closing-price column and using the "clipboard" command, we can specify the location of the file that includes the data in which we are interested. The ?read.csv command lists the available options at our disposal.

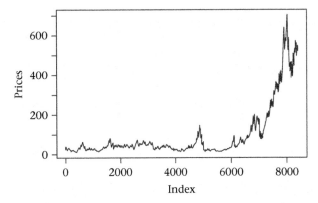

Figure 3.2 Elementary stock line chart.

```
# Load the .csv file
aapl_2 <- read.csv(file = "path/aapl.csv", header = TRUE,
  stringsAsFactors = FALSE)

# Reverse the entries
aapl_2 <- aapl_2[rev(rownames(aapl_2)), ]
```

This time around, we specified that headers are present in the input file. R knows to call the columns by their correct names, and if we want to extract the closing-price, the following command suffices:

```
aapl_close <- aapl_2[, "Close"]
```

To get some quick summary statistics in tabular format, we can utilize the summary() function.

```
summary(aapl_close)
## Min.   1st Qu. Median   Mean  3rd Qu.  Max.
## 11.00   25.50   40.50   96.29  77.00  702.10
```

The summary() function outputs the mean, median, first, and third quantiles, along with any missing value (NA) information. Summarizing and visualizing a particular data set should be one of the first steps conducted prior to performing any subsequent analysis. Most of the time, such summary statistics help uncover structural issues with the data.

Installing packages in R

Most of the functionality that we care about has probably already been created by another R user. Leveraging the work of others is something that is highly encouraged within the R community. There is no need to reinvent the wheel if it already exists and rolls just fine. Packages, or libraries are bundles of functions (usually written in R, C++, C or Fortran), data, and supporting documentation on a specific topic. A list of such specific topics can be found on the CRAN Task Views website: cran.r-project.org/web/views/. Some organizations also create their own packages in-house without making them publicly available. For a thorough discussion on how to create such a packaged bundle, the following reference serves as a good starting point.[2]

A package we will leverage later in this section is called **quantmod**. It is the brainchild of Jeffrey Ryan,[3] and it allows one to work with financial time series data in an intuitive manner.

To install **quantmod**, open up an R console and enter the following command: install.packages("quantmod"). Notice the quotes around the package name. Here is a full list of what the install.packages() function arguments are:

```
install.packages(pkgs, lib, repos = getOption("repos"),
    contriburl = contrib.url(repos, type),
    method, available = NULL, destdir = NULL,
    dependencies = NA, type = getOption("pkgType"),
    configure.args = getOption("configure.args"),
    configure.vars = getOption("configure.vars"),
    clean = FALSE, Ncpus = getOption("Ncpus", 1L),
    verbose = getOption("verbose"),
    libs_only = FALSE, INSTALL_opts, quiet = FALSE,
    keep_outputs = FALSE, ...)
```

During the installation process, **quantmod** automatically loads all the dependencies that it needs. If the local machine is connected to the Internet, R will use a default folder as the repository for the installed packages. This folder location can be changed by specifying a different path via the lib argument.

Installing a package is one thing. Using it, is another. Installation happens only once, but loading happens every time the script is called. The library() or require() commands are used to load packages into the R environment. They are equivalent for the most part.[4]

Storing and transmitting data

We have to figure out how to store and retrieve data efficiently before we can conduct any meaningful analysis. There are many ways to accomplish both objectives. As far as storage is concerned, some popular storage mediums are

- Comma separated value files (.csv).
- Excel spreadsheets (.xls or .xlsx).
- Relational databases

Many more storage and retrieval options exist,[5] but for 90 percent of the tasks that we are interested in, knowing how to work with these file types is more than enough.

As far as transmission from one computer to another is concerned (this also applies to storage), the .json data format is quite popular. The acronym JSON stands for Javascript Object Notation, and it uses a key-value paradigm to store information in a somewhat human readable format.

A sample .json file might look something like this:

```
{
  "CVX":
  {
    "Currency": "USD",
    "Sector": "Basic Materials",
    "Industry": "Major Integrated Oil & Gas"
  },
  "GOOG":
  {
    "Currency": "USD",
    "Sector": "Technology",
    "Industry": "Internet Information Providers"
  }
}
```

This file can be locally saved and then, via the **RJSONIO** package, parsed into a list object.

```
# Install and load the package
install.packages("RJSONIO")
library(RJSONIO)

# Read the file
out <- fromJSON(content = "path/sample_json_file.json" )
# Look at the structure of the resulting object
str(out)
## List of 2
## $ CVX : Named chr [1:3] "USD" "Basic Materials...
##   ..- attr(*, "names")= chr [1:3] "Currency"...
## $ GOOG: Named chr [1:3] "USD" "Technology"...
##   ..- attr(*, "names")= chr [1:3] "Currency"...
```

Another popular format that is used to encode and transfer data between applications is XML (Extensible Markup Language). YAML is yet another one. YAML is a recursive acronym for "YAML Ain't Markup Language." Both of these formats are similar in that they encode the data in human-readable form. R packages that parse XML and YAML are called **XML** and **yaml** respectively.

A more compact format can be obtained by saving the data as .rdata or .rds files. In R, this can be accomplished by using the save() and saveRDS() commands. These are functions that convert the underlying data objects into binary form. The objects can be reinstated back into the R framework via the load() and readRDS() commands respectively. The suffix used for the file names can actually be arbitrary. The only reason to stick with .rdata and .rds is for clarity and convention.

For comparison purposes, we can save the data frame of AAPL we obtained from Yahoo as a .csv file and query its size.

```
write.csv(aapl_2, file = "path/aapl_2.csv")
```

This file registers as 455 KB on disk.

```
save(aapl_2, file = "path/aapl_2.rdata")
```

By our saving the original data frame as a binary object, the file is now only 164 KB in size. This is approximately a 2.5 compression factor. To see that the files are indeed the same, we can load the saved version back into memory and compare it with the .csv version. Since the save() command restores everything back into the main environment, we will have to rename the old file so as not to override it. We could have used saveRDS() instead to accomplish the same thing. We do this by assigning it to a new variable and by deleting the old variable.

```
aapl_old <- aapl_2
rm(aapl_2)
load(file = "path/aapl_2.rdata")
```

The identical() command can be used to check whether the objects are the same.

```
identical(aapl_old, aapl_2)
## [1] TRUE
```

It is certainly preferable to work with these binary R-objects whenever possible. The compromise here is the portability of the data between different frameworks. Many applications already consume .csv and .json formats. Only R users, however, consume R serialized files.

Extracting data from a spreadsheet

Spreadsheets are ubiquitous in the financial industry. Traders, accountants, quants, and many other professionals rely on spreadsheets to manage portfolios of financial instruments, keep track of accounting metrics, and do quantitative analysis.

◇	A	B	C	D
1	time	signal1	signal2	
2	8:30:00	0.43	−0.2	
3	8:31:00	0.54	0.33	
4	8:32:00	0.32	−0.21	
5				
6				

Figure 3.3 Sample signals sheet.

◇	A	B	C	D
1				
2				
3				
4				
5		Intensity	score	
6		2	7.5	
7		3	8.4	
8		6	5.4	
9				
10				

Figure 3.4 Sample strength sheet.

The XLConnect package provides a platform-independent interface to Excel and allows us to cast the data into familiar R data frames [33]. According to the developer's website (http://www.mirai-solutions.com/), XLConnect is free software that does not require any registration or other obligation. It is also not necessary to have an installation of Microsoft Excel in order to use the functionality provided by this package. The only requirement, is that the latest version of the Java Runtime Environment (JRE) be installed.

To illustrate the functionality, we will use an .xlsx workbook consisting of two sheets. The first sheet is named *signals*, and the second sheet is named *strength*. The workbook itself is named *strategy.xlsx*.

```
library(XLConnect)

# Create a workbook object
book <- loadWorkbook("path/strategy.xlsx")

# Convert it into a data frame
signals = readWorksheet(book, sheet = "signals", header
= TRUE)

signals
##         time signal1 signal2
## 1 08:30:00    0.43   -0.20
## 2 08:31:00    0.54    0.33
## 3 08:32:00    0.32   -0.21
```

```
strength = readWorksheet(book, sheet = "strength", header
= TRUE)

strength
##  intensity score
## 1    2    7.5
## 2    3    8.4
## 3    6    5.4
```

It is also possible to create a workbook and populate it with data from R.

```
# Setup a new spreadsheet
book <- loadWorkbook("demo_sheet.xlsx", create = TRUE)

# Create a sheet called stock1
createSheet(book, name = "stock1")

# Creating a sheet called stock2
createSheet(book, name = "stock2")

# Load data into workbook
df <- data.frame(a = c(1, 2, 3), b = c(4, 5, 6))
writeWorksheet (book, data=df, sheet="stock1", header = TRUE)

# Save the workbook
saveWorkbook(book, file = "path/demo_sheet.xlsx")
```

For more information on how to work with Excel files in R, the post by Nicola Sturaro Sommacal on http://www.r-bloggers.com/read-excel-files-from-r/ is useful.

Accessing a database

At some point in their careers, quant/trader practitioners have to either extract data from, or enter data into, some kind of database. These databases, especially in finance and trading, are mostly relational in nature. The last few years have also seen the rise of the NoSQL family of databases.[6] R provides functionality for accessing both relational and NoSQL types. Generally speaking, a database is a storage medium that provides extra functionality for the fast and scalable storage and retrieval of data. Many databases have specific query languages associated with them. SQL is an example of such a language. SQL stands for Standard Query Language.[7] Databases that use some form of SQL come in many flavors. A few of the popular ones are listed in Table 3.1.

Table 3.1 Popular relational databases

Oracle	www.oracle.com/database
MySQL	www.mysql.com
Microsoft SQL Server	www.microsoft.com/sql-server
PostgreSQL	www.postgresql.com
Microsoft Access	www.office.microsoft.com/en-us/access
DB2	www.ibm.com/software/data/db2

In this next example, we will extract some data from a MySQL database. Creating and populating such a database is outside the scope of this book. The endnotes[8] explain how one might go about setting one up. This example assumes that a MySQL database already exists and is prepopulated with data.

We will explore three ways of accessing MySQL data from R. The first method utilizes the **RODBC** package, the second method uses the **RMySQL** package, and the third method explores the **dplyr** package.

The **RODBC** package is an R wrapper to the Open Database Connectivity (ODBC) programming interface. This interface allows third-party applications to seamlessly connect and manipulate data to/from relational databases via SQL calls. On a Windows machine, a registered data-source name can be set up in the ODBC Data Source Administrator menu. Once the appropriate driver for MySQL has been installed and the name defined, we can use the `odbcConnect()` command to initiate a connection to the MySQL instance. A MySQL instance can be comprised of multiple databases, each in turn having one or more tables. Each row in a table is considered a separate record. Each column in such a table is referred to as a field. The database I have set up for this demonstration is called `OptionsData`, and it includes a table called `ATMVolatilities`. This table includes some dummy implied volatility estimates for a few stocks. The fields in the table are the symbol, the expiration date of the option, the maturity in days, the delta of the option, whether it is a put or a call, and the implied volatility for each option.

```
# Load the RODBC package
require(RODBC)

# Establish a connection to MySQL
con <- odbcConnect("rfortraders")

# Choose the database name and table name
database_name <- "OptionsData"
table_name <- "ATMVolatilities"
symbol <- "SPY"
sql_command <- paste0("SELECT Symbol, Date, Maturity,
```

```
Delta, CallPut, ImpliedVolatility FROM ",
database_name, ".", table_name,
" WHERE Maturity = 91
AND Symbol IN ('", symbol, "');")

iv <- sqlQuery(con, sql_command)

# disconnect from database
odbcClose(con)
```

The above SQL-query extracts the implied volatilities of a 91-day maturity option for the SPY ETF for an arbitrary number of days. The output looks something like this:

```
head(iv)
## Symbol Date Maturity Delta CallPut ImpliedVolatility
## SPY 6/9/2014      91     55      C          0.115925
## SPY 6/9/2014      91     60      C          0.119577
## SPY 6/9/2014      91     65      C          0.123468
## SPY 6/9/2014      91     70      C          0.127629
## SPY 6/9/2014      91     75      C          0.132094
## SPY 6/9/2014      91     80      C          0.136776
```

The **RMySQL** package provides similar functionality to the **RODBC** one. It is custom tailored to MySQL, and many practitioners who work with such databases prefer to use this package instead. Here is some code that establishes a connection to the local instance, extracts the data in the form of a data frame, and then, closes the connection:

```
# Load the necessary package
require(RMySQL)

# Establish a connection
con <- dbConnect(MySQL(), user="your_login",
  password="your_password",
  dbname="OptionsData",
  host="location_of_database")

# List the tables and fields
dbListTables(con)

# Define the command and extract a data frame
sql_command <- paste0("SELECT Symbol, Date, Maturity,
  Delta, CallPut, ImpliedVolatility FROM ",
```

```
  database_name, ".", table_name,
  " WHERE Maturity = 91
  AND Symbol IN ('", symbol, "');")

result <- dbGetQuery(con, sql_command)

# Close the connection
dbDisconnect(con)
```

It is also possible to extract the tabular data in chunks if the data is voluminous.

```
results <- dbSendQuery(con, sql_command)
partial_results <- fetch(results, n = 100)
```

The **dplyr** package

The **dplyr** package is another contribution by Hadley Wickham and Romain Fran-cois [45, 44]. It evolved from the **plyr** package, which also happens to be very popular. The latest **dplyr** enhancements provide efficient methods for working with R data frames. The d in the name stands for data frame. A lot of thought has gone into the development of **dplyr**, and most of the time-sensitive components within the package have been directly implemented in C++. Expect to see the R community migrate to **dplyr** for many data manipulation tasks. The source code is currently maintained on github at: https://github.com/hadley/dplyr. To install the package, one can use either the CRAN version or the latest github development version:

```
# Get the CRAN version
install.packages("dplyr")
require(dplyr)

# Or, first load devtools
install.packages("devtools")
require(devtools)

# Get the github version
devtools::install_github("hadley/dplyr")
require(dplyr)
```

Hadley recommends that users of the package familiarize themselves with the principles of *tidy data* prior to doing any serious work with **dplyr**. The relevant information can be found here: http://vita.had.co.nz/papers/tidy-data.pdf

According to the github release notes, here are some of the formats that **dplyr** currently supports:

- data frames
- data tables
- SQLite
- PostgreSQL/Redshift
- MySQL/MariaDB
- Bigquery
- MonetDB
- data cubes with arrays

The beauty of the implementation is that the details of the underlying data containers are abstracted away from the user. The `tbl()` structure is used as a tabular proxy for the data extracted from the listed repos.

Here are some important commands to be aware of when dealing with **dplyr**:

- tbl()
- group_by()
- summarise()
- do()
- %>%

This next example will focus on some of the core functionality and will utilize a data set that is part of the **dplyr** installation. The full example can be found here: https://github.com/hadley/dplyr.

```
# Load the flight database that comes with dplyr
library(hflights)

# Look at number of rows and columns
dim(hflights)
## [1] 227496      21
```

A row in this data frame looks like this:

What we want to do at this point is calculate aggregate statistics on a certain subset of the data. As an initial step, the data will be coerced into a `data.table` [72].[9] We could have easily coerced the data into a data frame instead.

```
# First, coerce the data into a data.table
flights_dt <- tbl_dt(hflights)

# What type of object is this?
class(flights_dt)
## [1] "tbl_dt"  "tbl"    "data.table" "data.frame"
```

To find the median arrival delay time for all carriers, we begin by grouping the data by carrier:

Table 3.2 Sample data row from **dplyr**

Sample hflights row	
Year	2011
Month	1
DayOfMonth	2
DayOfWeek	7
DepTime	1401
ArrTime	1500
UniqueCarrier	AA
FlightNum	428
TailNum	N576AA
ActualElapsedTime	60
AirTime	40
AirDelay	−10
DepDelay	0
Origin	IAH
Dest	DFW
Distance	224
TaxiIn	7
TaxiOut	13
Cancelled	0
CancellationCode	0
Diverted	0

```
# Create a grouping by carrier
carrier_group <- group_by(flights_dt, UniqueCarrier)

# Now compute the summary statistics
summarise(carrier_group, avg_delay = mean(ArrDelay, na.rm
= TRUE))
```

The execution time for the aggregate summary is on the order ten milliseconds. This is pretty fast indeed. Here is what the summary looks like in Table 3.2.

The do() function allows one to apply an arbitrary function to a group of data. The %>% operator can be used to chain the results together. An example of this can be seen by typing ?do in the R console.

The mastering of **dplyr** is something I wholeheartedly recommend to all aspiring data analysts. It should be a part of any data filtering or data analysis workflow conducted in R. It can take a while, however, to get used to the *tidy data* paradigm of data manipulation. I do consider this an intermediate-level topic, and as such, I will leave it up to the reader to explore the full glory of **dplyr** in more detail.

Table 3.3 Output of `summarise` for **dplyr**

Mean Delay Example	
UniqueCarrier	Mean Delay
AA	0.89
AS	3.19
B6	9.85
CO	6.09
DL	6.08
EV	7.25
F9	7.66
FL	1.85
MQ	7.15
OO	8.69
UA	10.46
US	−0.63
WN	7.58
XE	8.18
YV	4.01

Using the xts package

In the beginning of this chapter, we looked at the price trajectory of AAPL. The data was downloaded from Yahoo in the form of a .csv file, and we read the contents into R. The plot we produced was fairly coarse, and apart from the line graph, it did not contain any useful information such as the time on the x-axis or other metrics that might be of interest to a stock trader.

One of our goals in this chapter will be to automatically extract financial time series from the web and also to produce better (more informative) plots. The **quantmod** package can do all this for us and much more.

One of the packages that **quantmod** relies on is **xts** [49]. This package provides functionality for working with time series data. The most important thing to know about **xts** is that it is used to create a new object that combines the core data with a time index. This is very useful, because one can eventually perform queries and apply transformations to the underlying data based on the time index.

The documentation on **xts** is fairly descriptive. The examples listed on the help page are a great way to gain exposure to some of the functionality that is available.

```
# load the library xts
library(xts)


# Load a small dataset that comes along with xts.
# We could have used our original .csv file as well.
```

```
data(sample_matrix)

# Look at the data
head(sample_matrix)
## [1] "matrix"

# What is the type of this object?
class(sample_matrix)
## [1] "matrix"

# Use the str() command to get more details about this object.
str(sample_matrix)

## num [1:180, 1:4] 50 50.2 50.4 50.4 50.2 ...
## - attr(*, "dimnames")=List of 2
## ..$ : chr [1:180] "2007-01-02" "2007-01-03"
## "2007-01-04" "2007-01-05" ...
## ..$ : chr [1:4] "Open" "High" "Low" "Close"
```

The output from str() can be somewhat daunting. It is telling us that the matrix has 180 rows and 4 columns. It is also displaying that the row names equal the dates and that the column names equal the strings: "Open", "High", "Low", and "Close". We can take this data and convert it into an **xts** object. To the user, everything will look the same as before. Underneath the hood, though, R will be doing some pretty neat indexing.

```
xts_matrix<-as.xts(sample_matrix, descr ='my new xts object')
```

A description is not required as part of the declaration. This is an optional parameter. Using the str() command one more time on xts_matrix

```
str(xts_matrix}
## An 'xts' object on 2007-01-02/2007-06-30 containing:
## Data: num [1:180, 1:4] 50 50.2 50.4 50.4 50.2 ...
## - attr(*, "dimnames")=List of 2
## ..$ : NULL
## ..$ : chr [1:4] "Open" "High" "Low" "Close"
## Indexed by objects of class: [POSIXct,POSIXt] TZ:
## xts Attributes:
## List of 3
## $ tclass: chr [1:2] "POSIXct" "POSIXt"
## $ tzone : chr ""
## $ descr : chr "my new xts object"
```

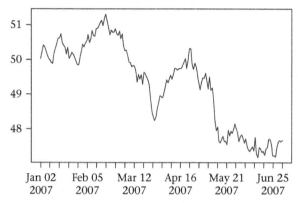

Figure 3.5 First **xts** plot.

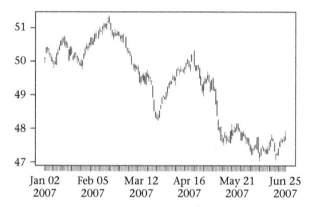

Figure 3.6 An **xts** candle plot.

The displayed information is different now. There are no more row names. They have been replaced by a *POSIX*[10] time-class [132]. The class(xts_matrix) command reveals that our object also inherits some of its attributes from the **zoo** class.

Here is a plotting example. The plot() function knows that it is now dealing with an **xts** input object and, as such, will produce a different graphical layout. This is polymorphic[11] behavior in action.

```
# Simple plot
plot(xts_matrix[,1], main = "Our first xts plot",
  cex.main = 0.8)


# Or we can try something fancier.
 plot(xts_matrix, main = "Candle plot on xts object",
   cex.main = 0.8, type = "candles")
```

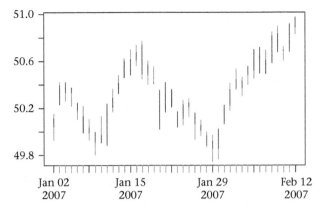

Figure 3.7 Subsetting an **xts** plot.

The main reason we want to turn a time series into an **xts** object is because we can take advantage of the indexing properties that come along with it. Given that we want to plot the price of a stock between two dates, how can this be accomplished? Here are some examples:

```
plot(xts_matrix["2007-01-01::2007-02-12"],
  main = "An xts candle plot with subsetting",
  cex.main = 0.8, type = "candles")
```

Notice the single string argument that is passed to the price matrix. This time-based formatting makes it easy to work with human readable dates as time boundaries.

```
range <- "2007-03-15::2007-06-15"
plot(xts_matrix(range))
```

The paste() function is useful for concatenating strings together. It takes the input arguments and pastes them together. By default, it will separate the strings with a space, unless one specifies sep = "".

```
start_date <- "2007-05-05"
end_date <- "2007-12-31"

plot(xts_matrix[paste(start_date, "::",
  end_date, sep = "")])

# Defaults to space separator
paste("Hello", "World", "in R")
## [1] "Hello World in R"

paste("Hello", "Again", sep = "**")
```

```
## [1] "Hello**Again"
```

A vector of strings can be pasted together with a specified separator between the elements of the vector as follows:

```
paste(c(1,2,3,4,5), collapse = "oooo")
## [1] "1oooo2oooo3oooo4oooo5"
```

We need to investigate a few more aspects of **xts** objects before we can conduct some interesting time series analysis. One question that typically comes up, is that of time stamp formatting. In particular, how does **xts** know what time is specified by an arbitrary string? In one of the previous examples we used the as.xts() command to convert a matrix into an **xts** object. The function knew that the row names should be used as a time index, and it also figured out that 2007-01-04 meant yyyy-mm-dd (four digit year - two digit month - two digit day). What if the time stamp had been provided as 04012007 or 01-04-2007 or even 2007/01/04? In most cases, the user has to specify what format the time index is in.

Here is an example that illustrates this point:

```
# Create a vector of 10 fictitious stock prices along with
# a time index in microsecond resolution.
price_vector <- c(101.02, 101.03, 101.03, 101.04, 101.05,
  101.03, 101.02, 101.01, 101.00, 100.99)

dates <- c("03/12/2013 08:00:00.532123",
  "03/12/2013 08:00:01.982333",
  "03/12/2013 08:00:01.650321",
  "03/12/2013 08:00:02.402321",
  "03/12/2013 08:00:02.540432",
  "03/12/2013 08:00:03.004554",
  "03/12/2013 08:00:03.900213",
  "03/12/2013 08:00:04.050323",
  "03/12/2013 08:00:04.430345",
  "03/12/2013 08:00:05.700123")

# Allow the R console to display the microsecond field
options(digits.secs = 6)

# Create the time index with the correct format
time_index <- strptime(dates, format = "%d/%m/%Y %H:%M:%OS")

# Pass the time index into the its object
xts_price_vector <- xts(price_vector, time_index)
```

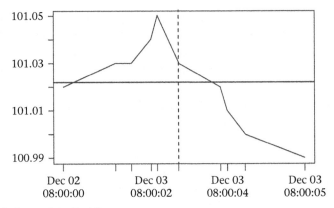

Figure 3.8 An **xts** plot with ablines.

The options(digits.secs) command controls the maximum number of dig-its to print on the screen when formatting time values in seconds. This will ensure that the microseconds in the time stamp show up when the xts_price_vector is referenced in the console. The strptime() function takes a string or a vector of strings as an input and converts them into the specified format. One important thing to keep in mind is that the specified time stamp has microsecond resolution. Therefore, a %OS symbol, and not %S (seconds), is required at the end of the time format. The documentation on ?strptime includes specific formatting details.

Given a perfectly valid **xts** time series object, we can plot it and also add some vertical and horizontal lines as we have done before. The vertical line can now be indexed by the time stamp. The only tricky part with the vertical line is that we have to define what format the time stamp is in. This can be done via the as.POSIXct() function.

```
# Plot the price of the fictitious stock
plot(xts_price_vector, main = "Fictitious price series",
  cex.main = 0.8)

# Add a horizontal line where the mean value is
abline(h = mean(xts_price_vector), lwd = 2)

# Add a vertical blue line at a specified time stamp
my_time <- as.POSIXct("03/12/2013 08:00:03.004554",
  format = "%d/%m/%Y %H:%M:%OS")

abline(v = my_time, lwd = 2, lty = 2)
```

So what is this POSIXct thing? It is a wrapper that converts a date-time object into the POSIX format I alluded to earlier. There exist quite a few packages in R that implement date and time constructs.[12]

To extract the data component of the price vector, we can use the `coredata()` command. The following example looks at manipulating the time index directly. To motivate this example, we will create a nonhomogeneous time series. Nonhomogeneity in time is something that is encountered a lot in practice. Important events tend to arrive at irregular time intervals. Take, for example, a subset of trades on the S&P 500 E-mini (ES) futures contract within a specified time interval. It might look something like this:

```
es_price <- c(1700.00, 1700.25, 1700.50, 1700.00, 1700.75,
   1701.25, 1701.25, 1701.25, 1700.75, 1700.50)

es_time   <- c("09/12/2013 08:00:00.532123",
   "09/12/2013 08:00:01.982333",
   "09/12/2013 08:00:05.650321",
   "09/12/2013 08:10:02.402321",
   "09/12/2013 08:12:02.540432",
   "09/12/2013 08:12:03.004554",
   "09/12/2013 08:14:03.900213",
   "09/12/2013 08:15:07.090323",
   "09/12/2013 08:16:04.430345",
   "09/12/2013 08:18:05.700123")

# create an xts time series object
xts_es <- xts(es_price, as.POSIXct(es_time,
   format = "%d/%m/%Y %H:%M:%OS"))

names(xts_es) <- c("price")
```

One metric of interest that comes up in high-frequency trading is the trade order-arrival rate. We can explore this metric by looking at the successive differences in time stamps between trades. The `difftime()` function computes the time difference between two date-time objects. This example sets the time unit explicitly to seconds. The default setting also happens to be the same.

```
time_diff <- difftime(index(xts_es)[2], index(xts_es)[1],
   units = "secs")

time_diff
## Time difference of 1.45021 secs
```

We can create a loop that will go through all the pairs and then store the results in a vector.

```
diffs <- c()
```

```
for(i in 2:length(index(xts_es))) {
  diffs[i] <- difftime(index(xts_es)[i], index(xts_es)[i - 1],
    units = "secs")
}
```

This will certainly work, but it is not the optimal way to obtain the answer. Here is a vectorized solution:

```
diffs <- index(xts_es)[-1] - index(xts_es)[-length(index(xts_e
```

```
diffs
## Time differences in secs
## [1]    1.4502099    3.6679881 596.7520001
## [4] 120.1381109    0.4641221 120.8956590
## [7]   63.1901100   57.3400221 121.2697780
## attr(,"tzone")
```

```
class(diffs)
## [1] "difftime"
```

The above line of code can further be optimized by calling the `index()` function once instead of three times.

```
es_times <- index(xts_es)
diffs <- es_times[-1] - es_times[-length(es_times)]
```

```
diffs
## Time differences in secs
## [1]    1.4502099    3.6679881 596.7520001
## [4] 120.1381109    0.4641221 120.8956590
## [7]   63.1901100   57.3400221 121.2697780
## attr(,"tzone")
```

We can also generate a graphical representation of the the time differences between consecutive trades for our fictitious ES future time series.

```
par(mfrow = c(2, 1))
diffs <- as.numeric(diffs)
plot(diffs, main = "Time difference in seconds for ES trades",
  xlab = "", ylab = "Time differences",
  cex.lab = 0.8,
  cex.main = 0.8)
grid()

hist(diffs, main = "Time difference in seconds for ES trades",
```

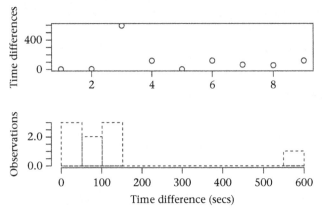

Figure 3.9 Plots of time differences between trades.

	AAPL.Open	AAPL.High	AAPL.Low	AAPL.Close	AAPL.Volume	AAPL.Adjusted
2007-01-03	86.29	86.58	81.90	83.80	44225700	80.54
2007-01-04	84.05	85.95	83.82	85.66	30259300	82.33
2007-01-05	85.77	86.20	84.40	85.05	29812200	81.75
2007-01-08	85.96	86.53	85.28	85.47	28468100	82.15
2007-01-09	86.45	92.98	85.15	92.57	119617800	88.97
2007-01-10	94.75	97.80	93.45	97.00	105460000	93.23

Figure 3.10 AAPL data from **quantmod**.

```
   xlab = "Time difference (secs)", ylab = "Observations",
   breaks = 20,
   cex.lab = 0.8,
   cex.main = 0.8)
grid()
```

Using the quantmod package

The **quantmod** package provides online and offline access to financial data in **xts** format. It also provides facilities for creating intricate graphs tailored to financial data.

Here is how we can extract some Apple stock data from Yahoo.

```
# Load the quantmod packages after installing it locally.
library(quantmod)
AAPL <- getSymbols("AAPL", auto.assign=FALSE)

head(AAPL)
```

AAPL is a now an **xts** object that contains open, high, low, close, volume, and adjusted-price data.

The `auto.assign` parameter allows for the returned object to be stored in a local variable rather than the R session's `.GlobalEnv`. Some of the other arguments to `getSymbols()` are: `src`, `time`, and `verbose`.

The `src` argument specifies the source of the input data. It can be set to extract information from sources such as:

- Yahoo
- Google
- Fred
- Oanda
- mysql
- .csv files

The time argument can be of the form "2011/" or "2010-08-09::2010-08-12".

Charting with quantmod

The `chartSeries` function can be directly applied to an **xts** object with open, high, low, and close data. There are many arguments to `chartSeries` that can assist in the further customization of a chart. As usual, we can reference `?chartSeries` for more information. Using our previously created AAPL object, this is what the function outputs:

```
# Adding some technical indicators on top of the original plot
chartSeries(AAPL, subset='2010::2010-04',
    theme = chartTheme('white'),
    TA = "addVo(); addBBands()")
```

The `reChart()` function can be used to update the original chart without specifying the full set of arguments:

```
reChart(subset='2009-01-01::2009-03-03')
```

The **quantmod** package exposes a range of technical indicators that can seamlessly be added on top of any chart. These technical indicators reside within the **TTR** package that was authored by Josh Ulrich [59]. **TTR** is one of those dependencies that is automatically loaded during the **quantmod** installation process.

```
chartSeries(AAPL, subset='2011::2012',
    theme = chartTheme('white'),
    TA = "addBBands(); addDEMA()")
```

Technical indicators can also be invoked after the chart has been drawn by using

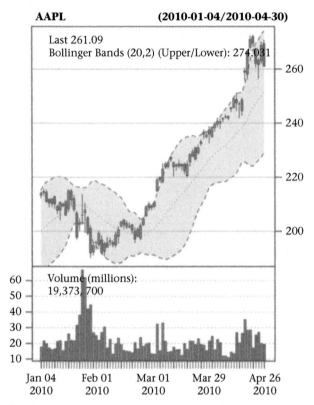

Figure 3.11 Chartseries of stock prices with indicators.

```
addVo()
addDPO()
```

Two more functions that are definitely worth exploring are `addTA()` and `newTA()`. These allow the creation of custom indicators that can be rendered in a subchart or overlaid onto the main plot.

In this next example, we will plot the price of AAPL without any technical indicators, and then we will create a custom indicator that uses the close price of the stock. The custom indicator simply adds 90 to the existing price. One can, of course, use this method to create arbitrarily complex indicators.

```
# Initial chart plot with no indicators
chartSeries(AAPL, theme = chartTheme('white'), TA = NULL)

# Custom function creation
my_indicator <- function(x) {
    return(x + 90)
}
```

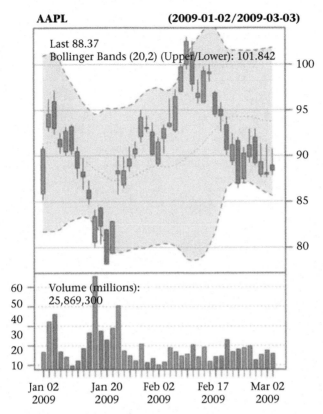

Figure 3.12 Chartseries of stock prices with indicators recharted.

```
add_my_indicator <- newTA(FUN = my_indicator, preFUN=Cl,
  legend.name = "My Fancy Indicator", on = 1)

add_my_indicator()
```

Graphing with ggplot2

Another useful set of graphing functionality is provided by **ggplot2** [40]. This package was also written by Hadley Wickham and is one of the most popular R packages to date. The **ggplot2** package is inspired by the *Grammar of Graphics.*[13]

In order to illustrate some of the functionality of **ggplot2**, we will create a plot of the volume distribution of AAPL for varying levels of percentage returns:

```
# Create a matrix with price and volume
df <- AAPL[, c("AAPL.Adjusted", "AAPL.Volume")]
names(df) <- c("price", "volume")
```

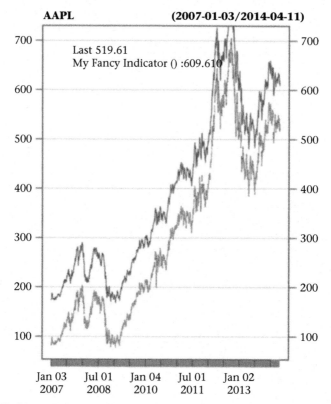

Figure 3.13 Chartseries of stock prices with custom indicator.

	price	volume	return	cuts	means
2007-01-04	82.33	30259300	0.0219816.6	2	29516561
2007-01-05	81.75	29812200	-0.007069752	1	19686094
2007-01-08	82.15	28468100	0.004881035	1	19686094
2007-01-09	88.97	119617800	0.079752390	3	45805683
2007-01-10	93.23	105460000	0.46770324	3	45805683
2007-01-11	92.08	51437600	-0.012411794	1	19686094

Figure 3.14 Cuts applied to a vector.

```
# Create
df$return <- diff(log(df[, 1]))
df <- df[-1, ]
```

Next, we will use the cut() function to create buckets of returns. We are specifically interested in the magnitude of the returns. A total of three buckets will be used for this demonstration:

```
df$cuts <- cut(abs(df$return),
```

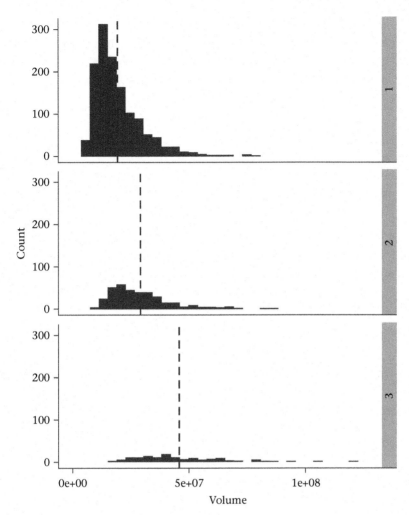

Figure 3.15 Volume profile with **ggplot2**.

```
  breaks = c(0, 0.02, 0.04, 0.25),
  include.lowest = TRUE)

# Create another column for the mean
df$means <- NA

for(i in 1:3) {
  group <- which(df$cuts == i)
  if(length(group) > 0) {
    df$means[group] <- mean(df$volume[group])
  }
}
```

Figure 4.13 displays the contents of our object `df`.

Buckets labeled as 1, group together the lowest returns, whereas buckets with the value of 3, include the highest returns. All other returns fall somewhere in-between. We want to graph the distribution of the volume for each of these buckets.

```
# Load ggplot2
library(ggplot2)
ggplot(df) +
geom_histogram(aes(x=volume)) +
facet_grid(cuts ~ .) +
geom_vline(aes(xintercept=means), linetype="dashed", size=1)
```

Upon initial inspection, **ggplot2** syntax can appear somewhat confusing. The `aes()` attribute specifies the aesthetics of how the data will be rendered on the x or y axis. The `geom` idiom defines the type of plot to be displayed. The + operator is used to concatenate the layers together into a coherent graph.

A great resource on all things **ggplot2** is the book by Hadley Wickham titled *ggplot2: Elegant Graphics for Data Analysis [40]*.

Summary

This chapter is devoted to some of the data-processing tasks that an R user might encounter on a daily basis. Various ways of importing financial price information into the R environment are explored, and the use of the popular file formats (.csv, .xml, .xls, .yaml. json) are explained. A few examples on accessing data from a relational database are also provided. The very important **xts** package is introduced, along with ample examples on time-based indexing. The excellent **dplyr** package is applied to a data munging example and typical use cases are given for the **quantmod** and **ggplot2** packages.

4 | Basic Statistics and Probability

We now know how to convert raw time series data into **xts** objects, how to use **quantmod** to retrieve data from local and remote repos, and how to create basic visualizations with **ggplot2**. The next logical step is to start looking for patterns in the data that might reveal exploitable trading opportunities. This course of action inevitably leads us to ask questions about the statistical nature of financial time series.

This chapter covers the basics of statistical analysis and attempts to demystify some of the statistical parlance.

What is a statistic?

From a practical, nonrigorous viewpoint, we can think of a statistic as a function (formula) that operates on a set of numbers. As an example, the formula for the arithmetic mean of N numbers is $\mu = \sum_{i=1}^{N} X_i/N$. The arithmetic mean is most certainly a statistic since it satisfies our basic definition. Another statistic might be $W = \prod_{i=1}^{N} X_i^2 \log(X_i)$. Once more, the formula is written out clearly, and the input is the set X_i. We have not said anything about the usefulness of the statistic at this point. Some familiar statistics include the *variance, standard deviation, kurtosis,* and *correlation.*

Population versus sample

Consider the set of numbers: 102, 103.2, 102, 101.2, 499, 103.2 101.23, 99.2. Here are some questions we might want to ask about these numbers:

1. Where do these numbers come from?
2. Are these all the numbers, or should we expect more to arrive?
3. Is there a predictable sequence present in the data?

One thing that becomes obvious based on the previous mental exercise, is that we need to make certain assumptions about the data, given limited information about its origin. If we knew that these were the only numbers present in our set, then we

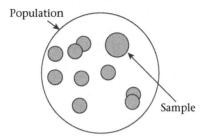

Figure 4.1 Population versus sample.

would say that we have access to the entire `population`. If the numbers were a sample from a larger set, then we would call this a `sample`.

Many times, it is not easy to tell whether we are working with sample or population data. When in doubt, it is safe to err on the side of assuming that the data at hand forms a `sample` set. Having access to all the data versus some of the data makes all the difference in the world. If, for example, we were tasked with figuring out the average height of all the mountains on earth, it would become straightforward to define the population as the heights of all the mountains on earth. A sample from this population would be a handful of these mountains. Picking samples from populations is a tricky matter.[1]

To answer the average mountain-height question conclusively, one would have to measure the height of every single mountain in the world. Even though we have access to the full population, it becomes prohibitively expensive to compute `statistics` on this data set. This is where samples come to the rescue. Properly chosen, unbiased samples will greatly assist us in answering questions about the population statistics we care about.

It helps to think of statistics as the mathematical machinery that transforms `sample` properties into `population` properties. This is an oversimplification, to say the least, but nevertheless, it provides a helpful heuristic to keep the basic concepts straight. By making a few assumptions about our underlying data, we can use sample average statistics to approximate population parameters. The number of observations we use and the method of selecting those observations will influence the outcome.

Intuitively, it makes sense that the more observations we place in our sample, the closer our sample average height will be to the true population average height. It also makes sense that the more samples of a given size we choose, the better our estimate for the true population average will become. Statisticians have given fancy names to these intuitive concepts. They are called the `Law of Large Numbers` and the `Central Limit Theorem` respectively [117, 126].

The example that follows will use R to generate 1,000,000 random numbers from a normal (Gaussian) distribution. This will be our population. Specifically, we will set the mean to be 2.33 and the standard deviation to 0.5. We will then extract

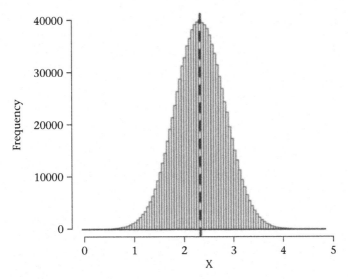

Figure 4.2 Gaussian population.

samples out of this population of varying size and compute the mean of each sample. The end result will be a plot of these sample means. Since we know exactly what the population mean is (we created it after all), the plot will help illustrate the convergence property of the **Law of Large Numbers.**

```
# Set the seed
set.seed(100)
X <- rnorm(1000000, mean = 2.33, sd = 0.5)
mu <- mean(X)
sd <- sd(X)
hist(X, breaks = 100)
abline(v = mu, lwd = 3, lty = 2)
```

The set.seed() function guarantees that we generate the same random numbers every time we use the same argument to the function:

```
set.seed(12)
rnorm(5)
## [1] -1.4805676  1.5771695 -0.9567445 -0.9200052 -1.9976421
```

Running rnorm(5) again without preceding it with set.seed(12) will produce a different set of numbers:

```
rnorm(5)
## [1] -0.2722960 -0.3153487 -0.6282552 -0.1064639  0.4280148
```

We will create three vectors of size 5, 10, and 50 from X:

```
sample5  <- sample(X, 5, replace = TRUE)
sample10 <- sample(X, 10, replace = TRUE)
sample50 <- sample(X, 50, replace = TRUE)


sample5
## [1] 2.497921 2.635927 2.291848 2.127974 2.268268

sample10
## [1] 2.064451 2.274464 2.468938 1.800007 2.557669
## [6] 2.535241 1.331020 1.159151 1.661762 2.285889

sample50
## [1] 2.581844 2.138331 3.003670 1.864148 2.049141
## [6] 2.808971 1.400057 2.527640 3.639216 3.311873

mean(sample5)
## [1] 2.364388

mean(sample10)
## 2.013859

mean(sample50)
## 2.447003

mean(sample(X, 1000, replace = TRUE))
## 2.323124

mean(sample(X, 10000, replace = TRUE))
## [1] 2.334109
```

Notice how the mean of samples with increasing size converges to the population mean.

Central Limit Theorem in R

This example will build on the previous one. This time, we will take repeated measurements from X, but we will keep the sample size the same:

```
mean_list <- list()
for(i in 1:10000) {
  mean_list[[i]] <- mean(sample(X, 10, replace = TRUE))
}

hist(unlist(mean_list), breaks = 500,
```

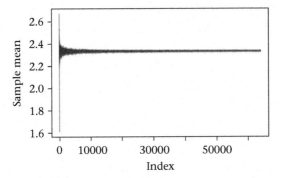

Figure 4.3 Convergence with large N.

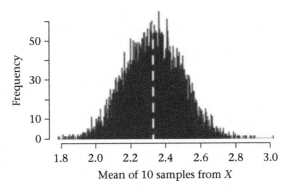

Figure 4.4 Convergence to a normal.

```
  xlab = "Mean of 10 samples from X",
  main = "Convergence of sample distribution",
  cex.main = 0.8)
abline(v = mu, lwd = 3, col = "white", lty = 2)
```

The distribution of the sample averages converges to a normal-looking distribution! To see how powerful the `Central Limit Theorem` is, consider a population that is highly nonnormal. We can create such a population by repeatedly picking either a 0 or a 1 with a 50 percent probability:

```
population <- sample(c(0, 1), 100000, replace = TRUE)
hist(population, main = "Non-normal", cex.main = 0.8)
abline(v = mean(population), lwd = 3, lty = 3)
```

By repeatedly extracting samples of size 10 from this highly nonnormal distribution, we still obtain a normal-looking distribution for the sample means:

```
mean_list <- list()
for(i in 1:10000) {
```

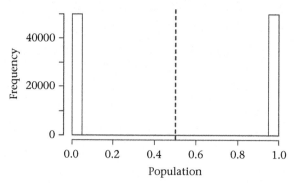

Figure 4.5 Nonnormal population.

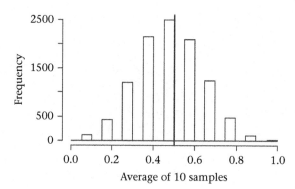

Figure 4.6 Nonnormal sample distribution.

```
   mean_list[[i]] <- mean(sample(population, 10, replace = TRUE
}
hist(unlist(mean_list), main = "Distribution of averages",
   cex.main = 0.8,
   xlab = "Average of 10 samples")
abline(v = 0.5, lwd = 3)
```

Unbiasedness and efficiency

Practitioners spend a lot of time asking questions about the properties of sample statistics, such as "How close is my sample statistic to the actual population statistic?" or "How many samples do I need in order to be very confident that my sample statistic is close to my population statistic?"

Good sample statistics should, ideally, have the following properties:

1. The expected value of the sample statistic should be equal to the true population statistic. The bias of an estimator is a number that captures this effect.

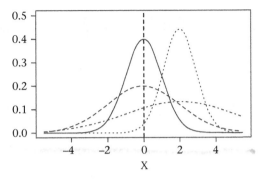

Figure 4.7 Bias versus efficiency.

2. The variance of the sample statistic should be as small as possible. This `efficiency` addresses this property.
3. The sample distribution should converge to the true population parameter as we increase the sample size. This is referred to as the `consistency` of an estimator.

The following illustration captures the difference between the bias and the efficiency of an estimator:

The true population parameter is 0. There are two distributions with an average that is equal to the population parameter. The one with the larger variance is unbiased and inefficient. The one with a lower variance is unbiased and efficient. Similarly, the other two displayed distributions are both biased (since their averages do not fall on the true parameter). One is more efficient than than other [123].

In one of our previous examples, we defined the population average as $\mu = \sum_{i=1}^{N} X_i/N$. Incidentally, the "best" sample estimator for the population average happens to be the sample average defined as: $\bar{x} = \sum_{i=1}^{n} X_i/n$, where $n < N$. In this case, the formulas are identical. Why does this happen to be the "best" estimator? Well, we can try to evaluate the first two criteria mentioned above and see for ourselves. What we want to show is that

$$E(\bar{x}) = \mu \tag{4.1}$$

Given the fact that the expectation operator is linear, we can pull the sum out of the E:

$$E(\bar{x}) = E\left(\frac{1}{N}\sum_{i=1}^{N} X_i\right)$$

$$= \frac{1}{N}E\left(\sum_{i=1}^{N} X_i\right) \tag{4.2}$$

$$= \frac{1}{N} \sum_{i=1}^{N} E(X_i)$$

$$= \frac{N\mu}{N} = \mu$$

A classic example that illustrates the bias of an estimator is that of the variance statistic. We can proceed as before and create an entire population of known mean μ and variance σ. By definition, the variance of a population is

$$\sigma^2 = \frac{\sum_{i=1}^{N}(X_i - \mu)^2}{N} \tag{4.3}$$

This next function computes the variance:

```
# Formula for population variance
population_variance <- function(x) {
  mean <- sum(x) / length(x)
  return(sum((x - mean) ^ 2) / length(x))
}

# Create a population
population <- as.numeric(1:100000)
variance <- population_variance(population)

variance
## [1] 833333333
```

What happens when we use the same formula on repeated samples from this population? We will call the population_variance() function repeatedly with a sample size set to 100.

```
output <- list()
for(i in 1:1000) {
   output[[i]] <- population_variance(sample(population,
   10, replace = TRUE))
}

variance_estimates <- unlist(output)
hist(variance_estimates, breaks = 100, cex.main = 0.9)
average_variance <- mean(variance_estimates)
abline(v = average_variance, , lty = 2, lwd = 2)
abline(v = variance, lwd = 2)
```

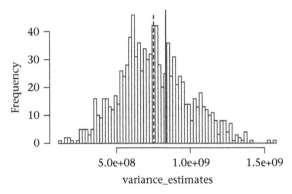

Figure 4.8 Estimating variance.

```
average_variance
## [1] 738123625
```

What happens when we use a sample statistic formula that is different from the population statistic formula? Will that distribution's mean be "closer" to the true variance? In other words, can we make the estimator less biased? The answer is yes, and the sample statistic formula to use is the following:

$$s^2 = \frac{\sum_i^N (X_i - \mu)^2}{N-1} \tag{4.4}$$

```
# Formula for unbiased variance estimator
sample_variance <- function(x) {
  mean <- sum(x) / length(x)
  return(sum((x - mean) ^ 2) / (length(x) - 1))
}

output <- list()
for( i in 1:1000 ) {
    output[[i]] <- sample_variance(sample(population,
    10, replace = TRUE))
}

sample_variance_estimates <- unlist(output)
average_sample_variance <- mean(sample_variance_estimates)

average_sample_variance
## [1] 836184961
```

This new formula with the $N - 1$ in the denominator seems to approximate the actual variance better than the population variance formula. It is certainly true that

836184961 is closer to 833333333 than is 738123625. But is this an artifact of our simulation? It turns out we can prove that this result holds true mathematically.

$$
\begin{aligned}
E[s^2_{biased}] &= E\left[\frac{1}{N}\sum_{i=1}^{N}(x_i - \bar{x})^2\right] = E\left[\frac{1}{N}\sum_{i=1}^{N}\left(x_i - \frac{1}{N}\sum_{j=1}^{N}x_j\right)^2\right] \\
&= \frac{1}{N}\sum_{i=1}^{N}E\left[x_i^2 - \frac{2}{N}x_i\sum_{j=1}^{N}x_j + \frac{1}{N^2}\sum_{j=1}^{N}x_j\sum_{k=1}^{N}x_k\right] \\
&= \frac{1}{N}\sum_{i=1}^{N}\left[\frac{N-2}{N}E[x_i^2] - \frac{2}{N}\sum_{j\neq i}E[x_ix_j] + \frac{1}{N^2}\sum_{j=1}^{N}\sum_{k\neq j}E[x_jx_k] + \frac{1}{N^2}\sum_{j=1}^{N}E[x_j^2]\right] \\
&= \frac{1}{N}\sum_{i=1}^{N}\left[\frac{N-2}{N}(\sigma^2+\mu^2) - \frac{2}{N}(N-1)\mu^2 + \frac{1}{N^2}N(N-1)\mu^2 + \frac{1}{N}(\sigma^2+\mu^2)\right] \\
&= \frac{N-1}{N}\sigma^2
\end{aligned}
\tag{4.5}
$$

By using $N-1$ in the denominator instead of the N, we eliminate the extra multiplicative term $\frac{N-1}{N}$.

$$
E[s^2] = E\left[\frac{1}{N-1}\sum_{i=1}^{N}(x_i - \bar{x})^2\right] = \sigma^2
\tag{4.6}
$$

We can reason that the $N-1$ term in the denominator serves to boost the numerical result enough to compensate for the degree of freedom[2] we give up in order to estimate the sample average that also happens to be present in the same formula. The above is an explanation that is often encountered in introductory statistics textbooks. It might help with simple examples, but when things get more complicated, this heuristic goes out the window. Consider the unbiased estimator of the population standard deviation. Here is a hint: it is not the square root of the unbiased variance estimator.

$$
s \neq \sqrt{\frac{\sum_i^N (X_i - \mu)^2}{N-1}}
\tag{4.7}
$$

The correct, unbiased standard deviation statistic for a normally distributed population is

$$
s = \frac{\sqrt{\frac{\sum_i^N (X_i - \mu)^2}{N-1}}}{c_4}
\tag{4.8}
$$

The formula for the correction factor c_4 is given by

$$c_4 = \sqrt{\frac{2}{N-1}} \frac{\Gamma\left(\frac{N}{2}\right)}{\Gamma\left(\frac{N-1}{2}\right)} \tag{4.9}$$

This formula is a consequence of Jensen's Inequality[3] and the definition of the expectation operator. Γ is the known gamma function given by

$$\Gamma(t) = \int_0^\infty x^{t-1} e^{-x} dx \tag{4.10}$$

Gamma

For positive integers N, the gamma function becomes

$$\Gamma(N) = (N-1)! \tag{4.11}$$

So far we have only investigated the bias of a statistical estimator. Bias can be expressed as $Bias(\hat{\theta}) = E(\hat{\theta}) - \theta$. Efficiency, $Var(\hat{\theta})$, of an estimator is also an important figure of merit, specifically, in the context of defining the Mean Square Error (MSE). The MSE is a measure of how accurate our estimator is. It can be shown that the MSE of a statistic $\hat{\theta}$ can be decomposed into the statistic's variance (efficiency) and bias [38].

$$MSE_{\hat{\theta}} = E(||\hat{\theta} - \theta||^2) = E\left(\sum_{i=1}^N \left(\hat{\theta}_i - \theta_i\right)^2\right) \tag{4.12}$$

Mean Square Error

$$= Var(\hat{\theta}) + Bias(\hat{\theta})^2$$

The above formulation is referred to as the bias-variance decomposition, and it shows us that for a given mean squared error, there is always a compromise between the bias and the variance. We also notice that the MSE of an unbiased estimator ($Bias(\hat{\theta}) = 0$) is simply the variance of the estimator $Var(\hat{\theta})$.

Consistency is another one of those properties that we would like our estimators to have. A consistent estimator is one in which its bias and variance approach 0 as the sample size approaches infinity. Consider the following graph. Notice how for small sample sizes, the sampling distribution is centered away from the true parameter θ. As the sample size increases, the mean of the distribution converges to the true parameter value and the variance of the distribution approaches zero. When the sample size N is equal to the total population, then there is no uncertainty left.

Why do we as quant/traders care about the concepts of bias, efficiency, and consistency? When we start thinking about how to develop models for a trading strategy, we will inevitably be faced with the task of estimating parameters for those models based on observable data. We will have to make assumptions about the

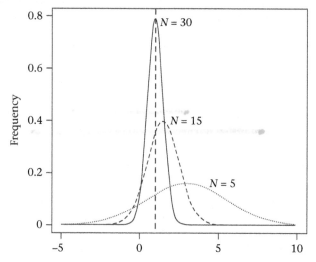

Figure 4.9 Estimator consistency.

data itself, as well as the parameters we are trying to fit. Coming up with relevant statistics to use as proxies for the hypothetical global parameters then becomes and important task. To solidify this point, consider the following scenario:

Say we have a market-making strategy in mind which, among other things, dynamically adjusts the amount of inventory it is willing to hold based on the current realized volatility of the market. How do we determine what the current realized volatility of the market is based on the recent observable market data? One way is to start off by making an assumption that an underlying mechanism exists that generates the observable prices, say, for example, a model such as the following one:[4]

$$\frac{dS}{S} = \sigma \, dW_t \tag{4.13}$$

This is a model with effectively one unknown parameter: the instantaneous variance σ^2. Consider this as the population parameter we want to estimate. Can we come up with estimators $\hat{\sigma}^2$ that will do a good job of nailing the true σ^2? All we have to go on is the recent price history of the financial instrument. It turns out that there are many proposals for such estimators. Some of the more popular ones go by the following names:

- Parkinson Estimator
- Yang Estimator
- Garman-Klass Estimator

The details of their derivation and statistical properties are beyond the scope of this book. Suffice it to say that they all attempt to balance bias and variance while

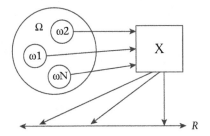

Figure 4.10 Random variable as a mapping.

keeping computational tractability in mind. A survey of these estimators can be found in the endnotes.[5]

Probability basics

`Probability Theory` is a branch of mathematics that attempts to quantify the uncertainty inherent in events. The concept of a probability is used as a proxy for uncertainty. We can think of a probability as a number between 0 and 1 that expresses the likelihood of a particular event occurring. The whole trick lies in being able to map uncertainties into probabilities. The laws of probability then take over and work with these probabilities to produce useful results. Here are some more definitions to keep in mind. These will not be rigorous definitions in the mathematical sense. However, they will serve to convey the important concepts of probability theory.

We can loosely define an `experiment` as a method of collecting data from some random process. A `sample space` is then the set of all possible outcomes of such an `experiment`. In this context, the word `sample` has a completely different meaning than what we saw in the previous discussion related to sample statistics.

If, for example, we define our experiment as the tossing of a coin, then the sample space is the set {Head, Tail}. If the experiment is defined as the tossing of two coins, then the sample space is the set {{Head, Head}, {Head, Tail}, {Tail, Head}, {Tail, Tail}}. If the experiment is the generation of stock prices, then the sample space can be thought of as all the possible real numbers in the interval $[0, \infty)$. It is certainly conceivable for the price of a given stock to drop to zero. It is also conceivable, albeit less likely, that the price of Google can go to $10,000,000 per share.

Random variables

A random variable is a mapping from the elements of a `sample space` into a real number. The following diagram illustrates this point:

It is typical to denote `random variables` with capital letters. The sample space itself is usually denoted by the capital Greek letter omega (Ω). An element of this sample space is denoted by the lower case omega (ω). In mathematical notation: $X(\omega) = r$ where $r \in R$.

For our single die-tossing experiment, we can define a random variable as

$$X(Head) = 32$$
$$X(Tail) = 65.2 \tag{4.14}$$

Why 32 and 65.2? Why not? There is nothing in the definition of a random variable that tells us what real numbers to assign to the right hand side. For the purpose of solving certain problems, though, it makes more sense to use specific numbers. Here is a mapping that might be more intuitive:

$$X(Head) = 1$$
$$X(Tail) = 0 \tag{4.15}$$

Yet another plausible alternative is the following:

$$X(Head) = 1$$
$$X(Tail) = -1 \tag{4.16}$$

What about the stock price process? What kind of mapping makes sense there? Since the sample space of possible stock prices is already comprised of real positive numbers, we can just use those as the mapping.

$$X(100.0) = 100.0$$
$$X(120.32) = 120.32$$
$$\cdots \tag{4.17}$$
$$X(\omega) = \omega$$

Probabilities

Next, we need to talk about probabilities. One can think of these as weights that we can assign to every occurrence of a random variable. A probability is a measure of the likelihood of a certain event occurring. Probabilities can take on any real value between zero and one. A probability of zero means that an event has absolutely no chance of occurring, whereas a probability of one implies that the event will most certainly occur.

For a more formal setting, we can consider the three fundamental properties that a probability needs to have according to Kolmogorov [63, 134].

1. E is an event in the sample space Ω, and its probability is a real number that is greater than or equal to zero.

$$P(E) \in R, P(E) \geq 0 \tag{4.18}$$

2. The sum of all the events in a sample space is equal to one.

$$P(\Omega) = 1 \tag{4.19}$$

3. For any set of mutually exclusive events, the total probability of the union of these events is equal to the sum of the individual event probabilities:

$$P(E_1 \cup E_2 \cup ... \cup E_N) = \sum_{i=1}^{N} P(E_i) \tag{4.20}$$

Probability distributions

A probability distribution is a function that assigns a probability to the outcome of a random variable. For random variables that take on discrete values, we use probability mass functions to denote the probabilities on the y-axis and the values of the random variable on the x-axis. Here is what a probability mass function looks like for the random variable that describes the single coin tossing experiment:

$$P(Head) = P(X = 1) = 0.5$$
$$P(Tail) = P(X = -1) = 0.5 \tag{4.21}$$

```
plot(c(-1, 1), c(0.5, 0.5), type = "h", lwd = 3,
    xlim = c(-2, 2), main = "Probability mass function of coin
    toss",
    ylab = "Probability",
    xlab = "Random Variable",
    cex.main = 0.9)
```

The probability mass function hints at a fair coin, given that the probability of each occurrence is 0.5. It also has the important property that the probabilities sum to one.

$$P(X = 1) + P(X = -1) = 1 \tag{4.22}$$

The notion of a probability mass function is only applicable to discrete distributions. For continuous distributions, defining a single probability for a real number

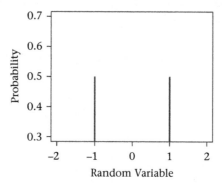

Figure 4.11 Coin toss mass function.

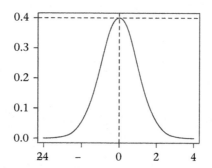

Figure 4.12 The normal distribution.

does not make sense since that number will always be zero. The workaround is to assign a probability to a range of values. One of the most important continuous probability distributions is the Gaussian. This probability density function has an area under the curve equal to one. Here is the mathematical formulation of this statement:

$$\int_{-\infty}^{\infty} \frac{1}{\sqrt{2\pi}} e^{-x^2} \, dx = 1 \tag{4.23}$$

It is interesting to note that the maximum of the normal distribution occurs at $x = 0$. A this point, $f(0) = \frac{1}{\sqrt{2\pi}}$. It is wrong, however, to say that $P(X = 0) = \frac{1}{\sqrt{2\pi}}$. The X random variable can take on any value from $-\infty$ to ∞. The probability of picking any one random X from this range is equal to 0. This is why $P(X = 0) = 0$. The following expression is more accurate: $P(X \leq 0) = 0.5$. This says that the area under the graph from $-\infty$ to 0 is equal to 0.5

When plotting probability distributions in R, it is possible for the y-axis to obtain values greater than one. This is confusing to some since they think of the y-axis as an actual probability. For discrete random variables, this is true. For continuous, it is not. For continuous random variables, the area under the curve needs to be equal

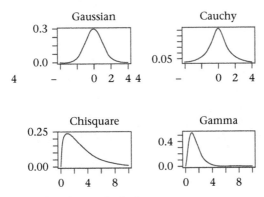

Figure 4.13 Examples of continuous distributions.

to one. Depending on the width of the bin used, the height adjusts in order to make the area equal to one.

The graphs of a few popular continuous distributions are illustrated below:

Bayes versus frequentist approach

Consider the coin-tossing experiment one more time. It is conceivable that a coin can also land on its edge when tossed. Furthermore, it is also conceivable that a coin can disappear into thin air prior to landing. We can certainly assign probabilities to these events as well. $P(X = Head) = 0.499$, $P(X = Tail) = 0.499$, $P(X = Edge) = 0.001$, $P(X = Disappears) = 0.001$. Despite the extremely rare occurrence of these edge cases, we still have to make sure that the total probabilities add up to 1. But how does one go about assigning probabilities to such events?

This is a highly subjective question with a highly subjective answer. Mathematicians have been arguing over this for hundreds of years, and we will not be exploring the nuances of these arguments here [135]. There are two schools of thought on the issue. The Frequentist approach defines a probability as the limit of its relative frequency after a large number of trials, whereas the Bayesian approach treats probabilities as malleable constructs based on the arrival of new data [115, 122].

In a Bayesian's mind, there is only data. The data shapes the probabilities, and not the other way around. The data implicitly sculpts the distribution of any parameters that might be used to fit a model of a particular phenomenon. The Baye's Rule provides a mechanism for updating such distributions. This rule can be expressed by the following equation:

$$P(Evidence|Data) = \frac{P(Data|Evidence)P(Evidence)}{P(Data)} \tag{4.24}$$

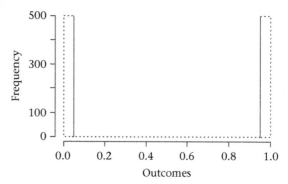

Figure 4.14 Coin flip density.

This formulation states that the probability of the evidence (our belief in the evidence) given some data is equal to the probability of the data given the evidence, multiplied by the probability of the evidence regardless of any data. The denominator in the equation is practically a scaling factor that makes the numbers work out. The mathematical terms for P(*Evidence*|*Data*) are the posterior distribution. The P(*Data*|*Evidence*) term is the likelihood function, and the P(Evidence) term is the prior distribution.

Simulations of coins

This next piece of R code simulates the tossing of a fair coin 1000 times. It generates a vector of 0's for supposed tails and a vector of 1's for heads. Notice the implicit mapping of the sample space {Head, Tail} to the numbers zero and one respectively. We will use this generated vector to get an estimate of the probabilities that are inherent in this experiment.

```
outcomes <- sample(c(0, 1), 1000, replace = TRUE)
```

Here is what a histogram of the outcomes looks like:
There are approximately 500 heads and 500 tails generated via the sample() function. A frequentist can claim that the probability one should assign to each event should be 500/1000 for heads and 500/1000 for tails. In effect, the number of observations for each side is divided by the total number of trials.

Next, let us consider an experiment that involves a biased coin. We will still use the sample() function, but we will override the default probabilities of {Heads} occurring.

```
set.seed(101)
biased_outcomes <- sample(c(0, 1), 1000,
    replace = TRUE, prob = c(0.4, 0.6))
```

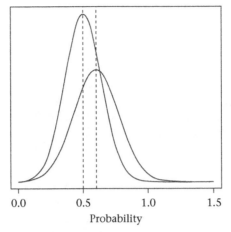

Figure 4.15 Bayesian prior to posterior.

Now, prior to obtaining any data, a Frequentist will make the claim that there is no way of defining the probability of a {Head} event occurring. Only after the data start coming in can the probability be estimated. On the other hand, a Bayesian starts off with an implicit assumption that the probability is somewhere in the 50 percent vicinity. This belief is expressed in terms of the prior distribution. The prior might even be different from that of a fair coin assumption. It depends on the Bayesian's mood and bias. The subtle difference here is that the Bayesian expresses an opinion prior to having seen any data, whereas the Frequentist does not. As data start to come in, both the Frequentist and the Bayesian will start to update their estimates on the probability of heads occurring. At the end of the run, the Frequentist will arrive at a point estimate of:

```
prob_estimate <- sum(biased_outcomes) /
    length(biased_outcomes)

prob_estimate
## [1] 0.603
```

The Bayesian prior will be modified as new information arrives. Eventually, its mean will converge to the true probability. The end result of this continuous updating process is a posterior distribution and not a point estimate. In the graph below, the mean shifts from 0.5 to 0.6. The variability in the posterior is a function of the variability in the prior and the characteristics of the data.

In the end, they both arrive at the same estimate for the probability of heads occurring. In many other estimation problems, however, the choice of prior can have a significant impact on the resulting parameter estimates.

A nice discussion on the Bayesian methodology as it pertains to the biased-coin example can be found here: http://www.win-vector.com/blog/2014/07/frequenstist-inference-only-seems-easy/.

On the use of RStan

This is an advanced topic, but one worth mentioning. In R it is possible to conduct a full Bayesian statistical inference by using the `Stan probabilistic language` [105]. The Stan project's main website can be found here: http://mc-stan.org/. Stan is multiteam collaboration from some of the top universities and institutions in the country. The project exposes very efficient MCMC sampling (Markov Chain Monte Carlo) and optimization routines that are written in C++. These algorithms are useful in Bayesian inference and luckily, there exists an R interface to Stan. The package is called **RStan**, and the installation instructions can be found here: https://github.com/stan-dev/rstan/wiki/RStan-Getting-Started. Note that **RStan** cannot be installed directly from CRAN. A C++ compiler is needed in order to compile the defined probabilistic models that Stan specifies. Those interested in further exploring Bayesian analysis and modeling techniques should definitely consider making **RStan** an integral part of their toolkit.

Summary

A nonrigorous overview of some useful and practical topics in introductory statistics and probability is provided in this chapter. A distinction is made between sample and population statistics, and the idea of a statistical estimator is presented. A general description of both the `Law of Large Numbers` and the `Central Limit Theorem` is provided along with R code examples that help demonstrate the concepts. The desirable properties of unbiasedness, efficiency, and consistency of statistical estimators are discussed, and the effects of these properties on their sampling distributions are illustrated. Lastly, the bias-variance decomposition of the MSE is explained, and the chapter ends with a brief mention of the Bayesian versus Frequentist interpretation of probability. The **RStan** package is also recommended to those advanced users who want to take their Bayesian analysis to the next level.

5 | Intermediate Statistics and Probability

This chapter will explore the statistical nature of stock prices and address the topics of stationarity, normality, and autocorrelation of stock returns. These are important concepts that will enable us to perform statistical inference[1] and pave the way for the construction of trading strategies.

Random process

In order to fit a model to data, we have to come up with a model. We will make the assumption that stock prices are generated by some type of `random process`. A random process, also known as a stochastic process, is a collection of random variables indexed by time. Some examples include

- the number of daily meteor strikes in the upper atmosphere,
- the average quantity per minute of buy-orders that arrive at an exchange's matching engine,
- bid-price updates of the S&P 500 E-mini contract every time a change in the top-of-book occurs,
- the daily closing price of IWM,
- the percentage return of GOOG on an hourly basis.

It helps to think of such a random process as a black box, the internal workings of which are not exposed to the observer. The only thing that the observer sees is a numerical output at a given point in time.

The collection $X_1, X_2, X_3, \ldots, X_N$, then, is a random process since every value is indexed by time. It is important to note that the time does not need to be in predefined discrete intervals. All that is required is that a value of the random process be accompanied by an increasing time index.

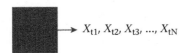

Figure 5.1 Random process.

From a quant's perspective, one of the ultimate goals is to be able to say something meaningful about the internal workings of the black box (random process) given only the output observations $X_1, X_2, X_3, \ldots, X_N$. This is not an easy problem by any means. Conceptually, if we knew the parameters the black box was using to generate today's stock prices, we could use this information to predict tomorrow's values. In reality, there is no single deterministic mechanism that generates stock prices or any other prices for that matter (interest rates, option quotes, bond prices, etc.) And even if such a mechanism did exist, it would probably be extremely complex and time-varying.

Reality, however, should not stop us from trying to use some of our math and programming tools to answer specific questions about the markets. It is the author's belief that even a simple model that is calibrated often, will do a decent job of approximating a more complex process. Instead of relying on a complex model to describe market events, it would be more beneficial to the quant/trader to use simpler techniques, but revisit those techniques and answers frequently. This requires that the practitioner have a solid grasp of the limitations of the simple model, as well as an understanding of the points of failure.

In order to fit the apparently complex market mechanics into our statistical framework, we have to make a few simplifying assumptions:

1. There exists a random process that we can model. This random process generates random variables we can record and analyze (prices, returns, and volumes).
2. The parameters of this random process are non time-varying for the most part.

Stock price distributions

We know from experience that stock prices cannot be negative, and we also know that they can theoretically go to infinity. The theoretical probability distribution should be capped at zero, and have tails that never touch the x-axis on the right-hand side. As a reminder, the reason why we concern ourselves with the probability distribution of stock prices is because we ideally want to ask questions of the form: what is the probability that the SPY ETF will have a closing price greater than $210 by tomorrow?

This next graph displays the histogram of prices for all the price history we have available in-memory. The mean and standard deviation of these prices are also computed and displayed on the graph:

```
# Extract prices and compute statistics
prices <- SPY$SPY.Adjusted
mean_prices <- round(mean(prices), 2)
sd_prices <- round(sd(prices), 2)

# Plot the histogram along with a legend
hist(prices, breaks = 100, prob=T, cex.main = 0.9)
```

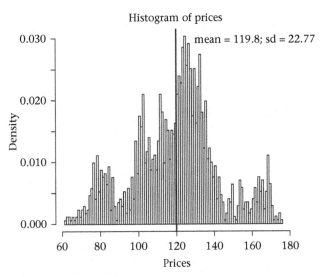

Figure 5.2 Price distribution.

```
abline(v = mean_prices, lwd = 2)
legend("topright", cex = 0.8, border = NULL, bty = "n",
  paste("mean=", mean_prices, "; sd=", sd_prices))
```

We can take a look at a similar price distribution, but this time, over a different time range. Before we move on, though, and in order to make our lives easier, we can encapsulate the above code into a function and run it multiple times with different date ranges. Here is the function definition:

```
plot_4_ranges <- function(data, start_date, end_date, title){

  # Set the plot window to be 2 rows and 2 columns
  par(mfrow = c(2, 2))

  for(i in 1:4) {
    # Create a string with the appropriate date range
    range <- paste(start_date[i], "::", end_date[i], sep = ""

    # Create the price vector and necessary statistics
    time_series <- data[range]

    mean_data <- round(mean(time_series, na.rm = TRUE), 3)
    sd_data <- round(sd(time_series, na.rm = TRUE), 3)

    # Plot the histogram along with a legend
    hist_title <- paste(title, range)
```

SPY prices for: 2007-01-01::2008-06-05   SPY prices for: 2008-06-06::2009-09-09

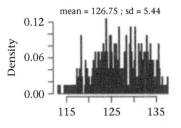

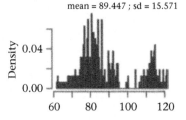

SPY prices for: 2009-10-10::201012-30   SPY prices for: 2011-03-03::2013-01-06

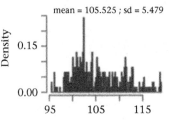

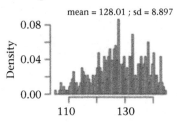

Figure 5.3 Four price distributions.

```
    hist(time_series, breaks = 100, prob=TRUE,
      xlab = "", main = hist_title, cex.main = 0.8)
    legend("topright", cex = 0.7, bty = 'n',
      paste("mean=", mean_data, "; sd=", sd_data))
  }

  # Reset the plot window
  par(mfrow = c(1, 1))
}
```

Having defined the function, we can now use it as follows:

```
# Define start and end dates of interest
begin_dates <- c("2007-01-01", "2008-06-06",
  "2009-10-10", "2011-03-03")
end_dates <- c("2008-06-05", "2009-09-09",
  "2010-12-30", "2013-01-06")

# Create plots
plot_4_ranges(prices, begin_dates,
  end_dates, "SPY prices for:")
```

One thing that becomes apparent from our plot is that the statistics we care about (mean and standard deviation) change with time. Different time ranges produce vastly different results. Over time, it appears that the price distribution of SPY is nonstationary.

Stationarity

A random process is called `strictly stationary` when the probability distribution of that process does not change shape and location with time. Consider a random process X_t indexed by time. The realization of this process is a time series that looks like $X_{t_1}, X_{t_2}, \ldots, X_{t_N}$. The equality in the equation below means that the distributions look the same. For strict stationarity,

$$X_{t_1}, X_{t_2}, \ldots, X_{t_N} = X_{t_1+\tau}, X_{t_2+\tau}, \ldots, X_{t_N+\tau} \tag{5.1}$$

Stationarity, in the strict sense, is rather difficult to come by in real life. In practice, we mostly care that at least the first few moments of the distribution are stationary. The mean and the covariance are two such moments.[2] This weaker form of stationarity is called `covariance stationary`, `weak-sense stationary`, or `second-order stationary`.

If the following hold, our process is covariance stationary:

$$E(X_t) = E(X_{t+\tau}) = \mu \tag{5.2}$$

and

$$cov(X_t, X_{t+\tau}) = f(\tau) \tag{5.3}$$

This second equation states that the covariance can be expressed as a function of only one parameter, namely τ.

Why do we care about stationarity? We care because in order to predict the future, we need to make the simplifying assumption that the future is going to look like the past. Imagine a black box that takes in a vector of closing price history and makes a prediction for what the next day's closing price is going to be. If the black box has never seen the recent price input before (say, during the calibration phase), how can it possibly draw any conclusions about what the future price will be? If, however, during the training phase, the new inputs are similar to the older inputs, then the black box has something to go on and can potentially make an educated guess on the future values. As a general rule, we want our inputs to any prediction algorithm to be stationary.

Financial price data are mostly `nonstationary`. In order to work with this information, it is important to make it stationary. There are a few ways to accomplish this. One way is to look at the price returns rather than the raw prices themselves. Another way is to form a cointegrated[3] spread where the inputs are nonstationary, but the combination is stationary.

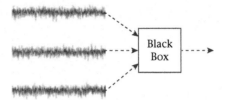

Figure 5.4 Stationary inputs to black box.

Here is a look at the same time ranges as before for the SPY stock. Rather than looking at prices though, we will investigate the natural logarithm of the successive price differences. This metric is known as the `log returns`. For small enough percentage returns, log returns provide a decent approximation. Mathematically, we can see this below:

$$R_t = \frac{P_t - P_{t-1}}{P_{t-1}}$$
$$= \frac{P_t}{P_{t-1}} - 1 \tag{5.4}$$

The Taylor expansion for $log(1+x)$ is

$$log(1+x) = x - \frac{x^2}{2} + \frac{x^3}{3} + O(x^4) \tag{5.5}$$

Consider what happens when x in the above equation is a small number:

$$log(1+x) \approx x \tag{5.6}$$

Substituting R_t for x gives us $log(1+R_t) \approx R_t$.

$$= log\left(1 + \frac{P_t}{P_{t-1}} - 1\right) \approx R_t$$
$$= log\left(\frac{P_t}{P_{t-1}}\right) = log(P_t) - log(P_{t-1}) \approx R_t \tag{5.7}$$

Why do we concern ourselves with the log difference of prices when we can just use regular old-fashioned returns? This is mostly due to the nice mathematical properties that log-prices have. We will soon see that percentage returns can be simplistically modeled as having a normal distribution, given that prices themselves follow a log-normal distribution.

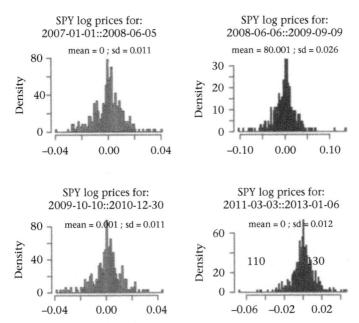

Figure 5.5 Stationary return distributions.

```
# Compute log returns
returns <- diff(log(prices))

# Use the same function as before to plot returns rather
than prices
plot_4_ranges(returns, begin_dates, end_dates, "SPY log
prices for:")
```

The means in the charts above appear to be close to zero, and the standard deviations are similar in value. From a preliminary visual inspection, we can conclude that the distribution of the returns is stationary, at least, in the first few moments of that distribution. We should keep in mind that this is by no means a sophisticated statistical analysis on the property of stationarity. There exist various statistical tests that attempt to answer the question of whether a particular distribution is stationary or not. A few of these tests go by the following names: KPSS unit root test, Elliot-Rothenberg Stock test, Augmented Dickey-Fuller (ADF) test, Phillips Peron test, Schmidt Phillips test, and Zivot Andrews test. A better explanation of these tests with implementations written in R can be found in Pfaff's book on cointegrated time series in R: quant.stackexchange.com/questions/2372/how-to-check-if-a-timeseries-is-stationary.

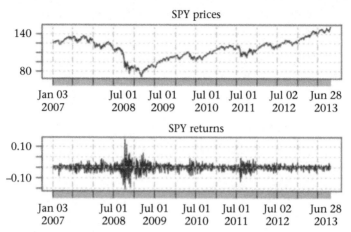

Figure 5.6 Stock prices and returns.

Determining stationarity with urca

The **urca** package can help us determine whether a hypothesized time series is indeed stationary or not. That is one of the use cases of **urca.** It is also used to model cointegration relationships between time series [4].

We will perform the stationarity test on the raw prices as well as the log returns of SPY.

Based on our previous discussion on the dynamics of prices and returns, we intuitively expect price distributions to be nonstationary. We also expect return distributions to be stationary.

There are multiple stationarity tests available in the literature. The **urca** package exposes a few of these to R users. The Kwiatkowski et al. Unit Root Test, or KPSS, is one such example. The idea behind KPSS is to assume a null hypothesis of stationarity around a deterministic trend. The resulting test statistic can then be compared against the critical values that this test outputs in order to either accept or reject the null hypothesis.

```
# Get SPY data and let's confirm that it is non-stationary
require(quantmod)
getSymbols("SPY")
spy <- SPY$SPY.Adjusted

# Use the default settings
require(urca)
test <- ur.kpss(as.numeric(spy))

# The output is an S4 object
class(test)
```

```
## [1] "ur.kpss"
## attr(,"package")
## [1] "urca"
```

```
# Extract the test statistic
test@teststat
## [1] 11.63543
```

```
# Look at the critical values
test@cval
##                  10pct  5pct 2.5pct  1pct
## critical values 0.347 0.463  0.574 0.739
```

The critical value is large enough that we can reject the null hypothesis that the time series is stationary. Can we say the same about the returns?

```
spy_returns <- diff(log(spy))
```

```
# Test on the returns
test_returns <- ur.kpss(as.numeric(spy_returns))
test_returns@teststat
## [1] 0.336143
```

```
test_returns@cval
##                  10pct  5pct 2.5pct  1pct
## critical values 0.347 0.463  0.574 0.739
```

We can barely reject the null at the 10 percent threshold in this case. How about subsetting the data to a period after January 2013, when things appear to be more calm?

```
test_post_2013 <- ur.kpss(as.numeric(spy_returns['2013::']))
test_post_2013@teststat
## [1] 0.06936672
```

Here we cannot reject the null hypothesis that we have a stationary time series.

Assumptions of normality

At this point, we will start to make simplifying assumptions about how prices and returns are distributed. Ignoring some of the obvious outliers and clustering of the returns during specific times, we will assume that the distribution of returns can safely be modeled as a Normal (Gaussian) distribution. Why? Because it will make the math easy.

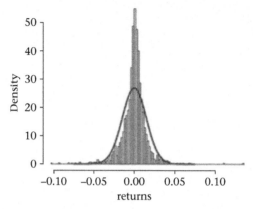

Figure 5.7 Normal histogram with density.

The formula for a Guassian distribution with a given mean μ and a standard deviation σ is

$$f(x) = \frac{1}{\sqrt{2\pi\sigma^2}} e^{\frac{(x-\mu)^2}{2\sigma}} \qquad (5.8)$$

We can try to superimpose such a normal distribution onto our empirical daily return data and see what that looks like. We start by generating random numbers that are normally distributed with the same mean and standard deviation as that of our stock returns. The two plots can then be superimposed via the following R code:

```
# Plot histogram and density
mu <- mean(returns, na.rm = TRUE)
sigma <- sd(returns, na.rm = TRUE)
x <- seq(-5 * sigma, 5 * sigma, length = nrow(returns))

hist(returns, breaks = 100,
  main = "Histogram of returns for SPY",
  cex.main = 0.8, prob=TRUE)
lines(x, dnorm(x, mu, sigma), col = "red", lwd = 2)
```

The dnorm() function creates a normal distribution given a range of x values, a mean, and a standard deviation. The lines() function creates a line plot on top of the existing histogram plot.

It becomes obvious from the plot that the data are not normally distributed. There appear to be more observations that fall around the 0 percent range. A normal distribution predicts fewer of these occurrences. There are also more outliers present in the tails of the distribution. We call such an empirical distribution a

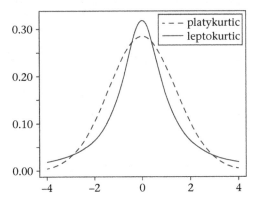

Figure 5.8 Leptokurtic and platykurtic.

leptokyrtic distribution. The word *lepto* comes from the Greek word for "thin". The opposite of *lepto* is the Greek word for "thick", *platy*.

Another way to visualize the difference between the empirical data at hand and a theoretical normal distribution is via the qqnorm() and qqline() functions. Using the same data as before

```
# Set plotting window
par(mfrow = c(1, 2))

# SPY data
qqnorm(as.numeric(returns),
  main = "SPY empirical returns qqplot()",
  cex.main = 0.8)
qqline(as.numeric(returns), lwd = 2)
grid()

# Normal random data
normal_data <- rnorm(nrow(returns), mean = mu, sd = sigma)
qqnorm(normal_data, main = "Normal returns", cex.main = 0.8)
qqline(normal_data, lwd = 2)
grid()
```

The deviation of points from a straight line signifies a departure from normality. Various statistical tests for the determination of normality and the deviance from a provided empirical distribution have been developed over time. Most of these (Kolmogorov-Smirnov, Shapiro-Wilks, Cramer-von Mises, Anderson-Darling) are available in R.

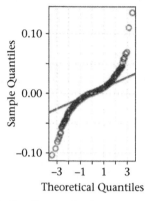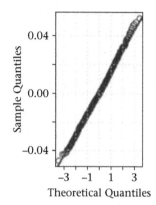

Figure 5.9 Quantile-quantile plots.

The Shapiro test, for example, is run by providing the raw returns to the shapiro.test() function as an argument. The resulting p-value[4] is a probability of sorts that specifies the likelihood of the data originating from a normal distribution.

```
answer <- shapiro.test(as.numeric(returns))

answer[[2]]
## [1] 5.118396e-34
```

According to this result, it is very unlikely that our data originated from an underlying Gaussian distribution.

The preceding analysis should be taken with a grain of salt. Before blindly trusting the output of any statistical test, it is important to understand the structure of the underlying data. Too much or too little data can dramatically skew the results of these statistical tests by making them too sensitive and by leading to more false positives than would otherwise be expected. Outliers can also skew the results. As a practical matter, it is important to visually inspect the data (whenever possible) prior to conducting any rigorous statistical analysis. This will save a lot of time and trouble down the road. To see how an outlier might skew the output of a statistical test, consider the following example. We will create a vector of normally distributed numbers and use the shapiro.test() function to investigate deviance from normality.

```
set.seed(129)
normal_numbers <- rnorm(5000, 0, 1)
ans <- shapiro.test(normal_numbers)

ans[[2]]
## [1] 0.9963835
```

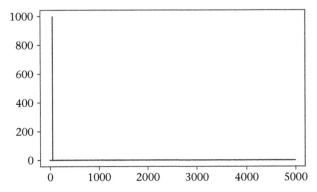

Figure 5.10 Erroneous value.

The high p-value hints at the fact that our sample does indeed originate from a normal distribution. What if we had one outlier present in our sample, an abnormally large value that was due to a data entry mistake, for example?

```
# Corrupt a single data point
normal_numbers[50] <- 1000
ans <- shapiro.test(normal_numbers)

ans[[2]]
## [1] 1.775666e-95
```

This p-value is practically zero in this case. The Shapiro-Wilks test is not robust enough to filter out the effect of the outlier. A simple plot of the data prior to conducting the test would have revealed the presence of the erroneous value.

Plotting the data is not always a practical approach. We can either automate the detection and handling of outlier data, or we can apply statistical tests that are robust to outliers.[5]

Correlation

Dealing with outliers is more of an art than a science. In order to motivate the next section, let us again consider the SPY and VXX log returns. This time, we want to see how correlated these returns are on a daily basis.

Correlation is a statistical measure of linear dependence between two random variables. The most common flavor of correlation used by practitioners is the Pearson Correlation. Another popular measure is the Rank Correlation.[6] The formula for the Pearson correlation coefficient is the following:

$$\rho_{X,Y} = \frac{E[(X - \mu_X)(Y - \mu_Y)]}{\sigma_X \sigma_Y} \tag{5.9}$$

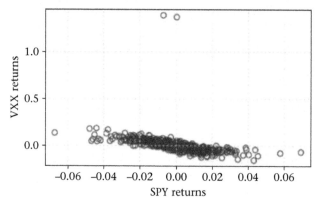

Figure 5.11 Typical scatter plot of returns.

The numerator $E[(X - \mu_X)(Y - \mu_Y)]$ is an important mathematical construct that is ubiquitous in finance. It is referred to as the covariance between random variables X and Y. When dealing with two or more random variables, we can express this construct as a matrix. This is called the covariance matrix, and is one of the cornerstones of modern finance. The correlation and the covariance in this formulation reveal pretty much the same information. The scaling is the only thing that differs between the two. A positive value for $\rho_{X,Y}$ alludes to the fact that the random variables X and Y might be related in a linear manner. Keep in mind that the correlation coefficient formula presented above is a population statistic. Different sample statistics exist that attempt to produce unbiased and efficient estimators of $\rho_{X,Y}$.[7]

```
sv <- as.xts(returns_matrix[, c(1, 6)])

head(sv)
##                   SPY.Close     VXX.Close
## 2009-02-02 -0.003022794 -0.003160468
## 2009-02-03  0.013949240 -0.047941603
## 2009-02-04 -0.004908132  0.003716543
## 2009-02-05  0.014770965 -0.006134680
```

The scatter plot between the SPY and VXX time series looks like this:

The correlation in R can be obtained by passing a matrix of time series as an argument to the cor() function:

```
cor(sv)

##                SPY.Close   VXX.Close
## SPY.Close    1.0000000 -0.4603908
## VXX.Close   -0.4603908  1.0000000
```

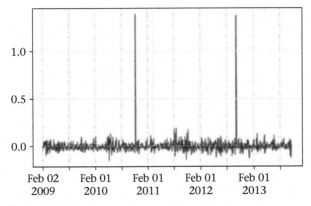

Figure 5.12 Outliers in VXX.

The result is a matrix that lists all the possible pairwise correlations. It is comforting to see that the SPY returns are correlated with themselves. The SPY and VXX returns appear to be negatively correlated. This also makes sense given that the VXX is an stock that tracks volatility. How confident are we that the correlation between SPY and VXX is indeed -0.46? Also, how sensitive is this correlation estimate in the presence of outliers? A plot of the VXX returns reveals the presence of two outliers:

Filtering data

What happens to the correlation estimate if we remove these outliers? We now have one of three choices to make. We can completely ignore the outliers and proceed with our statistical analysis, we can delete the outliers from the sample, or we can transform the outliers into more sensible values. We will opt for deleting the erroneous entries.

```
# Find the outliers
outliers <- which(sv[, 2] > 1.0)

# If any outliers exist, remove them
if(length(outliers) > 0) {
  sv <- sv[-outliers, ]
}

cor(sv)
##                SPY.Close   VXX.Close
## SPY.Close    1.0000000  -0.8066466
## VXX.Close   -0.8066466   1.0000000
```

Notice the dramatic change in the correlation estimate and subsequent scatter plot:

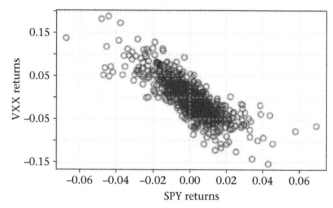

Figure 5.13 Removal of outliers.

A strong linear relationship between the SPY and VXX returns is indeed present. One way to quantify the strength of such a relationship is to consider the R^2 of a linear regression between these two time series. The concept of correlation is closely tied to that of linear regression. It turns out that the square root of the R^2 of a linear regression in two variables is equal to the Pearson correlation coefficient. The R^2 is a measure of how well the variability in the dependent variable can be explained by the variability in the independent variable.

$$\rho = \sqrt{R^2} \tag{5.10}$$

Going back to our two time series of interest, the output of a linear regression can be thought of as the best-fit, straight line through a scatter plot of points in a two-dimensional space. Such a linear relationship can be established by obtaining an estimate of the slope and intercept of this line. This is what the lm() function returns. The lm() function also returns certain statistics that describe how "plausible" these parameters actually are. When we have more than two variables in a regression (multivariate regression), the estimated coefficients still form a line, but in a higher dimensional space. Here is the mathematical model that a linear regression attempts to fit:

$$Y = \alpha + \beta_1 X_1 + \beta_2 X_2 + \cdots + \beta_N X_N + \epsilon \tag{5.11}$$

The coefficients of interest are the α and the β's. The ϵ term is a catch-all term that includes the variability not captured by the linear model. Ideally, this term is normally distributed with no autocorrelation or other discernible structure.

R formulas

Before we proceed with a linear regression example, an explanation of formulas is in order. Certain functions (lm(), glm(), nls()) can accept symbolic expressions as part of their argument list. R uses the ~ operator to create such constructs. Given two variables y and x, we can create a symbolic expression or a formula as follows:

```
# Create a formula
my_formula <- as.formula("y ~ x")

# What is the output?
my_formula
## y ~ x

# What is the class of my_formula?
class(my_formula)
## [1] "formula"
```

This effectively tells R that we want to establish a linear relationship between the dependent variable y and the independent variable x. It also tells R that we want both the slope and intercept of such a linear relationship. By changing the right-hand side of this formula to y ~ x − 1, we are instructing the model to ignore the intercept. For more than one independent variable, we can specify a formula that looks something like this: y ~ x + z + w + z*w − 1. This captures the linear relationship between the variables y, x, z, and w, and also includes the interaction term between z and w. The I() function can be used to perform mathematical operations within a formula. For instance: y ~ x + z + I(w*x) will create a new independent variable that is equal to the product of w and x. The help pages in R for ?formula have more detailed examples on how to structure such formulations.

```
# Create a linear regression object
reg <- lm(VXX.Close ~ SPY.Close, data = sv)

# Here is the output
summary(reg)

## Call:
## lm(formula = VXX.Close ~ SPY.Close, data = sv)

## Residuals:
##      Min        1Q    Median        3Q       Max
## -0.085607 -0.012830 -0.000865  0.012188  0.116349

## Coefficients:
```

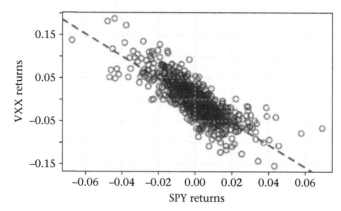

Figure 5.14 Regression output on plot.

```
##                Estimate Std. Error t value Pr(>|t|)
## (Intercept) -0.0024365  0.0006641  -3.669 0.000254 ***
## SPY.Close   -2.5848492  0.0552193 -46.811  < 2e-16 ***
## ---
## Signif. codes:  0 '***' 0.001 '**' 0.01 '*' 0.05 '.' 0.1

## Residual standard error: 0.02287 on 1187 degrees of freedom
## Multiple R-squared:  0.6486,   Adjusted R-squared:  0.6483
## F-statistic:  2191 on 1 and 1187 DF,  p-value: < 2.2e-16
```

The slope and intercept are listed under the coefficients section of the summary output. In our case, the intercept is -0.0024365 and the slope is -2.5848492. The numbers under the `Pr(>|t|)` heading are the p-values of the estimated parameters. A `p-value` is defined as the probability of observing the estimated parameter given that the `null hypothesis` is true. The null hypothesis is the assertion that the parameters (slope and intercept) are zero. The fact that the p-values are very small leads us to conclude that we can reject the null hypothesis. This is just a fancy way of saying that we are are confident our estimates are nonzero.

The coefficients can be programmatically extracted as follows:

```
b <- reg$coefficients[1]
a <- reg$coefficients[2]
```

The linear model is telling us that the relationship between VXX returns and SPY returns, at time t is: $VXX_t = aSPY_t + b + \epsilon_t$. The noise term ϵ_t is also referred to as the `residuals` of the regression. Superimposing the result of a linear regression onto a scatter plot of points is something that practitioners do often. The `abline()` function can be used to accomplish this.

The fit on contemporaneous returns looks pretty good. Here is what the residuals look like:

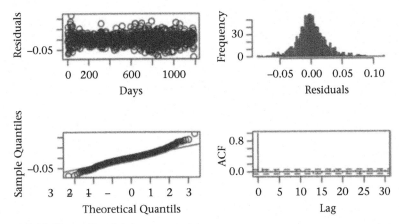

Figure 5.15 Diagnostics plots.

```
par(mfrow = c(2, 2))
plot(reg$residuals,
  main = "Residuals through time",
  xlab = "Days", ylab = "Residuals")
hist(reg$residuals, breaks = 100,
  main = "Distribution of residuals",
  xlab = "Residuals")
qqnorm(reg$residuals)
qqline(reg$residuals)
acf(reg$residuals, main = "Autocorrelation")
```

These four plots show different aspects of the residuals. At first glance, the time and histogram plots seem to indicate that the residuals are normally distributed. They do, however, have fatter tails than what a normal distribution would imply. This can also be seen in the quantile-quantile plot generated by qqplot(). The acf() function computes the autocorrelation of a particular time series. It asks the question, is there a correlation between the current observation and any of the previous observations? In a looser sense, can we use the previous values to say something about the next values? The way this is accomplished is by shifting the time series back by one step at a time and by recomputing the correlation with the original series. For a lag of zero, the correlation should be one. Any other lag will produce a different number. The autocorrelation plot above shows that there is no significant autocorrelation structure present in the residuals of our simple linear regression model. If there were, we would have to revisit the assumptions of using a linear regression to capture the relationship between the two variables. In an ideal world, we want the residuals to be as "noisy" as possible. We want them to be normally distributed with no inherent structure (neither a linear or a nonlinear dependence).

Looking at contemporaneous returns is one way in which to analyze relationships between different securities. A more interesting question to ask, is whether there exists a linear relationship between yesterday's returns and today's returns. If this is so, we can make the case that a linear regression model would be a good first attempt at predicting the market for the dependent regressor.

```
vxx_lag_1 <- lag(VXX$VXX.Close, k = 1)

head(vxx_lag_1)
##                 VXX.Close
## 2009-01-30            NA
## 2009-02-02        104.58
## 2009-02-03        104.25
## 2009-02-04         99.37
## 2009-02-05         99.74
## 2009-02-06         99.13

head(VXX$VXX.Close)
##                 VXX.Close
## 2009-01-30        104.58
## 2009-02-02        104.25
## 2009-02-03         99.37
## 2009-02-04         99.74
## 2009-02-05         99.13
## 2009-02-06         97.70
```

The `lag()` function shifted the prices over by one step, in effect, lagging the time series by one day. Now, let us go back to our filtered VXX matrix of returns and look at the linear regression between a lagged SPY and VXX. In the following example, we are implicitly making the assumption that SPY returns lead the VXX returns:

```
# Merge returns with lagged returns
sv <- merge(sv, lag(sv))

# Scatter plot of lagged SPY vs. VXX
plot(as.numeric(sv[, 3]), as.numeric(sv[, 2]),
main = "Scatter plot SPY lagged vs. VXX.",
xlab = "SPY lagged",
ylab = "VXX"
cex.main = 0.8,
cex.axis = 0.8,
cex.lab = 0.8)
grid()
```

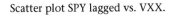

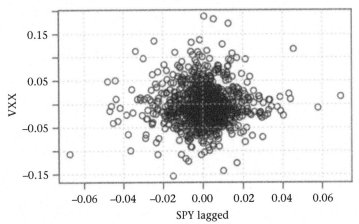

Figure 5.16 Scatter plot with lag.

No surprises here. The scatter plot suggests that there is no discernible linear relationship between lagged SPY returns and VXX returns. The output of a linear regression will confirm this suspicion:

```
reg2 <- lm(VXX.Close ~ SPY.Close.1, data = sv)

summary(reg2)
## Coefficients:
##               Estimate Std. Error t value Pr(>|t|)
## (Intercept) -0.004140    0.001121  -3.694 0.000231 ***
## SPY.Close.1  0.104119    0.093154   1.118 0.263918

## Residual standard error: 0.03857 on 1186 degrees of freedom
## (1 observation deleted due to missingness)
## Multiple R-squared:  0.001052, Adjusted R-squared:  0.00021
## F-statistic: 1.249 on 1 and 1186 DF,  p-value: 0.2639
```

What about making the assumption that VXX returns lead the SPY returns? We can easily switch up the regression by lagging VXX and by using SPY as the independent regressor. The results are the same.

The function ccf() (cross correlation function) performs a similar analysis by independently lagging both time series and by computing pairwise correlations. It is analogous to the acf() function, but it operates on two different time series instead of one.

```
ccf(as.numeric(sv[, 1]), as.numeric(sv[, 2]),
    main = "Cross correlation between SPY and VXX",
```

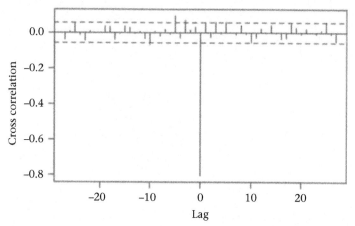

Figure 5.17 Cross correlation of returns.

```
ylab = "Cross correlation", xlab = "Lag", cex.main = 0.8,
cex.lab = 0.8, cex.axis = 0.8)
```

The linear in linear regression

As discussed above, a linear regression is a mathematical model that attempts to identify linear relationships between regressors. The qualifier "linear" is an important one to keep in mind. It is possible for two variables to be very related and yet, a linear regression might completely fail to identify this fact.

The classic example that is used to illustrate this point is that of a parabola. The function $f(x) = x^2$ is purely deterministic, and it clearly outlines the true dependence between x and $f(x)$. Here's what the output of a linear regression looks like on this data:

```
x <- seq(1:100)
y <- x ^ 2

# Generate the plot
plot(x, y)

# Fit the regression
reg_parabola <- lm(y ~ x)

# Superimpose the best fit line on the plot
abline(reg_parabola, lwd = 2)

# Look at the results
summary(reg_parabola)
```

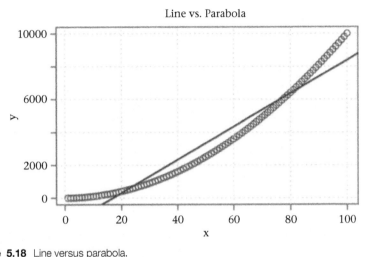

Figure 5.18 Line versus parabola.

```
## Coefficients:
##                 Estimate   Std. Error t value Pr(>|t|)
## (Intercept)   -1717.000    151.683   -11.32   <2e-16 ***
## x               101.000      2.608    38.73   <2e-16 ***
## ---
## Signif. codes:  0 '***' 0.001 '**' 0.01 '*' 0.05 '.' 0.1

## Residual standard error: 752.7 on 98 degrees of freedom
## Multiple R-squared:  0.9387,    Adjusted R-squared:  0.9381
## F-statistic:  1500 on 1 and 98 DF,  p-value: < 2.2e-16
```

Clearly a linear regression is not the ideal choice for detecting nonlinear relationships. A small tweak to one of the variables, however, allows us to once again use the lm() function.

```
plot(x, sqrt(y))
reg_transformed <- lm(sqrt(y) ~ x)
abline(reg_transformed)

summary(reg_transformed)
## Coefficients:
##                 Estimate Std. Error    t value     Pr(>|t|)
## (Intercept) -5.684e-14  5.598e-15  -1.015e+01    <2e-16 ***
## x            1.000e+00  9.624e-17   1.039e+16    <2e-16 ***
## ---
## Signif. codes:  0 '***' 0.001 '**' 0.01 '*' 0.05 '.' 0.1
```

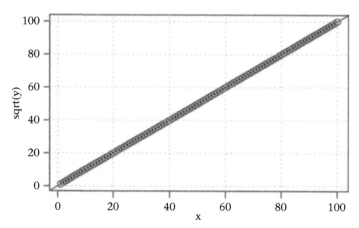

Figure 5.19 Square root transformation.

```
## Residual standard error: 2.778e-14 on 98 degrees of freedom
## Multiple R-squared:      1,     Adjusted R-squared:      1
## F-statistic: 1.08e+32 on 1 and 98 DF,  p-value: < 2.2e-16
```

The mathematical transformation of variables is a technique that can be used successfully in conjunction with linear regression. Finding transformations that work well in a linear regression model is certainly not a trivial task.

Volatility

Volatility is a measure of dispersion of a set of numbers around their average value. Given any set of numbers, we can come up with an estimate of this dispersion. A commonly used metric for the volatility of a random process is the standard deviation statistic that we have seen before.

$$\sigma = \sqrt{\frac{\sum_{i=1}^{N} (X_i - \mu)^2}{N}} \qquad (5.12)$$

Another popular alternative is the sum of absolute deviations from the average:

$$D = \sum_{i=1}^{N} |X_i - \mu| \qquad (5.13)$$

Volatility of returns is an important metric that traders and quants study in great detail.

For the purposes of developing certain trading strategies, what we really care about is how much and how frequently the returns of financial instruments oscillate around their mean values. We will not concern ourselves with the direction of a particular move. Rather, we will focus on the relative magnitude of such moves. Why do we not care about direction? The answer is, it is difficult to predict direction. Saying something about the magnitude is significantly easier.

Notice that the formula for volatility includes the squared returns as a building block. When dealing with daily or intraday return distributions, we will find that the mean value is close to zero. The formula for variance can thus be approximated as:

$$\sigma^2 = \sum_{i=1}^{N} r_i^2 \qquad (5.14)$$

We have already seen that on a daily time scale, at least, there is no significant autocorrelation between returns. What about in the higher-order moments of the return distribution? Consider the following simulation:

```
# Generate 1000 IID numbers from a normal distribution.
z <- rnorm(1000, 0, 1)


# Autocorrelation of returns and squared returns
par(mfrow = c(2, 1))
acf(z, main = "returns", cex.main = 0.8,
  cex.lab = 0.8, cex.axis = 0.8)
grid()
acf(z ^ 2, main = "returns squared",
  cex.lab = 0.8, cex.axis = 0.8)
grid()
```

By construction, the above artificially generated returns should exhibit no autocorrelation. Indeed, this seems to be the case from the graph. How about the squared returns?

This should come as no surprise. Since the initial vector of numbers z is iid (independent and identically distributed), we expect the resulting squared vector to also be iid.

Now, here is what the autocorrelation profile for real squared returns looks like. Remember that squared returns, when summed together, form a proxy for dispersion or variance.

```
par(mfrow = c(1, 1))
acf(sv[, 1] ^ 2, main = "Actual returns squared",
  cex.main = 0.8, cex.lab = 0.8, cex.axis = 0.8)
grid()
```

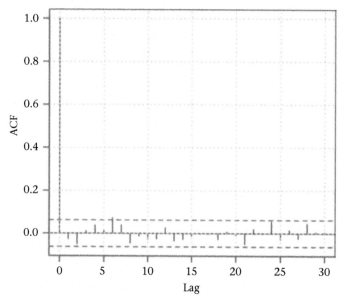

Figure 5.20 Autocorrelation of returns.

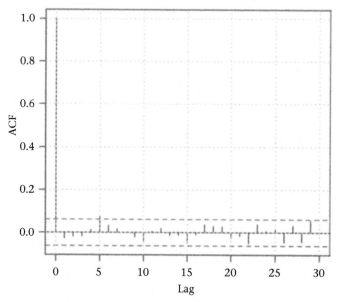

Figure 5.21 Autocorrelation of theoretical squared returns.

Statistically significant autocorrelation exists at various lags for daily squared returns. Higher order moments for empirical distributions also exhibit autocorrelation effects, and so do the absolute values of returns:

```
par(mfrow = c(1, 2))
```

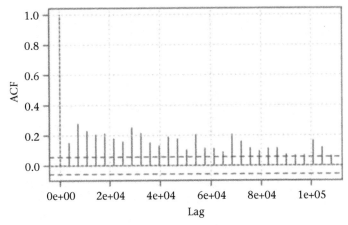

Figure 5.22 Autocorrelation of actual squared returns.

```
acf(sv[, 1]^3)
acf(abs(sv[, 1]))
```

Various hierarchies of econometric models have been proposed to account for this autocorrelation structure in higher-order moments [50]. The three main categories of such models go by the following names:

- ARIMA
- GARCH
- Stochastic Volatility

This behavior in volatility is often referred to as heteroscedastic. It is especially noticeable when looking at returns plotted through time. A normal-looking series with no autocorrelation would have no clustering present. The fact that real financial data does, implies that there is a memory effect in the higher-order moments of such time series.

Summary

This chapter builds on the previously covered introductory probability and statistics material. A `Random Process` is defined, and the connection between financial time series and such processes is made. The important concept of `Stationarity` is addressed, and various R statistical tests for evaluating the presence of stationarity and normality are presented. The notion of correlation between time series is illustrated, and outlier detection and filtering techniques are explored. A digression is made to discuss the implementation of linear regression and autocorrelation studies within R, and the chapter ends with a demonstration of the autocorrelation in squared returns. This finding inevitably leads to the consideration of advanced econometric modeling techniques for explaining the heteroscedastic behavior in volatility.

This page intentionally left blank

6 | Spreads, Betas and Risk

In the previous chapter, we concluded that no noticeable autocorrelation exists for daily returns. This implies that knowing the level of the previous day's return does not help us in forecasting today's return. The hypothesis we will formulate in this section is that we can artificially create a time series that is somewhat forecastable. We will refer to this new time series as a spread. The claim we are making is that a stock spread has a better chance of being tradable than an individual outright does. This, of course, is a subjective and suspicious statement in and of itself. Bear with me, though for the remainder of the chapter. I am mostly interested in conveying a methodology of thinking rather than a concrete fact about price behavior.

Defining the stock spread

A binary stock spread (pair) consists of a long position in one stock and a short position in a second stock. Some pairs can even be constructed by going long (buying) or going short (selling) both stocks. For example, if one stock tracks the inverse of a certain index (such as the SDS ETF), then we can buy both ETF's and still create a spread that might work for our purposes. Pairs trading is a trading technique that was reportedly first applied by Tartaglia[1] during his stint at Morgan Stanley in the '80s [131].

From a business perspective, if two companies sell similar widgets, then they should be influenced by the same underlying business and economic factors. If the general economy falters, then so will their sales. If a common resource that is utilized in the production of the widgets becomes scarce, then the manufacturing costs of both companies will increase, and inventories might decrease. If company A dramatically lowers their prices, then so will company B. From a high level view, companies A and B are linked together through common external factors, as well as complex feedback mechanisms.

We will not venture to explain stock A and stock B returns via common factor models.[2] Rather, we will only investigate the relative price behavior of both stocks. That is to say, the dynamics of the stock spread.

On any given day, we might not know whether Coke stock and Pepsico stock will go up or down. We do, however, believe that the common underlying factors that affect both companies will be reflected in their respective stock prices. If Coke goes up on a particular day, then so should Pepsico. This is the relationship we will attempt to model.

Consider the price changes of Coke in dollar terms and the price changes of Pepsico in dollar terms. If we wanted to create a dollar-neutral portfolio, then how many shares of Coke should we purchase and how many shares of Pepsico should we sell in order to accomplish this? A dollar-neutral portfolio is a portfolio with a monetary value close to zero.

This is what the spread-beta attempts to answer. We can think of a beta as the slope of the best-fit line between the scatter plot of price changes of both stocks. Betas are typically computed between percent returns and not price changes. Price changes do, however, provide a more intuitive answer from a trading perspective. Betas can also be computed between raw prices or the logarithm of prices. We call these resulting betas a cointegrating vector.[3] Regressions applied to nonstationary time series, such as stock prices, will yield nonsensical results. The only time this regression makes sense is if the stock pair is cointegrated. The check for cointegration relies on the statistical analysis of the resulting residuals.

Here is a scatter plot of Coke versus Pepsico price changes over a year:

```
pepsi <- getSymbols('PEP', from = '2013-01-01',
   to = '2014-01-01', adjust = T, auto.assign = FALSE)


coke <- getSymbols('COKE', from = '2013-01-01',
   to = '2014-01-01', adjust = T, auto.assign = FALSE)
Sys.setenv(TZ = "UTC")


prices <- cbind(pepsi[, 6], coke[, 6])
price_changes <- apply(prices, 2, diff)
plot(price_changes[, 1], price_changes[, 2],
   xlab = "Coke price changes",
   ylab = "Pepsi price changes",
   main = "Pepsi vs. Coke",
   cex.main = 0.8,
   cex.lab = 0.8,
   cex.axis = 0.8)
grid()


ans <- lm(price_changes[, 1] ~ price_changes[, 2])
beta <- ans$coefficients[2]
```

Over this time frame, on average, if Coke moves by ΔS, then Pepsico will move by $\beta \Delta S$. If we purchase 1,000 shares of Coke, how many shares of Pepsico do we need to sell in order to remain dollar neutral? The answer is $1000/\beta$.

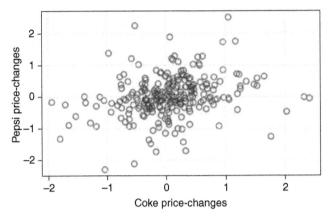

Figure 6.1 Pepsi versus Coke price changes.

So, what does this beta tell us? We are making the assumption that Coke price changes are nonrandom variables and that Pepsico price changes are random variables. The implicit claim is that the variability between these two time series is solely due to Pepsico. What if we assumed that all the variability was due to Coke? Then we would get a different beta.

```
ans2 <- lm(price_changes[, 2] ~ price_changes[, 1])
beta2 <- ans2$coefficients[2]

beta
## [1] 0.2614627

beta2
## [1] 0.2539855
```

Ordinary Least Squares versus Total Least Squares

Notice how these two betas differ. They are not inverses as one would intuitively expect. This inconsistency in betas has led some traders to adopt a total least squares[4] beta rather than an Ordinary Least Squares (OLS) beta.

Total least squares regression attempts to explain the variability of a system in terms of both time series. It does so by minimizing the sum of the perpendicular squared distance between every point on the scatter plot and the best-fit line through those points. OLS, in turn, minimizes the squared vertical or horizontal distance between the scattered points and the best fit line.

TLS betas can be derived by utilizing Principal Component Analysis (PCA)[5]. In R, we can run a PCA analysis by invoking the `prcomp()` function. The whole idea behind PCA is to convert a set of correlated observations into a set of linearly uncorrelated observations. These new observations are called the `principal`

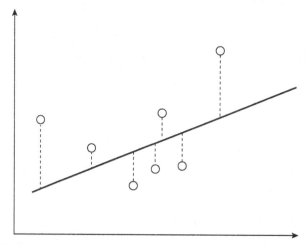

Figure 6.2 Ordinary least squares distance minimization.

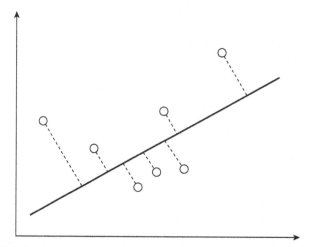

Figure 6.3 Total least squares distance minimization.

components. This approach is elegantly outlined in Paul Teetor's presentation: http://quanttrader.info/public/CRUG_MeetUp.pdf.

A mental recipe for finding these components is the following:

1. Find the direction on the scatter plot that has the highest variance associated with it.
2. Find the second best direction that is orthogonal (perpendicular) to the first.

These directions (vectors) will be the principal components. Here is some code that calculates these components:

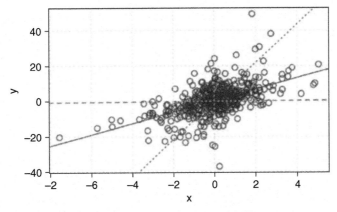

Figure 6.4 Total least squares regression between SPY and AAPL.

```
# Get the data
SPY <- getSymbols('SPY', from = '2011-01-01',
  to = '2012-12-31', adjust = T, auto.assign = FALSE)
AAPL <- getSymbols('AAPL', from = '2011-01-01',
  to = '2012-12-31', adjust = T, auto.assign = FALSE)

# Compute price differences
x <- diff(as.numeric(SPY[, 4]))
y <- diff(as.numeric(AAPL[, 4]))

plot(x, y, main = "Scatter plot of returns. SPY vs. AAPL",
  cex.main = 0.8, cex.lab = 0.8, cex.axis = 0.8)
abline(lm(y ~ x))
abline(lm(x ~ y), lty = 2)
grid()

# Total least squares regression
r <- prcomp( ~ x + y )
slope <- r$rotation[2, 1]  /  r$rotation[1, 1]
intercept <- r$center[2] - slope * r$center[1]

# Show the first principal component on the plot
abline(a = intercept, b = slope, lty = 3)
```

Constructing the spread

In this next example, we will set up a stock spread and look at the number of buy and sell signals we obtain from a naive trading strategy. The strategy will be to buy the spread when it is below a certain lower threshold and to sell the spread when it is above a certain upper threshold. To make our lives easier, we will split this task into separate functions.

```r
# Function to calculate the spread
calculate_spread <- function(x, y, beta) {
  return(y - beta * x)
}

# Function to calculate the beta and level
# given start and end dates
calculate_beta_and_level <- function(x, y,
  start_date, end_date) {
  require(xts)

  time_range <- paste(start_date, "::",
    end_date, sep = "")
  x <- x[time_range]
  y <- y[time_range]

  dx <- diff(x[time_range])
  dy <- diff(y[time_range])
  r <- prcomp( ~ dx + dy)

  beta <- r$rotation[2, 1] / r$rotation[1, 1]
  spread <- calculate_spread(x, y, beta)
  names(spread) <- "spread"
  level <- mean(spread, na.rm = TRUE)

  outL <- list()
  outL$spread <- spread
  outL$beta <- beta
  outL$level <- level

  return(outL)
}

# Function to calculate buy and sell signals
# with upper and lower threshold
calculate_buy_sell_signals <- function(spread, beta,
  level, lower_threshold, upper_threshold) {

  buy_signals <- ifelse(spread <= level -
    lower_threshold, 1, 0)
```

```
sell_signals <- ifelse(spread >= level +
    upper_threshold, 1, 0)

# bind these vectors into a matrix
output <- cbind(spread, buy_signals,
    sell_signals)
colnames(output) <- c("spread", "buy_signals",
    "sell_signals")

return(output)
}
```

In the above example, we wrote three functions that broke up the signal calculation task into manageable components. The first function, `calculate_spread()` does exactly what the name implies. Given two stock price time series and a beta, it returns the spread. This helper function is used as an input to the next function which returns the spread, the beta, and the mean level of the spread. We use a list to return all three objects from the function. The third function, `calculate_buy_sell_signals()`, creates a matrix of the spread in the first column, the buy signals in the second column, and the sell signals in the third column.

Here is how we can use the functions that we defined above:

```
# Implementation
# Pick an in-sample date range
start_date <- "2009-01-01"
end_date <- "2011-12-31"
x <- SPY[, 6]
y <- AAPL[, 6]

results <- calculate_beta_and_level(x, y,
    start_date, end_date)
results$beta
## [1] 4.923278

results$level
## [1] -239.0602

plot(results$spread, ylab = "Spread Value",
    main = "AAPL - beta * SPY",
    cex.main = 0.8,
    cex.lab = 0.8,
    cex.axis = 0.8)
```

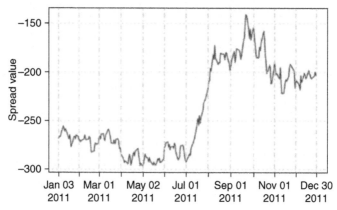

Figure 6.5 The AAPL versus SPY spread.

This does not look like a particularly attractive spread to trade, at least in its current form. There seem to be periods of stability characterized by mean reversion, sprinkled with sudden jumps to the upside. We will, nonetheless, proceed with this particular spread in order to highlight some of the issues that arise in practice.

So now we know what the in-sample beta is, and we also observe that the mean level of the spread is around −239.06 for the same period. Let us apply these values to the out-of-sample period and determine our trading signals.

```
# Out of sample start and end dates
start_date_out_sample <- "2012-01-01"
end_date_out_sample <- "2012-10-22"
range <- paste(start_date_out_sample, "::",
  end_date_out_sample, sep = "")

# Out of sample analysis
spread_out_of_sample <- calculate_spread(x[range],
  y[range], results$beta)

plot(spread_out_of_sample, main = "AAPL - beta * SPY",
  cex.main = 0.8,
  cex.lab = 0.8,
  cex.axis = 0.8)
abline(h = results$level, lwd = 2)
```

Signal generation and validation

The plot of the out-of-sample results reveals that the entire spread is above the in-sample level. There is no buy signal at all, only sell signals. At this point, do we trust our spread enough that we are willing to sell large quantities of AAPL and

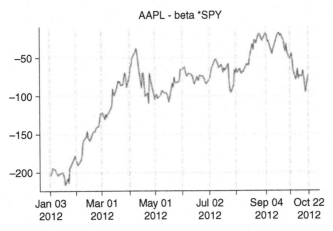

Figure 6.6 Out of sample AAPL versus SPY spread.

buy βSPY for as long as the spread is above its mean value? The answer is no. There seems to be a fundamental flaw in either the way we calculated the spread or in the way we selected the stocks to pair up in the first place. Is there any way to salvage the situation? Maybe. What if the betas we are calculating are way too stale by the time we look at our out-of-sample data? After all, AAPL is a dynamic company, and the stock price will certainly reflect that. SPY is a proxy for the S&P 500, and it might not respond as fast to such fluctuations. It certainly feels like we could do better by pairing AAPL with a comparable company in the same sector at least.

But we got this far. Why give up now? Let us compute some dynamic (rolling) betas. We will assume that the relationship between AAPL and SPY is still a tradable one, albeit on a more refined timescale. The following R code calculates a rolling beta on a ten day window and then plots the new spread. For trading purposes, we would update the beta on a daily basis (say, at the close of the market) and use that new beta during the next trading day.

Again, this exercise focuses on creating a stock spread that looks mean reverting and that can potentially be traded. We have said nothing about the correct position sizing or the trading rules per se. If the betas keep changing, then the positions will probably change as well. This is something that has to be addressed later on. For now, we are only concerned with the dynamics of the modified spread for signal-generation purposes.

```
# Rolling window of trading days
window_length <- 10

# Time range
start_date <- "2011-01-01"
end_date <- "2011-12-31"
range <- paste(start_date, "::",
```

```
  end_date, sep = "")

# Our stock pair
x <- SPY[range, 6]
y <- AAPL[range, 6]

dF <- cbind(x, y)
names(dF) <- c("x", "y")

# Function that we will use to calculate betas
run_regression <- function(dF) {
  return(coef(lm(y ~ x - 1, data = as.data.frame(dF))))
}

rolling_beta <- function(z, width) {
  rollapply(z, width = width, FUN = run_regression,
  by.column = FALSE, align = "right")
}

betas <- rolling_beta(diff(dF), 10)

data <- merge(betas, dF)
data$spread <- data$y - lag(betas, 1) * data$x
```

Let us take a look at what the equivalent spread on returns looks like. The only thing we have to change is to compute the betas between the returns rather than the price differences.

```
returns <- diff(dF) / dF
return_beta <- rolling_beta(returns, 10)
data$spreadR <- diff(data$y) / data$y -
  return_beta * diff(data$x) / data$x
```

The end result of this code is the data frame data that looks like this:

```
tail(data)
##                betas      x       y     spread      spreadR
## 2011-12-22 2.770586 119.60 383.07 138.70795 -0.002322110
## 2011-12-23 3.094533 120.67 387.66  53.33343  0.003311904
## 2011-12-27 3.450416 120.76 390.74  17.04417  0.007083611
## 2011-12-28 3.364819 119.18 387.00 -24.22055  0.004194527
## 2011-12-29 3.004804 120.41 389.38 -15.77781 -0.003361064
```

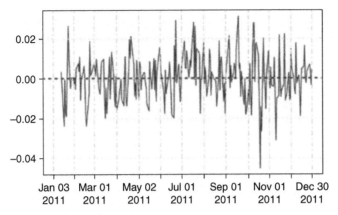

Figure 6.7 Rolling beta spread.

Visually, the spread looks more mean reverting than it did before. In order to determine decent buy and exit points, we can keep going with a ten day rolling window and compute what the spread standard deviation was over that historical time period. We will make the assumption that going forward, the variability of the spread will remain the same.

The spread we will use will be the one based on price differences.

```
threshold <- sd(data$spread, na.rm = TRUE)

threshold
## [1] 143.7734
```

Here is the plot one more time with a one sigma move superimposed above and below the mean of the spread, which we assume to be centered at zero.

```
plot(data$spread, main = "AAPL vs. SPY In-Sample",
  cex.main = 0.8,
  cex.lab = 0.8,
  cex.axis = 0.8)
abline(h = threshold, lty = 2)
abline(h = -threshold, lty = 2)
```

How profitable would this spread be? A way to assess this is to write a simple backtester that tracks the hypothetical entry and exit points. We will assume that we only maintain a single long or short position in the spread at any one time. If we buy one unit of the spread and we keep getting buy signals, we will not purchase more units. Rather, we will wait for a sell signal, in which case we will reverse the position. This is a naive approach. Nevertheless, this exercise is meant to cover the basics of spread trading. A better strategy will certainly require a different scaling-in and scaling-out approach. Here is the code:

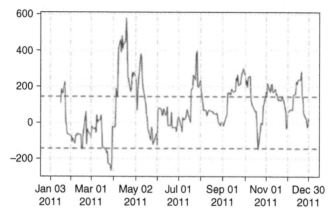

Figure 6.8 Price difference spread for SPY versus AAPL.

```
# Construct the out of sample spread
# Keep the same 10 day rolling window
window_length <- 10

# Time range
start_date <- "2012-01-01"
end_date <- "2013-12-31"
range <- paste(start_date, "::",
  end_date, sep = "")

# Our stock pair
x <- SPY[range, 6]
y <- AAPL[range, 6]

# Bind these together into a matrix
dF <- cbind(x, y)
names(dF) <- c("x", "y")

# Calculate the out of sample rolling beta
beta_out_of_sample <- rolling_beta(diff(dF), 10)

# Buy and sell threshold
data_out <- merge(beta_out_of_sample, dF)
data_out$spread <- data_out$y -
  lag(beta_out_of_sample, 1) * data_out$x

# Plot the spread with in-sample bands
plot(data_out$spread, main = "AAPL vs. SPY out of sample",
```

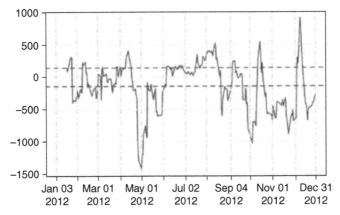

Figure 6.9 Out of sample spread with bands.

```
    cex.main = 0.8,
    cex.lab = 0.8,
    cex.axis = 0.8)
abline(h = threshold, lwd = 2)
abline(h = -threshold, lwd = 2)
```

The trading logic can be summarized by the following vectorized commands:

```
# Generate sell and buy signals
buys <- ifelse(data_out$spread > threshold, 1, 0)
sells <- ifelse(data_out$spread < -threshold, -1, 0)
data_out$signal <- buys + sells
```

Here is a look at where these buy and sell signals fall on the spread. We will make the buy signals circles and the sell signals triangles.

```
plot(data_out$spread, main = "AAPL vs. SPY out of sample",
    cex.main = 0.8,
    cex.lab = 0.8,
    cex.axis = 0.8)
abline(h = threshold, lty = 2)
abline(h = -threshold, lty = 2)

point_type <- rep(NA, nrow(data_out))
buy_index <- which(data_out$signal == 1)
sell_index <- which(data_out$signal == -1)

point_type[buy_index] <- 21
point_type[sell_index] <- 24
points(data_out$spread, pch = point_type)
```

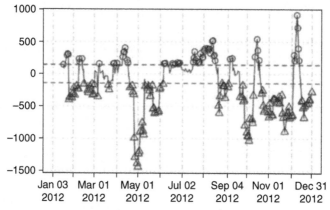

Figure 6.10 Buy and sell signals superimposed.

How many potential buy and sell signals do we have?

```
num_of_buy_signals <- sum(buys, na.rm = TRUE)
num_of_sell_signals <- sum(abs(sells), na.rm = TRUE)

num_of_buy_signals
## [1] 303
num_of_sell_signals
## [1] 189
```

Trading the spread

Now that our entry and exit signals have been calculated, we need to consider how much of our capital to invest in every trade. Can we afford to pile up buys on every buy signal and sell on every sell signal, or is that overkill? If we already have a buy signal and we get another one, should we trade the same size or increase our exposure? Do we exit a trade when the spread goes back to the mean or when it goes to the opposite threshold? These are all valid questions, and one can obtain the answers buy tweaking the backtesting logic to explore these scenarios.

We will keep our trading size at 100 shares for AAPL and $100 * \beta$ shares for SPY. The quantities traded will be placed in the same data_out table we have been using up to now to keep track of all the variables of interest. Aside from the quantities, we also need to keep track of how much money each trade is costing/making us. We need to account for both the realized and unrealized profit and loss (P&L) of each trade. This will eventually help us in calculating an equity curve for the strategy.

The equity curve is a graphical representation of the profit and loss profile of a trading strategy. The equity curve is very important in determining the risk versus reward trade-off inherent in a trading approach. The most desirable profile would, of course, be an upward sloping line with no downward fluctuations. In the real world, every strategy exhibits periods of negative returns, and this will be reflected in the equity curve as a downward movement through time. Figures of merit that we need to pay attention to include the volatility of the equity curve and the maximum drawdown of the equity curve over a certain time frame.

And now for some accounting logic. We will make the simplifying assumption that we enter or exit a trade the day after we receive a valid buy or sell signal. In reality, these execution decisions can be made at any point throughout the trading day. Since we are dealing with daily closing prices, it does not hurt to consider this worst-case execution scenario.

Here is what our current **data_out** table looks like:

```
##        beta_out_of_sample       x       y       spread signal
## 2011-01-13          NA 128.37 345.68          NA     NA
## 2011-01-14   1.7511157 129.30 348.48          NA     NA
## 2011-01-18   1.1630714 129.52 340.65 113.84550      1
## 2011-01-19   1.2803161 128.25 338.84 189.67609      1
## 2011-01-20   1.2286891 128.08 332.68 168.69711      1
## 2011-01-21   0.8045108 128.37 326.72 168.99319      1
## 2011-01-24   2.4936855 129.10 337.45 233.58766      1
## 2011-01-25   2.7762163 129.17 341.40  19.29065      0
## 2011-01-26   3.0802946 129.67 343.85 -16.14196      0
```

Notice how we have multiple buy signals in a row. In order to simplify our strategy, we only initiate a single long or short position at a time. Consecutive signals of the same side will be ignored. Here is how to come up with sizes for stock X and Y (SPY and AAPL) in our example:

```
prev_x_qty <- 0
position <- 0
trade_size <- 100
signal <- as.numeric(data_out$signal)
signal[is.na(signal)] <- 0
beta <- as.numeric(data_out$beta_out_of_sample)

qty_x <- rep(0, length(signal))
qty_y <- rep(0, length(signal))

for(i in 1:length(signal)) {
  if(signal[i] == 1 && position == 0) {
    # buy the spread
    prev_x_qty <- round(beta[i] * trade_size)
    qty_x[i] <- -prev_x_qty
    qty_y[i] <- trade_size
    position <- 1
```

```
  }

  if(signal[i] == -1 && position == 0) {
    # sell the spread initially
    prev_x_qty <- round(beta[i] * trade_size)
    qty_x[i] <- prev_x_qty
    qty_y[i] <- -trade_size
    position <- -1
  }

  if(signal[i] == 1 && position == -1) {
    # we are short the spread and need to buy
    qty_x[i] <- -(round(beta[i] * trade_size) +
      prev_x_qty)
    prev_x_qty <- round(beta[i] * trade_size)
    qty_y[i] <- 2 * trade_size
    position <- 1
  }

  if(signal[i] == -1 && position == 1) {
    # we are long the spread and need to sell
    qty_x[i] <- round(beta[i] * trade_size) + prev_x_qty
    prev_x_qty <- round(beta[i] * trade_size)
    qty_y[i] <- -2 * trade_size
    position <- -1
  }
}
```

At the end of the out-of-sample period, we will still have a residual quantity left over for both stocks. We can offset this quantity by zeroing out the positions on the last trading day.

```
qty_x[length(qty_x)] <- -sum(qty_x)
qty_y[length(qty_y)] <- -sum(qty_y)
```

Let us append these columns to our data_out table and see what we have accomplished thus far:

```
data_out$qty_x <- qty_x
data_out$qty_y <- qty_y

data_out[1:3, ]
##  beta_out_of_sample        x       y   spread signal qty_x qty_y
## 2012-01-17   2.1511279  123.48  408.20     NA     NA     0     0
## 2012-01-18   2.5890817  124.85  412.44  143.87168   1  -259   100
```

```
## 2012-01-19  2.0711505 125.51 411.13   86.17435  0   0    0
```

```
tail(data_out, 3)
##    beta_out_of_sample      x       y  spread signal qty_x qty_y
## 2012-12-27  6.5051194 138.15 499.45 -404.90307  -1    0    0
## 2012-12-28  5.6770827 136.66 494.14 -394.84962  -1    0    0
## 2012-12-31  6.3934172 138.98 516.04 -272.96095  -1 -668  100
```

The above values look realistic given the betas we have calculated. We have also managed to ignore consecutive buy and sell signals. The strategy carries forward 1 spread position at a time.

Now that we have the necessary quantities to buy and sell for each leg of the spread, we would like to know how much our realized and unrealized P&L is going to be.

If we purchase a 100-lot on day one and close out the position five days later, our realized P&L will be the difference between the entry and exit prices multiplied by the total quantity. During days 2, 3, and 4, however, even though the position has not been closed out, there is still a potential profit or loss associated with the position. We call this the unrealized component. A way to calculate the unrealized P&L is to mark the position to the current market price.

We will do a similar analysis for the spread above. The end result of the analysis will be the inclusion of two more columns that will include the equity curve for both stocks.

```
# function for computing the equity curve
compute_equity_curve <- function(qty, price) {

  cash_buy <- ifelse(sign(qty) == 1,
    qty * price, 0)
  cash_sell <- ifelse(sign(qty) == -1,
    -qty * price, 0)
  position <- cumsum(qty)
  cumulative_buy <- cumsum(cash_buy)
  cumulative_sell <- cumsum(cash_sell)

  equity <- cumulative_sell - cumulative_buy +
    position * price
```

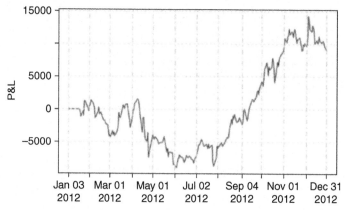

Figure 6.11 The SPY versus AAPL equity curve.

```
    return(equity)
}


# Add the equity curve columns to the data_out table
data_out$equity_curve_x <- compute_equity_curve(
  data_out$qty_x, data_out$x)
data_out$equity_curve_y <- compute_equity_curve(
  data_out$qty_y, data_out$y)
```

Figure 6.11 shows what the equity curve for the AAPL versus SPY spread looks like:

```
plot(data_out$equity_curve_x +
  data_out$equity_curve_y, type = 'l',
  main = "AAPL / SPY spread", ylab = "P&L",
  cex.main = 0.8,
  cex.axis = 0.8,
  cex.lab = 0.8)
```

Here are some observations:

1. The overall trend is upward sloping. This strategy would have made a positive return over the tested time period.
2. There are volatile periods in which the strategy loses money, but also periods in which the P&L increases rapidly.
3. It would be nice to quantify the risk of this strategy.

Here are a few more issues to consider:

1. How is position sizing a function of the risk-profile of the strategy?
2. How are signals a function of the strategy?

3. Is there forward-looking bias, and if so, how can we address this?
4. Have transaction fees been taken into account?
5. Is the spread something that is tradable?
6. Do price difference versus return betas make sense?

In the next chapter, we will do things the right way. We will leverage the **quantstrat** package to do most of the heavy lifting for us. Creating trade accounting and execution logic is a tedious and error-prone process. We would rather hand this off to **quantstrat** and, instead, focus on the signal generation and trade logic. The purpose of our spread example was to expose the reader to the basics and to get the creative juices flowing.

Considering the risk

We are at the point where we can come up with a few statistics that will help us capture both the good and the bad attributes of a trading strategy. These statistics will be used to compare alternative strategies on an equal footing. The formulas for such comparative statistics will, for the most part, include the "good stuff" (i.e., reward, return) in the numerator and the "bad stuff" (risk) in the denominator.

One cannot talk about the reward of a strategy without considering the associated risk. Risk is a very broad term and as a concept, it encompasses most of the things that can go wrong with a trading strategy. Traders are faced with two types of primary risk in their day-to-day activities. Market risk and operational risk. We will only consider the former type.

Operational risk addresses issues such as buggy software, faulty equipment, loss of exchange connectivity, trader error, inadequate internal oversight, litigation, and fraud [129]. The Basel II[6] accords define operational risk as, "the risk of a change in value caused by the fact that actual losses, incurred for inadequate or failed internal processes, people and systems, or from external events (including legal risk), differ from the expected losses."

Market risk refers to the performance of a particular strategy due to fluctuations in the prices of tradable instruments. These fluctuations might be due to external factors such as economic announcements, company-specific events, government mandates, weather patterns, prolonged droughts, and a myriad of other reasons. The important thing to realize, at least within the context of a trading strategy, is that the effects of these factors manifest themselves in the market prices and volume profiles of the underlying instruments. Analyzing the fluctuations of these observable random variables (price and volume) should give us enough information to say something about the market risk component of any strategy we come up with. Market price fluctuations, in and of themselves, are not necessarily a good proxy for risk. Consider the scenario in which we are long a certain stock and the market tanks by 20 percent. This certainly feels like a risky investment. However, when the market goes up by 20 percent, our concept of risk is different. Volatility and

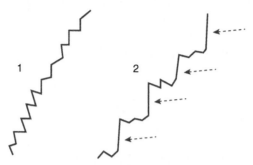

Figure 6.12 Two equity curves with same ending value.

variance are risk metrics that treat upward and downward moves in the same manner. Other metrics such as conditional variance, for example, make a distinction between "good" and "bad" volatility.

As alluded to before, volatility does not care about the direction of a particular price move. It is only concerned with the magnitude of such a move. This is evident in the formula for volatility. The square term removes any positive or negative directional bias.

$$\sigma = \sqrt{\frac{\sum_{i=1}^{N}(X_i - \mu)^2}{N}} \tag{6.1}$$

We can argue that a small volatility in the returns of a stock which we are long in is a good thing since the chance of a big drop in price is small. This, however, also precludes us from making a decent profit since the chance of an upward move is also small. This risk/reward trade-off is something that is very well understood in academia. Modern Portfolio Theory deals with these types of trade-offs in great detail. The covariance relationship between instruments, which includes the effects of volatility and correlation, is used as the primary risk barometer in most of the examples presented in the literature. The reason the covariance matrix is so popular among both academics and practitioners is because it is easy to implement and interpret. This does not mean that it is the way actual markets behave. For the purposes of analyzing the volatility of our simple spread, we will certainly take a look at volatility, but we will also investigate other risk metrics such as the maximum drawdown, the equity curve shape, and the conditional variance.

More on the equity curve

Consider the equity curves in figure 6.12.

They are both upward sloping, but the second graph has a higher volatility than the first graph. The volatility in the second graph is due to the sporadic upward bursts that could end up greatly benefiting the strategy in the long run. This is not a concrete example by any means. The purpose of the graphic is to illustrate the point

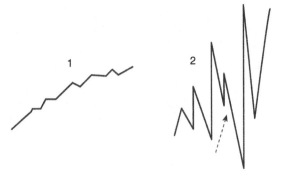

Figure 6.13 Two equity curves with different ending values.

Figure 6.14 Two equity curves with a different number of trades.

that volatility, the right kind of volatility, might not be a bad thing after all. What about the graphs displayed in figure 6.13? Which one would you prefer?

In this example, even though the second equity curve ends up at a higher final value, the large drawdown that occurs in the middle of the time period provides cause for concern.

How about the curves illustrated in figure 6.14?

The second equity curve was generated by a strategy that traded 11 times, whereas the first strategy only had 3 trades. One can argue that the strategy with fewer trades has not yet had the chance to showcase its true performance. Judging the merit of any statistic on a small sample size is not a prudent approach. As a general rule, the more data we have to base our decisions on, the better our inference will be.

The `Sharpe ratio` is a figure of merit developed by William F. Sharpe in 1966 [140]. It is calculated by using the average returns of a strategy adjusted by the risk-free interest rate in the numerator and the volatility in the denominator. A large Sharpe ratio is considered a good thing by most traders. A large Sharpe ratio, however, does not mean that the strategy is not risky.

$$s = \frac{E(R) - r_f}{\sigma} \tag{6.2}$$

Consider a trader that sells naked out-of-the-money call options on a weekly basis. Most of the time, the seller will collect all of the outstanding premium. Some days the seller will experience a small loss as the position goes against him. But most of the time, the seller will either scratch or win a portion of the total premium. This strategy will have a very high Sharpe ratio due to the consistent returns and the low volatility. A small denominator will tend to inflate the Sharpe ratio considerably. Is this a great strategy? Not at all. One abnormal move in the underlying contract might be enough to wipe out all of his previous gains and potentially much more than that. Since naked call selling is a strategy with unlimited risk, this can be a catastrophic outcome for the seller of premium.

Nevertheless, the Sharpe ratio is popular in both industry and in academia. When developing trading strategies or when presenting the results of a backtest or a track record to others, the Sharpe ratio should be presented along with other relevant risk metrics. Here is how to calculate the Sharpe ratio and the drawdown statistics in R:

```
# Calculates the Sharpe ratio
sharpe_ratio <- function(x, rf) {
  sharpe <- (mean(x, na.rm = TRUE) - rf) /
    sd(x, na.rm = TRUE)
  return(sharpe)
}

# Calculates the maximum drawdown profile
drawdown <- function(x) {
  cummax(x) - x
}
```

We can apply both of these to our previous spread.

```
par(mfrow = c(2, 1))

equity_curve <- data_out$equity_curve_x + data_out$equity
_curve_y

plot(equity_curve, main = "Equity Curve",
  cex.main = 0.8,
  cex.lab = 0.8,
  cex.axis = 0.8)

plot(drawdown(equity_curve), main = "Drawdown of equity curve"
  cex.main = 0.8,
  cex.lab = 0.8,
  cex.axis = 0.8)
```

We notice that the maximum drawdown is approximately $10,450. The average drawdown is approximately $3,760. The Sharpe ratio for the strategy is:

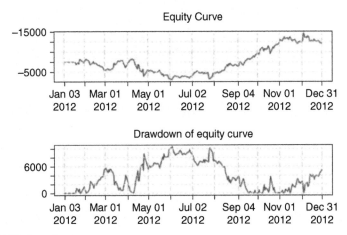

Figure 6.15 Drawdown curves.

```
equity <- as.numeric(equity_curve[, 1])
equity_curve_returns <- diff(equity) / equity[-length(equity)]

# Remove any infinities and NaN
invalid_values <- is.infinite(equity_curve_returns)
  | is.nan(equity_curve_returns)

sharpe_ratio(equity_curve_returns[!invalid_values], 0.03)
[1] 0.0658528
```

We are looking at a 0.065 Sharpe ratio over a 691-day period. Since Sharpe scales with the square root of time, we can multiply the result by a $\sqrt{250/691}$ scaling factor.

$$Sharpe_{Annualized} = 0.0658528\sqrt{250/691} = 0.03961003 \tag{6.3}$$

There exist hundreds of other risk measures. Here are a few more to consider:

1. The `Sortino ratio` is very similar to the Sharpe ratio. The difference appears in the denominator. Whereas Sharpe uses the full volatility, the Sortino ratio applies only the volatility of the negative returns.

$$Sortino = \frac{E(R) - r_f}{\sigma_-} \tag{6.4}$$

2. `Drawdown duration`. We have already seen the maximum drawdown statistic cited as an important risk metric. The drawdown duration is also another

dimension that should be analyzed. This measure tells us how long the strategy is in a slump. Smaller values are obviously better.

3. Omega ratio is a risk measure that takes the entire distribution into account. The formula weighs the positive returns over the negative returns of the strategy. It does so by taking the area under the cumulative distribution function above a threshold return of T and dividing this by the area between $-\infty$ and T [128].

$$\Omega(r) = \frac{\int_T^\infty (1 - F(r))dr}{\int_{-\infty}^T F(r)dr} \tag{6.5}$$

It turns out there is a very nifty decomposition of the above formula into the ratio of a European Call option and a European Put option.

$$\Omega(r) = \frac{C(r, T)}{P(r, T)} \tag{6.6}$$

The R code for evaluating this metric is:

```
omega_ratio <- function(r, T) {
    omega <- mean(pmax(r - T, 0)) / mean(pmax(T - r, 0))
    return(omega)
}
```

4. Straightness measure of the equity curve. The ideal equity curve would be an upward sloping one with no drawdowns and very low volatility. A theoretical line can be created between two extreme points, and then performance of the actual equity curve can be judged against this theoretical construct. Desirable traits would then be
   a. More values of the equity curve lying above the straight line.
   b. Less excursion below the straight line
   A discussion of this is approach is presented here:
   http://qusma.com/2013/09/23/equity-curve-straightness-measures/

5. Ulcer Index. Technical indicators can be applied to equity curves as well. The Ulcer index looks at the most recent high price and considers a value below that, a retracement of r_i [142]. The formula is the following:

$$r_i = \frac{p_i - p_{max}}{p_{max}} \tag{6.7}$$

$$Ulcer = \sqrt{\frac{r_1^2 + r_2^2 + \cdots + r_N^2}{N}} \tag{6.8}$$

Strategy attributes

A single number is not enough to express the desirable characteristics of a particular trading strategy. Rather than looking for the strategy with the highest Sharpe ratio or the smallest max-drawdown, it might be preferable to trade P&L variability for scalability. A strategy might have a great-looking risk profile when the traded size is small compared to what the market can support. When the participation rate of the strategy in the market increases, however, the performance could significantly degrade. This scalability and liquidity profile measure is important and needs to be taken into account when designing strategies that can potentially absorb a significant amount of capital.

Another strategy attribute that traders pay attention to is the frequency of order placement into the market. A rapid-fire approach might be desirable to certain traders, but less so to others. The perceived risk level from the frequency of order placement is a function of how comfortable the trader is with the technological platform that facilitates the trading. There is also the matter of capital allocation that comes into play. For smaller capital allocations, high throughput strategies might make sense. Large mutual funds will probably shy away from such endeavors.

Strategies that tend to get flat at the end of the day might also be preferable to strategies that require positions to be carried overnight. Not only will capital requirements be larger for the latter type, but the risk will also scale accordingly.

The `g-score` of a strategy is another attribute worth mentioning. It is a subjective measure that I developed to help keep the regulatory grey line in perspective. Traders often come up with trading ideas that might inadvertently trigger regulatory scrutiny under some circumstances. It is always nice to know that a trading strategy has a high g-score and thus a very low probability of being flagged by some external entity. A recommended calibration for the g-score is the following: a trading strategy that makes money entirely based on insider-trading information is completely illegal, and receives a g-score of 0. A buy-and-hold for the long-term investment approach, gets a 10. If there is any doubt that a proposed strategy has a g-score of 8, 9, or 10, then it is probably not worth the investment of time nor effort on the trader's behalf. Again, this is a subjective measure, and the point of the g-score is to make the quant/trader think about the legal implications of any proposed trading approach.

A way to measure the order arrival rate of trades coming into the market is to look at the successive time differences. This "trade duration" statistic is another strategy performance parameter that is often quoted in the literature and ties into the point we made earlier about high versus low frequency strategies. Here is some R code that calculates the length of time between trades:

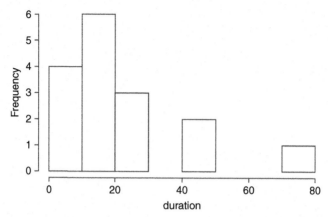

Figure 6.16 Histogram of trade duration.

```
# Find out where the trades occur
trade_dates <- data_out$qty_x[data_out$qty_x != 0]

# The trade_dates object is an xts object whose index
# contains the necessary time information
duration <- as.numeric(diff(index(trade_dates)))

# Summary statistics
summary(duration)
## Min. 1st Qu.  Median    Mean 3rd Qu.    Max.
## 1.00   13.50   21.00   31.84   44.00  128.00

# 4. Histogram of trade duration
hist(duration, breaks = 20,
  main = "Histogram of trade durations",
  cex.main = 0.8,
  cex.lab = 0.8,
  cex.axis = 0.8)
```

How would a simple buy-and-hold strategy have performed over the same time frame? This is a sensible question to ask since we can use the performance of such a buy-and-hold strategy as a baseline for comparison purposes. Many mutual fund managers get judged on how much they beat a particular benchmark return by. We can use the SPY exchange traded fund as a proxy for the market and evaluate how a long only strategy would have performed.

Summary

This chapter introduces the notion of constructing and trading a spread between two stocks. Ordinary Least Squares and Total Least Squares regression techniques are used to create suitable betas between the time series of interest.

A naive spread-trading strategy is defined, and suitable buy-sell logic is implemented in R code. The main purpose of this chapter is to expose a methodology of thinking about the evaluation of a trading hypothesis. The idea of `in-sample` versus `out-of-sample` analysis is also outlined. The section on risk is dedicated to addressing the concepts of a suitable equity curve, as well as desirable strategy attributes. Various risk metrics such as the `Sharpe ratio`, the `Omega ratio`, and others are also presented.

This page intentionally left blank

7 | Backtesting with Quantstrat

`Backtesting` is one of those activities in quantitative finance and trading that takes up a significant amount of time. It refers to the systematic methodology of testing out a particular hypothesis about market dynamics on a subset of historical data. It is akin to the scientific method in that it attempts to reconcile hypotheses with empirical observations. The end goal is to form predictions that result in profitable outcomes. The implicit assumption in all of this is that the historical patterns will, with high probability, manifest again in the future. The ultimate goal is to be ready to capitalize on those patterns when they are again detected. In a broad sense, we can think of the backtesting approach as follows:

1. Begin by asking a question about an observed or hypothesized market phenomenon.
2. Perform some background research in order to identify the data that will be required to satisfactorily answer the posed question.
3. Construct a hypothesis about how the phenomenon should work.
4. Codify the hypothesis and run it through real historical market data.
5. Observe the outcome and try to reconcile theory with observation.

Backtesting diverges from the scientific method in that we have limited historical data with which to work. Market dynamics are also not bound by the laws of physics. Most patterns exist for a limited time, and are most likely not due to immutable underlaying physical laws.

Backtesting methodology

The first component of a backtesting workflow deals with the generation of a trading signal based on historical data. This undoubtedly requires the most effort, and often involves econometric and other sophisticated data analysis work that needs to be carried out.

The second component involves the implementation of the trade entry and exit rules. Not all generated signals will warrant a trade. What determines whether a trade is executed is a set of rules that consider the current positions, equity constraints, portfolio constraints, current market data, and other variables that the trader deems important.

The third component of a backtesting framework requires the machinery that handles the accounting lifecycle of a trade. This is an important part of the system since it allows the trader to gauge the overall effectiveness of the strategy. This is where the P&L of the portfolio is calculated along with other relevant risk metrics that can be fed back into the second component. This part of the system needs to handle the nitty-gritty details of marking positions to the correct theoretical values, incorporating transaction costs, and calculating the relevant per-trade and aggregate statistics. Trading costs and slippage (i.e., buying the offer price vs. buying the bid price) need to properly be accounted for in any backtest.

The fourth component, the execution framework, is arguably the most difficult one to integrate. This is the part of the system that interacts with the outside world. When the trading strategy determines either to buy or sell a certain amount of stock, it needs to send the order out to an electronic exchange. The trader might have a direct connection to these exchanges or use a proxy connection through a broker. In either case, there are certain latencies and other restrictions between the path to and from the exchange that inevitably impact the strategy. These effects need to be accounted for in any realistic backtest. Unless the full path is exercised, it is difficult to reconcile a backtest with the actual performance of a strategy. This becomes more pronounced with high-frequency or low-latency trading strategies. For low frequency trading, the execution framework impact is much less relevant.

The **quantstrat** package was written by a professional team of quants to research proprietary trading strategies in an efficient and streamlined manner. The designers of this package put great care in implementing sound logic to account for most of the modules mentioned above. Not only is **quantstrat** free, but it also provides most of the functionality any trader/quant would ever need to fully test out a trading idea. One thing to note is that **quantstrat** is not an execution platform in and of itself. At the institutional level, there are custom tools for doing that. At the retail level, Interactive Brokers[1] is probably the best bet.

Quantstrat is a library for creating signal-based trading systems (i.e., buy when the 13-minute moving average crosses above the 48-minute moving average) in very few lines of code. Furthermore, the added advantage that **quantstrat** has above other backtesting systems is that it is still part of the R language. This means that customizing indicators, signals, and parts of rules is just a few function calls away. This chapter will be a quick overview on how to get off the ground with **quantstrat**. The R/Finance 2013[2] presentation provides a much more comprehensive overview for the interested reader [48].

We will analyze two strategies as part of our exploration. The first one will be a simple trend-following strategy devised by Andreas Clenow [1].[3] The second one will be an oscillator-based strategy devised by Laurence Connors [65].[4]

About blotter and PerformanceAnalytics

The **blotter** package is a powerful accounting analytics engine that handles all the nuances of trade monitoring. Under the hood, **quantstrat** leverages **blotter** a great deal. Whenever a **quantstrat** rule fires up an order, it is **blotter** that takes care of all of the heavy lifting by keeping track of the overall profitability of each trade through time. This granular tracking allows us to generate detailed analytics and summary statistics at the individual trade level.

According to the authors Peter Carl and Brian Peterson, "**PerformanceAnalytics** is a library of functions designed for evaluating the performance and risk characteristics of financial assets or funds. The goal of **PerformanceAnalytics** is to make it simple for someone to ask and answer questions about performance and risk as part of a broader investment decision making process [83].

The graphing capability and statistical-summary functionality of **PerformanceAnalytics** is leveraged by **quantstrat**. It is great at processing both normal and nonnormal return streams and it should be the primary tool of choice when considering the reward versus risk metrics of any strategy. Under the hood, the package uses the **xts** time-series functionality to make processing of such data efficient and convenient. The main focus of the package is on performance, style, and risk analysis. A reference to the contents and implementation of these modules can be obtained in the endnotes.[5]

Functionality also exists for value at risk (VAR) computations, as well as moment and co-moment analysis. The robust data cleaning and tabular summary functions are also great tools that come in handy, especially when dealing with messy data.

Initial setup

Perhaps the only drawback to **quantstrat** is the little bit of "boilerplate" code necessary to set up a trading strategy. While mildly annoying, it can be easily be packaged in a single file that is simply sourced at the beginning of any strategy.

This next snippet of code considers all the ETFs that had inception dates prior to 2003. We can place this code in a separate file named demoData.R and source it in as needed. This is what it looks like:

```
# Suppresses warnings
options("getSymbols.warning4.0" = FALSE)

# Do some house cleaning
rm(list = ls(.blotter), envir = .blotter)

# Set the currency and the timezone
currency('USD')
Sys.setenv(TZ = "UTC")
```

```r
# Define symbols of interest
symbols <- c("XLB", #SPDR Materials sector
  "XLE", #SPDR Energy sector
  "XLF", #SPDR Financial sector
  "XLP", #SPDR Consumer staples sector
  "XLI", #SPDR Industrial sector
  "XLU", #SPDR Utilities sector
  "XLV", #SPDR Healthcare sector
  "XLK", #SPDR Tech sector
  "XLY", #SPDR Consumer discretionary sector
  "RWR", #SPDR Dow Jones REIT ETF
  "EWJ", #iShares Japan
  "EWG", #iShares Germany
  "EWU", #iShares UK
  "EWC", #iShares Canada
  "EWY", #iShares South Korea
  "EWA", #iShares Australia
  "EWH", #iShares Hong Kong
  "EWS", #iShares Singapore
  "IYZ", #iShares U.S. Telecom
  "EZU", #iShares MSCI EMU ETF
  "IYR", #iShares U.S. Real Estate
  "EWT", #iShares Taiwan
  "EWZ", #iShares Brazil
  "EFA", #iShares EAFE
  "IGE", #iShares North American Natural Resources
  "EPP", #iShares Pacific Ex Japan
  "LQD", #iShares Investment Grade Corporate Bonds
  "SHY", #iShares 1-3 year TBonds
  "IEF", #iShares 3-7 year TBonds
  "TLT" #iShares 20+ year Bonds
 )

# SPDR ETFs first, iShares ETFs afterwards
if(!"XLB" %in% ls()) {
  # If data is not present, get it from yahoo
  suppressMessages(getSymbols(symbols, from = from,
    to = to,  src = "yahoo", adjust = TRUE))
 }
```

```
# Define the instrument type
stock(symbols, currency = "USD", multiplier = 1)
```

Here is a rundown of what this code does.

The `options("getSymbols.warning4.0" = FALSE)` line simply suppresses the getSymbols warning that comes from using Yahoo (the default getSymbols source) for more than five symbols, as well as the original highly verbose warning. This is not a mandatory line.

The `rm(list = ls(.blotter), envir = .blotter)` clears the blotter environment so as to have a clean workspace. Again, this is not a mandatory line, but as the blotter environment's contents are not displayed without a special call to `ls(.blotter)`, it is generally a good idea not to leave things there.

The next two lines (the currency and sys env lines) feed **blotter** some initialization settings regarding what type of currency and time zone we will be working in. Currencies have to be provided before any other instrument can be defined. USD should be plenty sufficient for anybody working with financial instruments quoted in USD. The time zone line is just something that needs to be set.

The `getSymbols(symbols, from = from, to = to, src = "yahoo", adjust = TRUE)` line gets the specified symbols (that long vector of symbols) from Yahoo. The `from` and `to` dates are not included in this file as these inputs can be kept within the actual strategy files. Finally, the if statement exists so that we can just type `rm(XLB)` in order to get the data all over again (say, for a different time period.) In this manner, the code does not need to start downloading symbols that are already located in the working environment.

Lastly, the line `stock(symbols, currency = "USD", multiplier = 1)` initializes the instruments with which we will be working. Although these are ETFs and not stocks per se, the stock argument functions as a sort of "default," which when specified with a multiplier of 1, will just take the time series as downloaded by `getSymbols()` in an "as-is" state. This is what we want.

The first strategy: A simple trend follower

It is time to backtest our first strategy. This strategy will utilize the demo data file that we saw in the previous section (since it contains most of the setup and initialization code), and will be based off of a simple trading strategy by Andreas Clenow.

We will leverage daily data for this strategy. The indicators/signals/rules are straightforward. The indicator will be generated by R's `lag()` function. The signal will be to go long(short) if the price is higher(lower) than it was a year ago. In order to equalize risk across instruments, we are going to size our order with a lagging ten day ATR (that is, we use yesterday's ATR to place our order sizes), and we will risk around 2 percent per trade. ATR stands for `Average True Range` and is an indicator that can be found in the **TTR** package.

Here is the code for the order sizing functionality:

```r
"lagATR" <- function(HLC, n = 14, maType, lag = 1, ...) {
  ATR <- ATR(HLC, n = n, maType = maType, ...)
  ATR <- lag(ATR, lag)
  out <- ATR$atr
  colnames(out) <- "atr"
  return(out)
}

"osDollarATR" <- function(orderside, tradeSize, pctATR,
  maxPctATR = pctATR,  data, timestamp,
  symbol, prefer = "Open", portfolio, integerQty = TRUE,
  atrMod = "", rebal = FALSE, ...) {

    if(tradeSize > 0 & orderside == "short"){
      tradeSize <- tradeSize * -1
     }

     pos <- getPosQty(portfolio, symbol, timestamp)
     atrString <- paste0("atr", atrMod)
     atrCol <- grep(atrString, colnames(mktdata))

    if(length(atrCol) == 0) {
      stop(paste("Term", atrString,
      "not found in mktdata column names."))
    }

     atrTimeStamp <- mktdata[timestamp, atrCol]
     if(is.na(atrTimeStamp) | atrTimeStamp == 0) {
       stop(paste("ATR corresponding to", atrString,
       "is invalid at this point in time.  Add a logical
       operator to account for this."))
     }

     dollarATR <- pos * atrTimeStamp
     desiredDollarATR <- pctATR * tradeSize
     remainingRiskCapacity <- tradeSize *
       maxPctATR - dollarATR

     if(orderside == "long"){
       qty <- min(tradeSize * pctATR / atrTimeStamp,
         remainingRiskCapacity / atrTimeStamp)
```

```
  } else {
    qty <- max(tradeSize * pctATR / atrTimeStamp,
      remainingRiskCapacity / atrTimeStamp)
  }

  if(integerQty) {
    qty <- trunc(qty)
  }
  if(!rebal) {
    if(orderside == "long" & qty < 0) {
      qty <- 0
    }
    if(orderside == "short" & qty > 0) {
      qty <- 0
    }
  }
  if(rebal) {
    if(pos == 0) {
      qty <- 0
    }
  }
  return(qty)
}
```

In short, the first (smaller) function computes a lagged ATR. The second function finds the output of the first, and sizes the order by rounding to the lowest(highest) amount of integer shares when we go long(short), depending on our trade size and the amount risked. So if we risk 2 percent of a 10,000 trade size, we will get 200 ATRs worth of the security long, or -200 short.

Here is the strategy setup:

```
require(quantstrat)
require(PerformanceAnalytics)

initDate = "1990-01-01"
from = "2003-01-01"
to = "2013-12-31"
options(width = 70)


# To rerun the strategy, rerun everything below this line
# demoData.R contains all of the data-related boilerplate.
source("demoData.R")
```

```
# Trade sizing and initial equity settings
tradeSize <- 10000
initEq <- tradeSize * length(symbols)

strategy.st <- "Clenow_Simple"
portfolio.st <- "Clenow_Simple"
account.st <- "Clenow_Simple"
rm.strat(portfolio.st)
rm.strat(strategy.st)

initPortf(portfolio.st, symbols = symbols,
  initDate = initDate, currency = 'USD')

initAcct(account.st, portfolios = portfolio.st,
  initDate = initDate, currency = 'USD', initEq = initEq)

initOrders(portfolio.st, initDate = initDate)

strategy(strategy.st, store=TRUE)
```

This is about as straightforward as things get. We first load the required
quantstrat and **PerformanceAnalytics** packages. Three dates have to be initial-
ized after that: the `initDate` (which must be before the first date covered by the
data), the beginning date `from` and the ending date `to`. Next, we initialize our trade
size (`tradeSize`) (i.e., our notional capital per instrument), and our initial equity,
which will be used to compute returns later on. Finally, we initialize the names
(strategy.st, portfolio.st, and account.st), clear the strategy environment (there will
be errors if we try to rerun the same strategy with a strategy of that same name in
existence), then initialize the portfolio, account, and orders in that specific order.
Lastly, we store the strategy object for subsequent retrieval.

Backtesting the first strategy

This next part shows how to turn R into a fully fledged backtesting research environment. Through the application of indicators, signals, and rules, it is possible to
quickly construct trading strategies, run them, and produce analytics.

To start with, here are the parameters and the function that we will use as our
signal-generating indicator.

```
nLag = 252
pctATR = 0.02
period = 10

namedLag <- function(x, k = 1, na.pad = TRUE, ...) {
  out <- lag(x, k = k, na.pad = na.pad, ...)
```

```
    out[is.na(out)] <- x[is.na(out)]
    colnames(out) <- "namedLag"
    return(out)
}
```

We will use a 252-day lag, a 2 percent risk on our capital, and size our orders according to the 10-day running ATR.

The function, is a wrapper that does two things: first, it creates a lagged version of the time series with the NAs set to the current price, and second, it gives the output a consistent column name. The following examples demonstrate this:

```
add.indicator(strategy.st, name = "namedLag",
    arguments = list(x = quote(Cl(mktdata)), k = nLag),
    label = "ind")

add.indicator(strategy.st, name = "lagATR",
    arguments = list(HLC = quote(HLC(mktdata)), n = period),
    label = "atrX")

test <- applyIndicators(strategy.st, mktdata = OHLC(XLB))
head(round(test, 2), 253)
```

The last two columns are called `namedLag.ind` and `atr.atrX` . Why atrX? There is no particular reason beyond the fact that it provides an easy way for the order-sizing function to find the appropriate column to use in order to properly size up the number of units the strategy will trade.

The arguments for adding an indicator are very straightforward. Every single indicator addition takes the form of a call to the `add.indicator()` function, with four key arguments:

1. The strategy to which to apply the indicator. For all intents and purposes, this should be named `strategy.st`.
2. The name of the function that will generate the computations. This is the indicator itself.
3. The arguments to the above function. They go inside the `arguments = list` parentheses. One of them will always be some form of the `mktdata` (market data) object.
4. The label of the indicator. This provides a column name that will allow the indicator to be located later on during the strategy execution.

Let us move onto signals. We will have four signals—a long entry, a long exit, a short entry, and a short exit. In **quantstrat**, exits take precedence over entries— so if an exit and entry happen at the same time, the exit will be executed first. In short, stop-and-reverse strategies (otherwise known as 100 percent in the market) will work. Basically, every strategy must have at minimum two rules per side—an entry and an exit. So a strategy that is both long and short demands at a minimum four rules. This is how signals are added to the backtest:

```
# Signals
add.signal(strategy.st, name = "sigCrossover",
  arguments = list(columns = c("Close", "namedLag.ind"),
  relationship = "gt"),
  label = "coverOrBuy")

add.signal(strategy.st, name = "sigCrossover",
  arguments = list(columns = c("Close", "namedLag.ind"),
  relationship = "lt"),
  label = "sellOrShort")
```

Signals have an identical format to indicators. They consist of the function call, the strategy name, the name of the desired function, its arguments, and a label. Similarly to indicators, signals can be customized, although most of the time, the signal functions found within **quantstrat** are sufficient. Later in this chapter, we will see the use of a signal function that will make some strategies more explicit. In this example, we will be using the sigCrossover function that lets the strategy know when the first column crosses over the second in a manner specified by the relationship argument. In this case, gt stands for greater than, and lt for less than. The first signal specifies the relationship of the price crossing over the lagged indicator, and the second signal vice versa.

Other types of signals are sigComparison (identical to sigCrossover, except the signal will be true for the entire time the relationship holds, rather than the first time), sigThreshold (basically sigCrossover for a static value. This is useful for oscillator-type strategies such as RSI-based trading systems), and the custom signal we will see later, called sigAND, which is simply an intersect operator.

Finally, the third aspect of the trading system trifecta is the add.rule function. Rules in **quantstrat** get highly involved, and their full depth is out of the scope of this chapter. However, these small examples will illustrate just a little bit of how rules are customizable within **quantstrat**.

```
# Long rules
add.rule(strategy.st, name = "ruleSignal",
  arguments = list(sigcol = "coverOrBuy",
  sigval = TRUE, ordertype = "market",
  orderside = "long", replace = FALSE,
  prefer = "Open", osFUN = osDollarATR,
  tradeSize = tradeSize, pctATR = pctATR,
  atrMod = "X"), type = "enter", path.dep = TRUE)
```

```
add.rule(strategy.st, name = "ruleSignal",
  arguments = list(sigcol = "sellOrShort",
  sigval = TRUE, orderqty = "all",
  ordertype = "market", orderside = "long",
  replace = FALSE, prefer = "Open"),
  type = "exit", path.dep = TRUE)

# Short rules
add.rule(strategy.st, name = "ruleSignal",
  arguments = list(sigcol = "sellOrShort",
  sigval = TRUE, ordertype = "market",
  orderside = "short", replace = FALSE,
  prefer = "Open", osFUN = osDollarATR,
  tradeSize = -tradeSize, pctATR = pctATR,
  atrMod = "X"), type = "enter", path.dep = TRUE)

add.rule(strategy.st, name = "ruleSignal",
  arguments = list(sigcol = "coverOrBuy",
  sigval = TRUE, orderqty = "all",
  ordertype = "market", orderside = "short",
  replace = FALSE, prefer = "Open"),
  type = "exit", path.dep = TRUE)
```

For rules, there is only one name that is used for the vast majority of **quantstrat** backtests, namely `ruleSignal`. Some noteworthy arguments are the following:

1. `sigcol`: The column containing the signal. Remember that label in the add.signal function? The add.rule function uses the named column to extract the necessary information.
2. `ordertype`: Will usually take the form of a market order. It can take the form of a limit order and a stop-limit order (only in the case of stop-loss orders.)
3. `prefer`: As quantstrat enters on the bar after the signal for all frequencies of data up to monthly and the default is to buy-on-close, it means buying the next day's close. Changing it to open usually makes more sense when talking about strategies that trade on daily bars.
4. `orderside`: Long or short, which is used in some of the order-sizing functions.
5. `replace`: Always set this to FALSE. If set to TRUE, any rule that gets executed will override any other rule at that time-stamp.
6. `osFUN`: This is the part that calls the ATR order sizing function (hence osFUN). osFUNs are functions that compute different order sizes depending on their inputs and what they were programmed to do. The arguments for osFUNs also go into the arguments list for ruleSignal.

7. `type`: Usually an enter or exit. There are other types that are outside the scope of this introduction.
8. `path.dep`: Always set to TRUE for ruleSignal.

Now that we have our strategy specified, let us run it. This is done via the following code:

```
# Get begin time
t1 <- Sys.time()
out <- applyStrategy(strategy = strategy.st,
  portfolios = portfolio.st)

# Record end time
t2 <- Sys.time()
print(t2 - t1)
```

The `applyStrategy()` function applies all of the indicators, signals, and rules to the strategy. This creates a stream of orders for the specified instruments. If everything works correctly, we will see a stream of orders that looks something like this:

```
## [1] "2007-10-22 00:00:00 XLY -655 @ 32.3578893111826"
## [1] "2007-10-22 00:00:00 XLY -393 @ 32.3578893111826"
## [1] "2007-10-23 00:00:00 XLY 393 @ 33.1349846702336"
## [1] "2007-10-23 00:00:00 XLY 358 @ 33.1349846702336"
## [1] "2007-10-25 00:00:00 XLY -358 @ 32.8639048938205"
## [1] "2007-10-25 00:00:00 XLY -333 @ 32.8639048938205"
## [1] "2009-09-30 00:00:00 XLY 333 @ 25.9947501843176"
## [1] "2009-09-30 00:00:00 XLY 449 @ 25.9947501843176"
## [1] "2009-10-02 00:00:00 XLY -449 @ 24.8800203565938"
```

Evaluating the performance

The next step is to analyze the effectiveness of the implementation. The following workflow will demonstrate how this is done:

```
updatePortf(portfolio.st)
dateRange <- time(getPortfolio(portfolio.st)$summary)[-1]
updateAcct(portfolio.st, dateRange)
updateEndEq(account.st)
```

These four lines issue the proper calls to update the P&L and to generate the transactional history needed for the analytics. Trade statistics include the percentage of correct trades, the profit factor (the ratio of money made to lost, aggregated by trades), the average win-to-loss ratio, and so forth.

```
tStats <- tradeStats(Portfolios = portfolio.st, use = "trades"
   inclZeroDays = FALSE)
tStats[, 4:ncol(tStats)] <- round(tStats[, 4:ncol(tStats)], 2)

print(data.frame(t(tStats[,-c(1,2)])))
aggPF <- sum(tStats$Gross.Profits) / -sum(tStats$Gross.Losses)
aggCorrect <- mean(tStats$Percent.Positive)
numTrades <- sum(tStats$Num.Trades)
meanAvgWLR <- mean(tStats$Avg.WinLoss.Ratio[
   tStats$Avg.WinLoss.Ratio < Inf], na.rm = TRUE)
```

This is what the tStats table looks like:

##	XLK	XLP	XLU	XLV	XLY
## Num.Txns	105.00	33.00	41.00	93.00	69.00
## Num.Trades	53.00	17.00	21.00	45.00	35.00
## Net.Trading.PL	6016.85	23438.64	20018.73	24191.83	16349.64
## Avg.Trade.PL	113.53	1378.74	953.27	537.60	467.13
## Med.Trade.PL	-97.78	-41.14	-114.53	-79.73	-136.29
## Largest.Winner	7203.51	5403.21	14892.92	1710.61	2287.43
## Largest.Loser	-1541.41	-231.73	-895.47	-1196.50	-786.39
## Gross.Profits	16494.40	24645.83	23631.91	31237.12	22885.87
## Gross.Losses	-10477.55	-1207.19	-3613.17	-7045.29	-6536.23
## Std.Dev.Trade.PL	1197.87	4154.99	3387.87	3619.68	3041.63
## Percent.Positive	35.85	35.29	33.33	37.78	31.43
## Percent.Negative	64.15	64.71	66.67	62.22	68.57
## Profit.Factor	1.57	20.42	6.54	4.43	3.50
## Avg.Win.Trade	868.13	4107.64	3375.99	1837.48	2080.53
## Med.Win.Trade	162.15	1287.61	2128.49	225.36	219.68
## Avg.Losing.Trade	-308.16	-109.74	-258.08	-251.62	-272.34
## Med.Losing.Trade	-172.44	-115.39	-193.79	-202.68	-209.24
## Avg.Daily.PL	51.89	428.46	894.51	3.13	-37.87
## Med.Daily.PL	-98.89	-48.45	-130.50	-82.54	-141.43
## Std.Dev.Daily.PL	1121.49	1428.19	3464.89	503.18	579.12
## Ann.Sharpe	0.73	4.76	4.10	0.10	-1.04
## Max.Drawdown	-8098.15	-3819.66	-8212.64	-5755.91	-7084.35
## Profit.To.Max.Draw	0.74	6.14	2.44	4.20	2.31
## Avg.WinLoss.Ratio	2.82	37.43	13.08	7.30	7.64
## Med.WinLoss.Ratio	0.94	11.16	10.98	1.11	1.05
## Max.Equity	6016.85	23457.62	21210.88	24220.69	16349.64
## Min.Equity	-5258.58	-330.75	-709.58	-3914.56	-4354.96
## End.Equity	6016.85	23438.64	20018.73	24191.83	16349.64

In essence, we can see that XLP has done exceptionally well by any stretch of the imagination (but particularly by the profit factor), meaning that the trading strategy has managed to mitigate most of the losses for this particular instrument. Note, however, that this is just an example in table reading. The main use for the tStats table for strategies with manageable amounts of instruments is to do a quick eyeball scan to look for particularly noteworthy instruments (i.e., the one instrument that lost money in an otherwise profitable strategy).

Here are the aggregate trading statistics for this strategy:

```
aggPF <- sum(tStats$Gross.Profits) / -sum(tStats$Gross.Losses)
## [1] 3.663545

aggCorrect <- mean(tStats$Percent.Positive)
## [1] 36.00233

numTrades <- sum(tStats$Num.Trades)
## [1] 1134

meanAvgWLR <- mean(tStats$Avg.WinLoss.Ratio[
   tStats$Avg.WinLoss.Ratio < Inf], na.rm = TRUE)
## [1] 9.871333
```

This strategy has the profile of a standard trend follower: A low win rate, coupled with large win-to-loss ratios. A 3.66 profit factor is also quite solid. However, it is also possible to look at returns analytics. These are only possible if we define an initial equity amount. Furthermore, all of the returns will be the P&L of individual instruments over our total equity, meaning that these returns are already weighted returns. This means that there is an implicit equal weighting applied to the return streams. For strategies that use asset rotation approaches, one would have to multiply all the returns by the number of symbols in the portfolio. Here is some code to run return analytics:

```
instRets <- PortfReturns(account.st)

portfRets <- xts(rowMeans(instRets) * ncol(instRets),
   order.by = index(instRets))
portfRets <- portfRets[!is.na(portfRets)]
cumPortfRets <- cumprod(1 + portfRets)
firstNonZeroDay <- as.character(index(portfRets)[
   min(which(portfRets != 0))])

# Obtain symbol
getSymbols("SPY", from = firstNonZeroDay, to = to)
SPYrets <- diff(log(Cl(SPY)))[-1]
cumSPYrets <- cumprod(1 + SPYrets)
comparison <- cbind(cumPortfRets, cumSPYrets)
colnames(comparison) <- c("strategy", "SPY")
chart.TimeSeries(comparison, legend.loc = "topleft",
   colors=c("green", "red"))
```

Figure 7.1 Clenow equity curve comparison.

```
# Calculate risk metrics
SharpeRatio.annualized(portfRets)
Return.annualized(portfRets)
maxDrawdown(portfRets)
```

The above code gets the instrument returns (instRets), computes the cumulative returns of the sums of all of the returns (as they are already weighted based on fraction of initial equity), and compares them to the cumulative returns of SPY over the same time frame. It plots both of these cumulative returns on one plot. This is also called an equity curve comparison.

In this case, we can see that the system looks like it works. Here are some aggregate portfolio characteristics:

```
SharpeRatio.annualized(portfRets)
## [1] 0.6424366

Return.annualized(portfRets)
## [1] 0.1392711

maxDrawdown(portfRets)
## [1] 0.278221
```

In other words, about a 14 percent return per year, at the cost of about twice that in max drawdown, and a Sharpe ratio of less than one. This is not the greatest, but definitely a return for the risk.

Finally, there is a function that allows one to view the position, P&L, drawdown, and even indicators overlaid (or underlaid) on a chart of a particular security. This is how it is done:

```
chart.Posn(portfolio.st, "XLB")
tmp <- namedLag(Cl(XLB), k = nLag)
add_TA(tmp$namedLag, col = "blue", on = 1)
```

This produces the Figure 7.2.

This allows us to see at an instrument level why the strategy may work, in that the rules are fairly intuitive (if the price is higher than it was a year ago, odds are, it is going to continue upwards), and why it may not (if the price trajectory mirrors itself from a year ago, we may be going long and short on pure noise, when the correct decision would have been to gauge the direction of the current price and stick with that decision).

Now that we have gone through a rough overview of a basic trend-following strategy, let us look at a strategy that tries to profit through mean reversion.

The second strategy: Cumulative Connors RSI

Rather than emulating a textbook example of a simple strategy (otherwise known as a toy strategy), this strategy will be something that looks somewhat more legitimate. The indicator in use will be the Connors RSI (3, 2, 100). This indicator takes an RSI-3 of the price action, an RSI-2 of the streak of the price differences (that is, if the price went up three days in a row, the streak would be 1, 2, 3), and a 100-day percentage ranking of the most recent returns. These quantities are averaged together. This makes for a more modern version of the classical RSI indicator. The strategy will buy when the cumulative sum exceeds a certain number of Connors RSIs.

For those not familiar with the indicator, here is a comprehensive introduction to it: http://www.qmatix.com/ConnorsRSI-Pullbacks-Guidebook.pdf

As we already demonstrated the fundamentals of strategy creation earlier, this section will go much faster than the last. Here is the description of the strategy: the strategy will go long (no shorting in this version) when the cumulative two-day Connors RSI is less than 40 and the closing price is above the 200-day SMA. It will sell when the one-day Connors RSI crosses above 75. Here are the new (refer to the first strategy for the prerequisite ATR order sizing) prerequisite functions:

```
# Compute Connor's RSI, depends on RSI TTR function
connorsRSI <- function(price, nRSI = 3, nStreak = 2,
  nPercentLookBack = 100 ) {
```

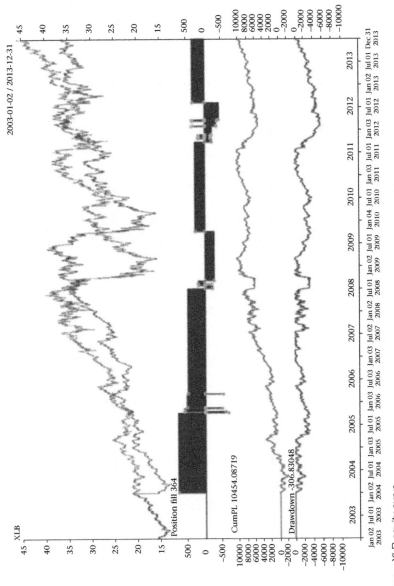

Figure 7.2 Clenow XLB equity curve.

```r
  priceRSI <- RSI(price, nRSI)
  streakRSI <- RSI(computeStreak(price), nStreak)
  percents <- round(runPercentRank(x = diff(log(price)),
    n = 100, cumulative = FALSE, exact.multiplier = 1) * 100)
  ret <- (priceRSI + streakRSI + percents) / 3
  colnames(ret) <- "connorsRSI"
  return(ret)
}


# Computes a running streak of positives and
# negatives of price changes
computeStreak <- function(priceSeries) {
  signs <- sign(diff(priceSeries))
  posDiffs <- negDiffs <- rep(0,length(signs))
  posDiffs[signs == 1] <- 1
  negDiffs[signs == -1] <- -1

  # Create vector of cumulative sums and cumulative
  # sums not incremented during streaks.
  # Zero out any leading NAs after na.locf
  posCum <- cumsum(posDiffs)
  posNAcum <- posCum
  posNAcum[posDiffs == 1] <- NA
  posNAcum <- na.locf(posNAcum, na.rm = FALSE)
  posNAcum[is.na(posNAcum)] <- 0
  posStreak <- posCum - posNAcum

  # Repeat for negative cumulative sums
  negCum <- cumsum(negDiffs)
  negNAcum <- negCum
  negNAcum[negDiffs == -1] <- NA
  negNAcum <- na.locf(negNAcum, na.rm = FALSE)
  negNAcum[is.na(negNAcum)] <- 0
  negStreak <- negCum - negNAcum

  streak <- posStreak + negStreak
  streak <- xts(streak, order.by = index(priceSeries))
  return (streak)
}

sigAND <- function(label, data=mktdata,
  columns,  cross = FALSE) {
  ret_sig = NULL
```

```
  colNums <- rep(0, length(columns))
  for(i in 1:length(columns)) {
    colNums[i] <- match.names(columns[i], colnames(data))
  }
  ret_sig <- data[, colNums[1]]
  for(i in 2:length(colNums)) {
    ret_sig <- ret_sig & data[, colNums[i]]
  }
  ret_sig <- ret_sig * 1
  if (isTRUE(cross))
    ret_sig <- diff(ret_sig) == 1
  colnames(ret_sig) <- label
  return(ret_sig)
}

cumCRSI <- function(price, nCum = 2, ...) {
  CRSI <- connorsRSI(price, ...)
  out <- runSum(CRSI, nCum)
  colnames(out) <- "cumCRSI"
  out
}
```

The sigAND function is a custom signal, created to be the intersection of two (or more) other signals. Beyond that, the Connors RSI works as described earlier, and the cumulative Connors RSI is simply a running sum of the indicator.

Here is all the strategy code:

```
rm(list = ls(.blotter), envir = .blotter)
initDate = '1990-01-01'
from = "2003-01-01"
to = "2013-12-31"
initEq = 10000

currency('USD')
Sys.setenv(TZ="UTC")
source("demoData.R")

strategy.st <- "CRSIcumStrat"
portfolio.st <- "CRSIcumStrat"
account.st <- "CRSIcumStrat"

rm.strat(portfolio.st)
rm.strat(strategy.st)
```

```r
initPortf(portfolio.st, symbols = symbols,
  initDate = initDate, currency = 'USD')

initAcct(account.st, portfolios = portfolio.st,
  initDate = initDate, currency = 'USD',
  initEq = initEq)

initOrders(portfolio.st, initDate = initDate)
strategy(strategy.st, store = TRUE)

# Parameters
cumThresh <- 40
exitThresh <- 75
nCum <- 2
nRSI <- 3
nStreak <- 2
nPercentLookBack <- 100
nSMA <- 200
pctATR <- .02
period <- 10

# Indicators
add.indicator(strategy.st, name = "cumCRSI",
  arguments = list(price = quote(Cl(mktdata)), nCum = nCum,
  nRSI = nRSI, nStreak = nStreak,
  nPercentLookBack = nPercentLookBack),
  label = "CRSIcum")

add.indicator(strategy.st, name = "connorsRSI",
  arguments = list(price = quote(Cl(mktdata)), nRSI = nRSI,
  nStreak = nStreak,
  nPercentLookBack = nPercentLookBack),
  label = "CRSI")

add.indicator(strategy.st, name = "SMA",
  arguments = list(x = quote(Cl(mktdata)), n = nSMA),
  label = "sma")

add.indicator(strategy.st, name = "lagATR",
  arguments = list(HLC = quote(HLC(mktdata)), n = period),
  label = "atrX")
```

```
# Signals
add.signal(strategy.st, name = "sigThreshold",
  arguments = list(column = "cumCRSI.CRSIcum",
  threshold = cumThresh, relationship = "lt", cross = FALSE),
  label="cumCRSI.lt.thresh")

add.signal(strategy.st, name = "sigComparison",
  arguments = list(columns = c("Close", "SMA.sma"),
  relationship = "gt"), label = "Cl.gt.SMA")

add.signal(strategy.st, name = "sigAND",
  arguments = list(columns = c("cumCRSI.lt.thresh",
  "Cl.gt.SMA"), cross = TRUE), label = "longEntry")

add.signal(strategy.st, name = "sigThreshold",
  arguments = list(column = "connorsRSI.CRSI",
  threshold = exitThresh, relationship = "gt",
  cross = TRUE), label = "longExit")

# Rules
add.rule(strategy.st, name = "ruleSignal",
  arguments = list(sigcol = "longEntry", sigval = TRUE,
  ordertype = "market", orderside ="long", replace = FALSE,
  prefer = "Open", osFUN = osDollarATR, tradeSize = tradeSize,
  pctATR = pctATR, atrMod = "X"), type = "enter", path.dep
  = TRUE)

add.rule(strategy.st, name = "ruleSignal",
  arguments = list(sigcol = "longExit", sigval = TRUE,
  orderqty = "all", ordertype = "market", orderside = "long",
  replace = FALSE, prefer = "Open"), type = "exit", path.dep
  = TRUE)

# Apply Strategy
t1 <- Sys.time()
out <- applyStrategy(strategy = strategy.st,
  portfolios = portfolio.st)
t2 <- Sys.time()
print(t2 - t1)

# Set up analytics
updatePortf(portfolio.st)
dateRange <- time(getPortfolio(portfolio.st)$summary)[-1]
```

```
updateAcct(portfolio.st,dateRange)
updateEndEq(account.st)
```

This strategy demonstrates the `sigThreshold` signal, which is the signal used for oscillator-type signals or other *scaled*-type signals that take on a fixed range of values. It also illustrates the use of `sigComparison`, which is identical to `sigCrossover` except that it is true for the entire time the relationship holds rather than the first point. The creation of custom signals is also explored through the use of `sigAND`. As with indicators, signals are simply R functions that take existing data and compute related quantities. Again, notice that the rules we created use our previously defined custom ATR order-sizing logic.

Evaluating the mean-reverting strategy

Here are the aggregate trade statistics for this strategy:

```
aggPF <- sum(tStats$Gross.Profits)/-sum(tStats$Gross.Losses)
## [1] 1.699368

aggCorrect <- mean(tStats$Percent.Positive)
## [1] 71.608

numTrades <- sum(tStats$Num.Trades)
## [1] 1500

meanAvgWLR <- mean(tStats$Avg.WinLoss.Ratio[
  tStats$Avg.WinLoss.Ratio < Inf], na.rm = TRUE)
## [1] 0.725
```

So far, not too bad. This is about par for the course for a mean-reverting type of strategy: a large percentage correct, a decently positive profit factor (albeit far from spectacular), and a win-to-loss ratio less than one (in other words, losers are going to hurt).

In this next section, we will look at a few more important performance metrics. The first bundle of statistics displays how the strategy performs on a daily basis while in the market. So, the profit factor of a strategy, for instance, rather than being computed on a per-trade basis, will now be aggregated on a per-day basis. If we had ten out of ten positive trades, our profit factor, according to tradeStats, would be infinite. But if each of those trades had only a few more up days than down days, our profit factor on daily statistics would be much closer to one. Here is an example of how daily statistics work:

```
dStats <- dailyStats(Portfolios = portfolio.st, use = "Equity"
rownames(dStats) <- gsub(".DailyEndEq", "", rownames(dStats))
```

```
print(data.frame(t(dStats)))
```

The output produces a table of columns (one per instrument):

```
##                            XLU        XLV        XLY
## Total.Net.Profit       2822.01    3844.99    4081.33
## Total.Days              384.00     314.00     344.00
## Winning.Days            206.00     168.00     191.00
## Losing.Days             178.00     146.00     153.00
## Avg.Day.PL                7.35      12.25      11.86
## Med.Day.PL               15.41      13.00      18.76
## Largest.Winner          725.62     690.22     632.56
## Largest.Loser          -950.62    -821.22    -782.98
## Gross.Profits         23038.84   21038.16   24586.03
## Gross.Losses         -20216.82  -17193.17  -20504.71
## Std.Dev.Daily.PL        155.96     166.35     178.05
## Percent.Positive         53.65      53.50      55.52
## Percent.Negative         46.35      46.50      44.48
## Profit.Factor             1.14       1.22       1.20
## Avg.Win.Day             111.84     125.23     128.72
## Med.Win.Day              92.74      95.73     102.38
## Avg.Losing.Day         -113.58    -117.76    -134.02
## Med.Losing.Day          -79.09     -79.56     -85.41
## Avg.Daily.PL              7.35      12.25      11.86
## Med.Daily.PL             15.41      13.00      18.76
## Std.Dev.Daily.PL.1      155.96     166.35     178.05
## Ann.Sharpe                0.75       1.17       1.06
## Max.Drawdown          -1845.00   -2201.70   -2248.18
## Profit.To.Max.Draw        1.53       1.75       1.82
## Avg.WinLoss.Ratio         0.98       1.06       0.96
## Med.WinLoss.Ratio         1.17       1.20       1.20
## Max.Equity             4344.64    3892.77    4081.33
## Min.Equity             -729.04   -1228.57    -631.80
## End.Equity             2822.01    3844.99    4081.33
```

The next set of analytics deals with duration measures. We will define a custom function that does a lot of the heavy lifting.

```
durationStatistics <- function(Portfolio, Symbols,
  includeOpenTrade = FALSE, ...) {

  tmp <- list()
  length(tmp) <- length(Symbols)
  for(Symbol in Symbols) {
```

```
    pts <- perTradeStats(Portfolio = Portfolio,
      Symbol = Symbol, includeOpenTrade = includeOpenTrade)
    pts$diff <- pts$End - pts$Start

    durationSummary <- summary(as.numeric(pts$diff))
    winDurationSummary <- summary(as.numeric(
      pts$diff[pts$Net.Trading.PL > 0]))
    lossDurationSummary <- summary(as.numeric(
      pts$diff[pts$Net.Trading.PL <= 0]))
    names(durationSummary) <-
      c("Min", "Q1", "Med", "Mean", "Q3", "Max")
    names(winDurationSummary) <-
      c("Min", "Q1", "Med", "Mean", "Q3", "Max")
    names(lossDurationSummary) <-
      c("Min", "Q1", "Med", "Mean", "Q3", "Max")
    names(winDurationSummary) <-
      paste0("W", names(winDurationSummary))
    names(lossDurationSummary) <-
      paste0("L", names(lossDurationSummary))

    dataRow <- data.frame(cbind(t(round(durationSummary)),
      t(round(winDurationSummary)),
      t(round(lossDurationSummary))))
    tmp[[Symbol]] <- dataRow
  }
  out <- do.call(rbind, tmp)
  return(out)
}
```

What this does is compile the five-number summary and mean of all trade statistics by instrument, and outputs these as a matrix. Here is the function call:

```
durStats <- durationStatistics(Portfolio=portfolio.st,
  Symbols=sort(symbols))
print(t(durStats))
```

And here is a sample of the output:

```
##          XLU XLV XLY
## Min        1   1   1
## Q1         5   4   3
## Med        8   6   6
## Mean      10   8   7
## Q3        14  10  10
```

```
## Max      27  33  22
## WMin      1   1   1
## WQ1       2   3   2
## WMed      6   5   5
## WMean     6   6   6
## WQ3       8   7   7
## WMax     21  20  20
## LMin      6   6   1
## LQ1      12   9   8
## LMed     16  16  12
## LMean    16  15  11
## LQ3      20  18  14
## LMax     27  33  22
```

The order of the statistics is aggregate, winners, and losers. From this small sample of output, one can already see one bit of potentially low-hanging fruit as to how to improve the strategy—by noticing that losers last a lot longer than winners. One way to potentially improve this strategy would be to set some sort of time-based exit that tracks whether or not the position is profitable yet. If it is not profitable after some small time frame (say, eight days), then we could exit the trade and wait for another setup.

The following is a quick way to compute market exposure, in other words, the proportion of the time the strategy spends in the market:

```
# Market exposure
tmp <- list()
length(tmp) <- length(symbols)
for(i in 1:nrow(dStats)) {
  totalDays <- nrow(get(rownames(dStats)[i]))
  mktExposure <- dStats$Total.Days[i] / totalDays
  tmp[[i]] <- c(rownames(dStats)[i], round(mktExposure, 3))
}
mktExposure <- data.frame(do.call(rbind, tmp))
colnames(mktExposure) <- c("Symbol", "MktExposure")
```

The output is:

```
print(mktExposure)
##      Symbol   MktExposure
## 1       EFA        0.113
## 2       EPP        0.122
## 3       EWA        0.137
## 4       EWC        0.137
## 5       EWG        0.126
```

```
## 6     EWH        0.136
## 7     EWJ        0.073
## 8     EWS        0.097
## 9     EWT        0.135
## 10    EWU        0.103
## 11    EWY        0.116
## 12    EWZ        0.108
## 13    EZU        0.123
## 14    IEF        0.155
## 15    IGE        0.144
## 16    IYR        0.127
## 17    IYZ        0.169
## 18    LQD        0.147
## 19    RWR        0.133
## 20    SHY        0.114
## 21    TLT        0.146
## 22    XLB        0.131
## 23    XLE        0.132
## 24    XLF        0.104
## 25    XLI        0.121
## 26    XLK        0.121
## 27    XLP        0.125
## 28    XLU        0.139
## 29    XLV        0.113
## 30    XLY        0.124
```

```
print(mean(as.numeric(as.character(mktExposure$MktExposure))))
## [1] 0.1257
```

On average, there is about a 12.5 percent exposure to the market. What kind of equity curve does this strategy produce, then? The answer is illustrated in Figure 7.3 below.

The returns are not spectacular when compared to being 100 percent exposed to SPY. The sharp drawdowns also appear to be cause for concern. This is clearly an area in which the strategy can improve. After all, low but steady returns can be leveraged (or put another way, the same strategy can be run with less capital due to its very small market exposure). However, if drawdowns are steep, then this puts the brakes on leveraging. This particular strategy has the potential for such steep drawdowns.

Here are the aggregate portfolio statistics:

```
SharpeRatio.annualized(portfRets)
## [1]   0.6973019
```

Figure 7.3 Connors equity curve comparison.

```
Return.annualized(portfRets)
## [1] 0.03370045

maxDrawdown(portfRets)
## [1] 0.09120687
```

The ratio of annualized returns to max drawdowns means that leverage will quickly become a problem, at least with this particular set of instruments. As a final step, here is a look at the equity curve of an individual instrument.

```
chart.Posn(portfolio.st, "XLB")
TA_CRSI <- connorsRSI(Cl(XLB), nRSI = nRSI,
  nStreak = nStreak, nPercentLookBack = nPercentLookBack)
add_TA(TA_CRSI, col = "red")

TA_cumCRSI <- cumCRSI(price = Cl(XLB),
  nCum = nCum, nRSI = nRSI, nStreak = nStreak,
  nPercentLookBack = nPercentLookBack)
add_TA(TA_cumCRSI, col = "blue")

TA_lagATR <- lagATR(HLC = HLC(XLB), n = period)
add_TA(TA_lagATR, col = "purple")
```

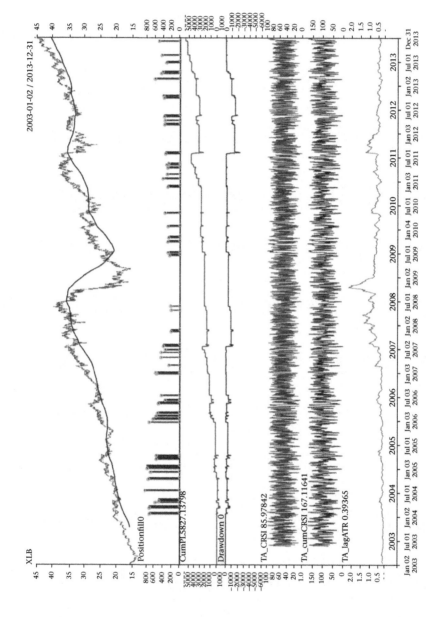

Figure 7.4 Connors XLB equity curve and indicators.

```
TA_SMA <- SMA(Cl(XLB), n = nSMA)
add_TA(TA_SMA, col = "blue", lwd = 2, on = 1)
```

The add_TA command with the argument on = 1 will plot the indicator on the same graph as the price series. Not including this argument will cause a new window pane to be created. Regarding the plot, it seems that the one time there was a massive drawdown was when the price crossed below the 200-day moving average. This is probably an oversight of the strategy. Had that price been completely above the same moving average, though, the same result would probably have held up. This is just another hint that a more sophisticated exit approach might be required to salvage this strategy.

Summary

A thorough introduction to the use of the **quantstrat** package as a backtesting framework is provided in this chapter. The demonstration includes detailed instructions for setting up the mandatory boilerplate code to get everything up and running. Two strategies (a trend follower and an oscillator) are defined, coded, and analyzed. The analysis leverages code from **quantstrat, blotter,** and **Performance-Analytics**. Custom analytics and strategy code are written on top of the **quantstrat** canned logic, and quite a few ways of dissecting a trading strategy are discussed.

This page intentionally left blank

8 | High-Frequency Data

Up to this point, we have only focused on daily equity data for our analysis. This low-granularity data comes with the nice property of being homogeneously spaced out in time. Homogeneity in time is a property that makes the mathematics of time series analysis much easier to handle. Tick data, on the other hand, is inherently nonhomogenous in time. Events such as book updates, trade updates, exchange messages and high-frequency news feeds, tend to arrive at arbitrary times.

High-frequency data has a lot to offer. There is a ton of information on the underlying microstructure[1] that can be be gleaned by analyzing all of the available information disseminated from an exchange. Most financial instruments trade multiple times per day. Some very liquid instruments can have hundreds of thousands of intraday market data and trade updates. A majority of these transactions occur within microseconds of each other. The SPY ETF is one such example. A typical trading day might result in 10 to 20 million book updates.[2] This figure includes the orderbook placement, modification and cancellation requests between humans, algorithms, and the exchange. Only a small subset of these book updates result in actual trades. This is also one of the main criticisms against high-frequency trading,[3] namely, the fact that all the messaging activity between vast networks of computers ends up only generating a small number of actual executions.

In terms of nomenclature, a book update refers to a change in either price, quantity, or count at a certain level of the orderbook. Most market makers and high-frequency traders concern themselves with the activity that occurs at the top of the book. This is where most of the valuable trading information bubbles up to.

Investors interact with the orderbook by either placing limit orders into it, by canceling or modifying these limit orders, or by issuing market orders. These orders are usually entered via a broker and eventually find their way to the exchange that hosts the centralized orderbook for the traded security. The exchange's matching engine is responsible for handling all the necessary matching and subsequent dissemination of order acknowledgments to the involved participants. The exchange also transmits the status of the orderbook whenever an update occurs. These updates are market data changes and trade information that traders and systems use to update their algorithms.

High-granularity or high-frequency data is hard to come by. Obtaining such data is a costly, time-consuming, and complex endeavor, to say the least. Hedge funds, banks, and proprietary trading firms, for the most part, have dedicated connections to the exchanges with which they trade. This makes it easier for them to capture, filter, and store such data in real time. Teams of developers and IT personnel are utilized to ensure the cleanliness, accuracy, and integrity of these data streams.

In this chapter, we will explore a few such high-frequency data sets. Such data has been graciously provided by **Tick Data, Inc.** for use in this book. The data comes in the form of preprocessed .csv files. This information should ideally be stored in a Time series database[4] that facilitates fast retrieval of information based on symbol, data-type, and time range. We will look at the data in its raw form.

High-frequency quotes

The provided stock quotes can be read into main memory via the `read.csv()` function:

```
spy_file <- "path/Stocks/QUOTES/SPY_2013_04_15_X_Q.asc"
spy_quotes <- read.csv(file = spy_file, header = FALSE,
    stringsAsFactors = FALSE)
```

The object spy_quotes is a data frame that takes up slightly over 1 GB of internal memory. There are more than 7.2 million lines with 21 columns in this data frame. Here is what the first few lines look like:

```
head(spy_quotes, 3)
##                        V1            V2   V3       V4   V5 V6 V7
## 1 04/15/2013 04:00:00.065   T 156.60     0.00     1  0  R
## 2 04/15/2013 04:00:00.626   P   0.00     0.00     0  0  R
## 3 04/15/2013 04:00:00.633   P 158.25   158.90     1 47  R

## V8 V9 V10 V11 V12 V13 V14 V15 V16 V17 V18 V19 V20 V21
## NA  1   T   T   1   2   A   C      NA  NA  NA  NA
## NA  2   P   P   0   2   A   C      NA  NA  NA  NA
## NA  3   P   P   1   2   A   C      NA  NA  NA  NA
```

The next step is to assign some appropriate column-names to our fields.

```
names(spy_quotes) <- c("date", "time", "exchange", "bid_price"
    "ask_price", "bid_size", "ask_size", "quote_condition",
    "mode", "market_maker_id", "sequence_number", "bid_exchange"
    "ask_exchange",  "national_bbo_indicator",
    "nasdaq_bbo_indicator", "quote_cancel_correction",
    "quote_source", "short_sale_restriction_indicator",
    "limit_up_down_bbo_indicator_cqs",
```

```
"limit_up_down_bbo_indicator_utp",
"finra_adf_mpid_indicator")
```

Here is what the field names mean according to the `Tick Data, Inc.` documentation:

- **Date:** Quote date.
- **Time:** Quote time. This number reflects the time at which the quote entered CTS. Milliseconds available: NYSE and AMEX from 2/7/06; NASDAQ from 12/5/05.
- **Exchange:** The Exchange that issued the quote. Arca, for example, is designated as P.
- **Bid Price:** Bid price truncated to eight implied decimal places.
- **Ask Price:** Ask price truncated to eight implied decimal places.
- **Bid Size:** Bid size in number of round lots (100 share units).
- **Ask Size:** Ask size in number of round lots (100 share units).
- **Quote Condition:** Condition of quote issued. For example, A means slow on the ask side.
- **Mode:** Sows Mode prior to 1/1/2004 if applicable.
- **Market Market Id:** For Nasdaq only. Identifies the Nasdaq market maker for each NASD quote.
- **Sequence Number:** For NYSE only. Market Data Systems (MDS) sequence number. This field applies only to NYSE trades. It will contain a zero if the trade is not an NYSE trade or if the sequence number is indeterminate.
- **Bid Exchange:** Exchange where the bid originated.
- **Ask Exchange:** Exchange where the ask originated.
- **National BBO Indicator:** Best bid and offer for Amex and NYSE only.
- **Nasdaq BBO Indicator:** Best bid and offer for Nasdaq only.
- **Quote Cancel/Correction:** Amex and NYSE only.
- **Quote Source:** C = CQS, N = Nasdaq.
- **Retail Interest Indicator (RPI):** Blank = Retail interest not applicable. A = retail interest on bid quote. B = Retail interest on offer quote. C = retail interest on both the bid and offer quotes.
- **Short sale restriction indicator:** Blank = Short sales restriction no in effect. A = short sales restriction activated. C = short sales restriction continued. D = short sales restriction deactivated. E = short sales restriction in effect.
- **Limit-up/Limit-down BBO Indicator CQS:** Blank = Limit up-limit down not applicable. A = Bid price above upper limit price band. Bid is nonexecutable.
- **Limit-up/Limit-down BBO Indicator UTP:** Same as above but for UTP.
- **Finra ADF MPID Indicator:** Options are 0, 1, 2, and 3.

Since the SPY's primary exchange is Arca, we will proceed by subsetting our data frame so as to only extract Arca quotes. The exchange code for Arca is designated as "P". Only the price and size fields will be used in this next example:

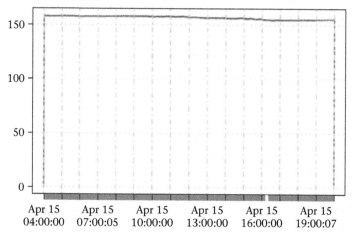

Figure 8.1 SPY bid price with outliers.

```
spy_quotes_arca <- spy_quotes[spy_quotes$exchange %in% c("P"),
  c("date", "time", "bid_price",
  "ask_price", "bid_size", "ask_size")]
```

The next step will be to transform the data into an **xts** object. This will require an appropriate time field.

```
require(xts)

# Setting to allow us to view the millisecond precision
options(digits.secs = 3)

time_index <- as.POSIXct(paste(spy_quotes_arca$date,
  spy_quotes_arca$time), format = "%m/%d/%Y %H:%M:%OS")
spy <- xts(spy_quotes_arca[, -c(1, 2)], time_index)
rm(time_index)
```

Now that we have a valid **xts** time series object, we can do some initial filtering on the data. A line plot of the bid prices is displayed below:

```
plot(spy$bid_price, type = 'l',
  main = "SPY bid price",
  cex.main = 0.8,
  cex.lab = 0.8,
  cex.axis = 0.8)
```

Notice the two extreme prices at the beginning and end of the time series. This is an artifact of reading in the ascii file directly from the **Tick Data, Inc.** raw file. The important takeaway from this graph is that it becomes vital to perform such visual

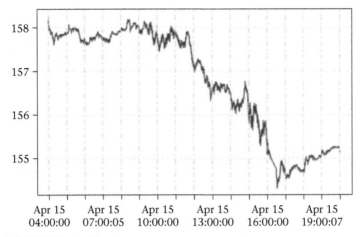

Figure 8.2 SPY bid price filtered.

inspection of the data whenever possible. This is especially true for high-frequency tick data. All sorts of artifacts can lurk in the darkness. We need to expose those early on and deal with them in an appropriate manner. In this case, the fix is simple. We will just omit the zero values.

```
spy_filtered <- spy[spy$bid_price > 0, ]
```

To see how many lines were removed:

```
rows_removed <- nrow(spy) - nrow(spy_filtered)

rows_removed
## [1] 2
```

The revised plot looks better:

```
 plot(spy_filtered$bid_price, type = 'l',
   main = "SPY filtered bid price",
   cex.main = 0.8,
   cex.lab = 0.8,
   cex.axis = 0.8)
```

This next filter will look for discrepancies in the ask price, as well as bid and ask sizes.

```
summary(as.numeric(spy_filtered$ask_price))
## Min. 1st Qu.  Median    Mean 3rd Qu.    Max.
## 154.3   156.1   156.7   156.8   157.7   158.9
```

The values look reasonable. Here are the summary statistics for the size columns:

```
summary(as.numeric(spy_filtered$bid_size))
## Min. 1st Qu.  Median  Mean 3rd Qu.   Max.
## 1.00 22.00 52.00 94.93 100.00 1565.00

summary(as.numeric(spy_filtered$ask_size))
## Min. 1st Qu. Median Mean 3rd Qu. Max.
## 1.0   24.0   59.0  110.8 118.0 1412.0
```

These values also look reasonable. At this point we should probably add a couple of extra filters to make sure that there are no significant gaps in the data and that there are no crossed prices. Crossed prices occur when the bid price at any point in time is greater than or equal to the offer price.

```
# Boolean vector where bid price >= the ask price
crossed_prices <- spy_filtered$bid_price >=
  spy_filtered$ask_price

any(crossed_prices)
## [1] FALSE
```

Inter-quote arrival times

This next step looks at the successive time differences between quote updates. We will define a quote update as any change in the top of the book.

```
# Extract the time index.
quote_times <- index(spy_filtered)

# Compute the consecutive time differences
time_differences <- as.numeric(diff(quote_times))

summary(time_differences)
## Min.   1st Qu. Median   Mean   3rd Qu.    Max.
## 0.0000 0.0000  0.0010  0.0645  0.0100  1010.0000
```

There are quite a few durations that are less than a millisecond apart. That is reasonable when dealing with tick-level data. The 1010-second difference (16.8 minutes) between two consecutive book updates, however, might be a concern. Let us explore this further.

```
# Identify times that seem abnormal
long_times <- which(time_differences > 1000)

long_times
## [1] 884312
```

```
# Show the data around the abnormally long time
spy_abnormal <- spy_filtered[(long_times - 2):(long_times + 2), ]
##                          bid_price ask_price bid_size ask_size
## 2013-04-15 16:13:00.987    155.00    155.02      289      270
## 2013-04-15 16:13:01.256    155.00    155.02      290      270
## 2013-04-15 16:13:01.282    155.00    155.02      295      270
## 2013-04-15 16:29:50.869    154.76    154.79        3        3
## 2013-04-15 16:29:50.887    154.76    154.77        3       10
```

From the output, it looks like no activity occurred between 16:13:01.282 and 16:29:50.869. Is this due to the exchange's being closed, an error in the feed or simply a slow trading period? A successful data-filtering operation requires us to have concrete answers to such questions. Some other questions are the following:

1. What are the valid trading times of the instrument on the exchange?
2. What are typical prices the instrument should be trading around?
3. Are there any upper and lower price limits imposed by the exchange?
4. What does the liquidity profile of the instrument look like?
5. What are the exchange holidays?

A 16-minute gap between two book updates might be normal for certain products that do not trade a lot. The only way to really know if this outlier is of any concern is to utilize prior knowledge of the product, along with some commonsense assumptions about the data.

Identifying liquidity regimes

In this next section, we will take a look at some of the statistical properties of the high-frequency SPY data. A typical metric that practitioners look at is the bid-ask spread. The bid-ask spread is the difference between the ask price and the bid price at the top level of the book. The following code plots this spread throughout the day.

```
# Calculate the bid-ask spread.
bid_ask_spread <- spy_filtered$ask_price -
  spy_filtered$bid_price

# Filter out abnormal value
outliers <- which(bid_ask_spread > 0.25)
if(length(outliers) > 0) {
  bid_ask_spread <- bid_ask_spread[-outliers, ]
}

# Plot the spread.
plot(bid_ask_spread, type = "l",
  main = "Bid ask spread",
```

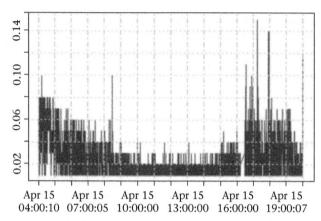

Figure 8.3 SPY intraday bid ask spread.

```
cex.main = 0.8,
cex.lab = 0.8,
cex.axis = 0.8)
```

The plot reveals three different liquidity regimes for SPY. It seems that we can broadly partition the trading day into an early-morning period, regular trading hours, and an after-hours period. We can separately visualize the price dynamics during these times by appropriately subsetting the data as follows:

```
# Create three time partitions for the SPY data
early_morning <- "2013-04-15 04:00:00::2013-04-15 08:29:00"
regular_trading <- "2013-04-15 08:30:00::2013-04-15 16:15:00"
after_hours <- "2013-04-15 16:15:01::2013-04-15 20:00:00"

# Create a histogram of the bid-ask spread for each period
par(mfrow = c(3, 1))

# Morning
data <- bid_ask_spread[early_morning]
hist(data, main = early_morning, breaks = 1000,
  xlim = c(0, 0.1))
abline(v = mean(data), lwd = 2, lty = 2)

# Afternoon
data <- bid_ask_spread[regular_trading]
hist(data, main = regular_trading, breaks = 1000,
  xlim = c(0, 0.1))
abline(v = mean(data), lwd = 2, lty = 2)
```

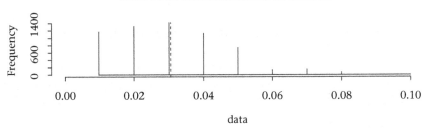

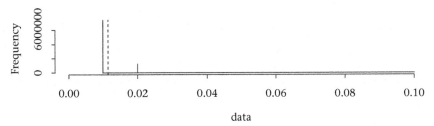

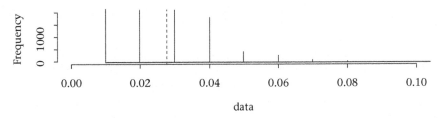

Figure 8.4 SPY intraday spread histograms.

```
# Evening
data <- bid_ask_spread[after_hours]
hist(data, main = after_hours, breaks = 1000,
   xlim = c(0, 0.1))
abline(v = mean(data), lwd = 2, lty = 2)
```

The second period is clearly more liquid given that the spread between bid and ask is 1-tick wide the vast majority of the time. For this next part of the analysis, we will only concentrate on this most liquid regime.

```
spy_day <- spy_filtered[regular_trading]
```

There is still a fairly large amount of information present in this data frame. This is expected, given that the bulk of the trading occurs between these hours.

The micro-price

At any given moment in time, what is the true theoretical price for the stock? Surprisingly, there is no correct answer to this question. One can argue that the theoretical price is the bid price. It is equally valid to claim that the ask price fills that role. Most practitioners favor something in-between. The midpoint price $(P_{bid} + P_{ask})/2$ is one such alternative. Can we do better? Since we already have both the price and the quantity information available to us, we will use the `micro-price` as a proxy for the true theoretical price. The micro-price is a weighted average of prices and quantities. If one deems that quantities at the top of the book contain relevant information, then it makes sense to incorporate these values into the theoretical price derivation. If, for example, the bid price is $150.00 with a 1,000 lot and the ask is $150.01 with a 1 lot, it follows that any theoretical price should lie somewhere between the bid-ask spread. This price should probably lie closer to the ask price since there seems to be greater buying pressure due to the larger size on the bid. What follows is both the mathematical equation and the R code for the micro-price:

$$Price_{micro} = \frac{Price_{bid} * Size_{ask} + Price_{ask} * Size_{bid}}{Size_{bid} + Size_{ask}} \tag{8.1}$$

```
spy_micro_price <- (spy_day$bid_price * spy_day$ask_size +
  spy_day$ask_price * spy_day$bid_size) /
  (spy_day$bid_size + spy_day$ask_size)
```

If the quantity is not deemed to be important (due to market fragmentation, hidden liquidity, or spoofing of the book), a mid-price will probably be an equally valid theoretical price.

The plot of the micro-price along with the bid and ask prices is shown below:

```
par(mfrow = c(1, 1))
range <- 10000:10100
title <- "Micro-price between bid-ask prices"
plot(spy_day$ask_price[range],
  ylim = c(min(spy_day$bid_price[range]),
  max(spy_day$ask_price[range])),
  main = title,
  cex.main = 0.8,
  cex.lab = 0.8,
  cex.axis = 0.8)
lines(spy_day$bid_price[range])
lines(spy_micro_price[range], lty = 2)
```

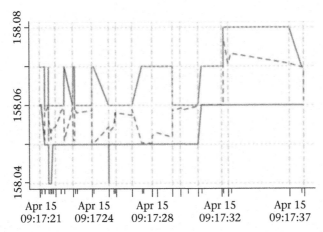

Figure 8.5 Micro-price between bid and ask.

Distributions and autocorrelations

Here is a look at the distribution of the micro-price returns:

```
spy_returns <- diff(log(spy_micro_price))

par(mfrow = c(2, 1))
plot(spy_returns,
  main = "Time series plot of micro-price returns",
  cex.main = 0.8, cex.lab = 0.8, cex.axis = 0.8)
hist(spy_returns, breaks = 1000,
  main = "Micro-price distribution",
  cex.main = 0.8, cex.lab = 0.8, cex.axis = 0.8)
```

Notice the extreme lepto-kurtocity in these returns. At this granularity, there are many more smaller returns than what a normal distribution of the same mean and variance would predict. We can use our old trick of superimposing a normal distribution onto the data in order to visualize the difference.

```
par(mfrow = c(1, 1))
mean_spy <- mean(as.numeric(spy_returns), na.rm = TRUE)
sd_spy <- sd(as.numeric(spy_returns), na.rm = TRUE)

hist(spy_returns, breaks = 10000, prob = TRUE,
  xlim = c(-0.00003, 0.00003),
  main = "Micro-price distribution vs. Normal",
  cex.main = 0.8,
  cex.lab = 0.8,
  cex.axis = 0.8)
```

Time-series plot of micro-price returns

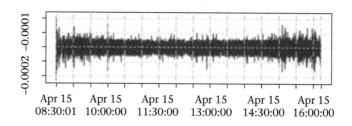

Micro-price distribution

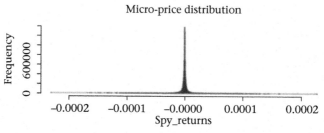

Figure 8.6 Micro-price distribution.

```
curve(dnorm(x, mean_spy, sd_spy), add = TRUE,
  yaxt = "n", lwd = 3, lty = 3)
```

What does the autocorrelation of the high-frequency returns look like? Recall that the daily return autocorrelation was nonexistent for lags greater than one.

```
spy_acf <- acf(as.numeric(spy_returns),
  na.action = na.pass,
  main = "Autocorrelation",
  cex.main = 0.8,
  cex.lab = 0.8,
  cex.axis = 0.8)
```

There exists a slight negative autocorrelation at lag 1. The micro-price tends to smooth out some of the bid-ask bounce effects.[5] This effect would have been more pronounced if we had used the bid-price, for example. The effect of the bid-ask bounce can be better observed by analyzing the autocorrelation of successive trades that occur in the SPY. This is due to the fact that multiple trades tend to occur between the bid and ask prices as market makers and other proprietary trades try to capture single-tick profits. This back and forth movement between bid and ask prices, coupled with the fact that the price changes are discrete in nature, due to the minimum 0.01 tick size of the SPY, leads to this artificial autocorrelation.

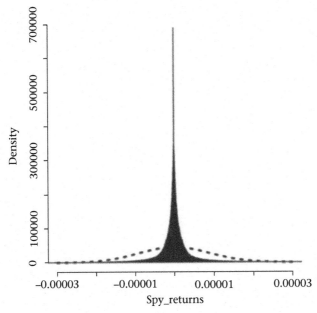

Figure 8.7 Micro-price distribution with normal superimposed.

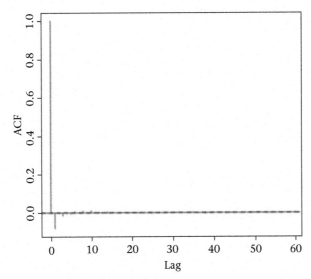

Figure 8.8 Micro-price autocorrelation of returns.

```
# Get the SPY traded prices from our tick data file
spy_trades_file <- "path/SPY_2013_04_15_X_T.asc"
spy_trades <- read.csv(file = spy_trades_file,
  header = FALSE, stringsAsFactors = FALSE)
```

```
names(spy_trades) <- c("date", "time", "price",
  "volume", "exchange", "sales_condition",
  "correction_indicator", "sequence_number",
  "trade_stop_indicator", "source_of_trade", "trf",
  "exclude_record_flag", "filtered_price")

# Extract only the ARCA trades
spy_trades_arca <- spy_trades[spy_trades$exchange %in% c("P"),
  c("date", "time", "price", "volume", "correction_indicator",
  "filtered_price")]

# Check if any filtered prices exist
any(!is.na(spy_trades_arca$filtered_price))
## [1] FALSE

# Check if there are any special correction indicators present
unique(spy_trades_arca$correction_indicator)
## [1] 0

# Drop the last two columns from the data frame
spy_trades_arca <- spy_trades_arca[, 1:4]

# Convert to an xts object for subsequent analysis
time_index <- as.POSIXct(paste(spy_trades_arca$date,
  spy_trades_arca$time), format = "%m/%d/%Y %H:%M:%OS")

spy_t <- xts(spy_trades_arca[, -c(1, 2)], time_index)
rm(time_index)

# First 6 entries
head(spy_t)
##                          price volume
## 2013-04-15 04:00:00.697 158.25    100
## 2013-04-15 04:00:00.697 158.24    200
## 2013-04-15 04:00:00.697 158.15    150
## 2013-04-15 04:01:42.190 158.06    200
## 2013-04-15 04:07:16.545 157.94    100
## 2013-04-15 04:12:45.265 157.92  10000

# Subset to regular trading hour range
regular_trading <- "2013-04-15 08:30:00::2013-04-15 16:15:00"
spy_t_day <- spy_t[regular_trading]
```

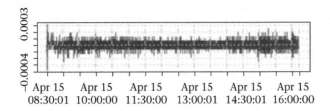

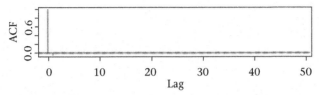

Figure 8.9 Trade price autocorrelation of returns.

```
# Look at the number of trade entries
dim(spy_t_day)
## [1] 93197      2
```

```
# Look at the amount of memory taken up
object.size(spy_t_day)
## [1] 2239080 bytes
```

We have managed to filter down the number of trade events to 93197 from an initial value of 517516. The spy_t_day object takes up approximately 22.4 MB of memory. It is time to look at the successive-trades autocorrelation:

```
# Compute returns
spy_t_day_returns <- diff(log(spy_t_day$price))[-1]
```

```
# Plot the distribution and the autocorrelation plot
par(mfrow = c(2, 1))
plot(spy_t_day_returns, main = "SPY returns on trades",
  cex.main = 0.8, cex.lab = 0.8, cex.axis = 0.8)
acf(as.numeric(spy_t_day_returns), main = "SPY trades acf",
  cex.main = 0.8, cex.lab = 0.8, cex.axis = 0.8)
```

The distribution of returns with a normal distribution superimposed is the following:

```
# Distribution of trade returns
par(mfrow = c(1, 1))
hist(spy_t_day_returns, breaks = 1000, prob = TRUE,
```

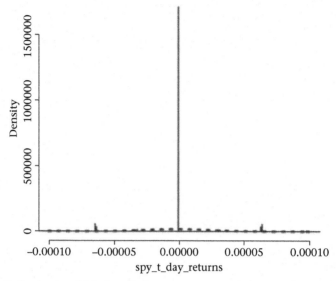

Figure 8.10 Trade price distribution of returns.

```
xlim = c(-0.0001, 0.0001),
main = "Distribution of SPY trade returns",
cex.main = 0.8,
cex.lab = 0.8,
cex.axis = 0.8)

curve(dnorm(x, mean(spy_t_day_returns),
  sd(spy_t_day_returns)),
  add = TRUE,
  yaxt = "n",
  lwd = 3,
  lty = 3)
```

It is interesting to note that the vast majority of consecutive trades occur at the same price levels. The distribution clearly shows a spike at zero. This overwhelms the y-axis and causes all the other occurrences to be displayed in the margins. What happens when we look at trades occurring at different prices? We can aggregate the volume on any single price level, and only take a look at trades that occur on those levels. By doing this, we can effectively preserve the volume information.

```
# Use the rle() function to find price sequences
prices_rle <- rle(as.numeric(spy_t_day$price))

# Here are the row indexes we want to keep
end_indexes <- cumsum(prices_rle$lengths)
```

```
# Here are the start indexes we want to sum the volumes from
start_indexes <- end_indexes - prices_rle$lengths + 1

# Create a vector of total volumes for each price
volume_list <- list()
volume_vector <- as.numeric(spy_t_day$volume)
for (i in 1:length(end_indexes)) {
  volume_list[[i]] <- sum(volume_vector[start_indexes[i]:
    end_indexes[i]], na.rm = TRUE)
}

# Create a reduced data set with distinct trade prices
spy_t_day_reduced <- spy_t_day[end_indexes, ]
spy_t_day_reduced$volume <- unlist(volume_list)
```

Here is a sample of the output:

```
head(spy_t_day_reduced, 10)
##                           price  volume
## 2013-04-15 08:30:01.964 158.17    510
## 2013-04-15 08:30:02.783 158.15   1000
## 2013-04-15 08:30:04.930 158.14    340
## 2013-04-15 08:30:11.964 158.12    100
## 2013-04-15 08:30:23.763 158.11   1100
## 2013-04-15 08:30:29.739 158.10   1720
## 2013-04-15 08:30:31.963 158.09    200
## 2013-04-15 08:30:45.164 158.08   4995
## 2013-04-15 08:30:46.888 158.07    100
## 2013-04-15 08:30:46.970 158.06   3330


head(spy_t_day, 10)
##                          price volume
## 2013-04-15 08:30:01.964 158.17    100
## 2013-04-15 08:30:01.964 158.17    410
## 2013-04-15 08:30:02.783 158.15   1000
## 2013-04-15 08:30:04.930 158.14    340
## 2013-04-15 08:30:11.964 158.12    100
## 2013-04-15 08:30:23.763 158.11   1000
## 2013-04-15 08:30:23.763 158.11    100
## 2013-04-15 08:30:28.153 158.10    400
## 2013-04-15 08:30:28.529 158.10    320
## 2013-04-15 08:30:29.739 158.10    180
```

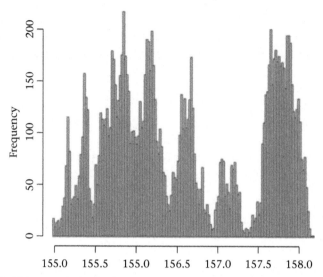

Figure 8.11 Histogram of price levels.

We can now explore a few more metrics on these filtered traded prices.

```
# Identify the most traded prices throughout the day
hist(as.numeric(spy_t_day_reduced$price), breaks = 200,
  main = "Histogram of traded prices for SPY on 2013-04-15",
  cex.main = 0.8,
  cex.lab = 0.8,
  cex.axis = 0.8)
```

We would not expect to find anything spectacular here. The clustering is another way of identifying levels where the bulk of the trading activity occurred.

The following plot displays the autocorrelation of trade returns on distinct consecutive prices.

```
acf(diff(log(as.numeric(spy_t_day_reduced$price))),
  main = "Autocorrelation of trades",
  cex.main = 0.8,
  cex.lab = 0.8,
  cex.axis = 0.8)
```

A very slight positive autocorrelation exists at lag 2. It is difficult to say whether this is significant or not without going through the process of fitting an autoregressive model[6] to the data.

Another question that often comes up is whether a particular trade was buyer or seller initiated. A trade record usually comes with an exact time-stamp, the price

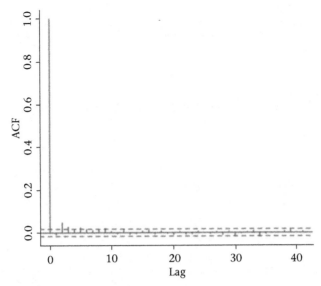

Figure 8.12 Autocorrelation of trade prices.

and the quantity of the trade. What we are missing, is whether it was a buyer-or a seller-initiated order. This information can, however, be gleaned from the combination of trade and market data. The result will not always be 100 percent accurate, but it will be a decent approximation. In 1991, Lee and Ready proposed to classify a trade as buyer initiated if it occurred on the ask price, and as a seller initiated if it occurred on the bid price. This requires the proper time-alignment of the quote and trade feeds. In the past, this used to be a hindrance. With the precision time-stamps available to us today, this analysis has become straightforward. The Lee and Ready algorithm has evolved since then [69]. Knowing what the liquidity makers and takers are doing is quite valuable information, especially in an intra-day, high-frequency setting. Consider the problem of attempting to detect the flow of informed liquidity. The VPIN model (volume synchronized probability of informed trading) is one example of an algorithm that tries to quantify this effect. One of the inputs is whether blocks of trades are buyer-or seller-initiated [26, 144].

Another question we may ask of the data is whether any nonlinear relationships exist between successive lags in returns space. One thing we might try, is to create a scatter plot of consecutive returns along with their respective lags and look at how the points move through time. In a random set of such points, we would expect there to be no discernible temporal relationship. The points would have the same chance of going toward the center of the cluster as away from it.

```
# Random return cloud with lag 1
n <- rnorm(50, 0, .20)
n_lag1 <- c(NA, n[-length(n)])
plot(n_lag1, n)
```

```
# Create arrows between the points
s <- seq(length(n)-1)
arrows(n_lag1[s], n[s], n_lag1[s+1], n[s+1])
```

In real data, code similar to the following might reveal point sequences that spend more time traveling around the edges of the cloud before diving back in toward the center.

```
# SPY return cloud with lag 1
spy_t_returns <- diff(log(as.numeric(
    spy_t_day_reduced$price[100:150])))
spy_t_returns_lag1 <- c(NA, spy_t_returns[
    -length(spy_t_returns)])
plot(spy_t_returns_lag1, spy_t_returns)

s <- seq(length(spy_t_returns)-1)
arrows(spy_t_returns_lag1[s], spy_t_returns[s],
    spy_t_returns_lag1[s+1], spy_t_returns[s+1])
```

The highfrequency package

Up to this point, we have created customized functionality for exploring some of the stylistic facts of high-frequency data. In terms of existing functionality that deals with these types of questions, the **highfrequency** package contains some helpful analytics [57]. The authors of this package are Jonathan Cornelissen, Kris Boudt, and Scott Payseur. Some of the functionality include:

- aggregation of price, quote and trade data,
- filtering of tick-data,
- calculation of liquidity measures,
- estimation and forecasting of volatility,
- analysis of microstructure noise and intraday periodicity.

The **highfrequency** package uses the **xts** framework for managing the underlying high-frequency time series. This makes it convenient to work with, and it should be a familiar pattern to the reader by now. The latest version of the source code for this package can be found here:

```
library("devtools")
install_github("highfrequency", "jonathancornelissen")
```

A nice tutorial on using **highfrequency** is referenced in the endnotes.[7]

Summary

This chapter looks at the dynamics of higher-frequency tick-data. All prior discussions and code examples have been based on daily data that were downloaded from free online repositories. A vendor specific data-formatting scheme for tick data is explored and simple filtering steps are applied to the raw files. Tick data is leveraged to explore the time-inhomogeneity of quote updates. The distribution of high-frequency returns is analyzed and intra-day bid-ask spreads are visualized. The notion of a micro-price is presented as a means of generating a theoretical price, which often falls between the bid-ask spread of an underlying instrument. A suggestion on exploring nonlinear relationships between disparate time points is provided along with a typical use case of generating buyer-versus seller-initiated trade indicators. A brief mention of the **highfrequency** package is also made.

This page intentionally left blank

9 | Options

Options are tradable derivate contracts that "derive" their value from other under-lying instruments. Wikipedia defines these instruments as follows: "An Option is a contract which gives the buyer (the owner) the right, but not the obligation, to buy or sell an underlying asset or instrument at a specified strike price on or before a specified date [130]." They are similar to futures contracts in that they provide a mechanism to purchase or sell a certain physical or financial asset sometime in the future at a price that is known in the present. Whereas futures obligate the contract holder to purchase or sell the underlying asset at the agreed-upon price, options provide the "option" to purchase or sell the underlying asset at the agreed-upon price. This added flexibility or optionality comes at a premium. No upfront exchange of funds is required in order for the buyer and seller to enter into a futures contract. To buy an options contract, however, the buyer has to pay a premium. Similarly, the person selling the option contract gets to collect the premium.

Option theoretical value

The premium of an option contract is a function of several variables. These vari-ables include the agreed-upon purchase or sell price K (also known as the strike price), the current price of the underlying asset (S), the time to expiration of the option contract (T), the stream of cash flows paid by the underlying asset in the form of dividends between time zero (now) and the expiration of the contract (d), the risk-free interest rate (r), and a fudge factor that makes everything work out nicely (σ). This fudge factor is called the *implied volatility* of the option.

Figure 9.1 Black Scholes inputs.

A history of options

Options, in one form or another, have been around since antiquity. Aristotle tells the tale of how Thales (the ancient Greek philosopher from Miletus) placed a deposit on a local olive-oil press to secure the rights to use the press during the next harvest. Thales believed that the subsequent harvest would be better than the last one. In effect, he had purchased a call option on the use of the press. He supposedly profited handsomely from this transaction [51]. Fast-forward a few thousand years, and in 1848, the Chicago Board of Trade (CBOT) first opened its doors for business. The CBOT is still one of the largest options exchanges in the world. It is also considered the world's oldest. The CBOT merged with the CME in 2007.

Even though options had been trading for a long time, it was not until 1973 when a monumental shift in the industry occurred. A seminal paper published by Fisher Black and Myron Scholes revealed an elegant mathematical formula for coming up with the theoretical value of an option. This formula is known as the **Black–Scholes** Partial Differential Equation (PDE), and it relates the above-referenced parameters (S, K, r, T, d, σ) to a market price (V) [27].[1]

$$\frac{\partial V}{\partial t} + rV\frac{\partial V}{\partial S} + \frac{1}{2}V^2\sigma^2\frac{\partial^2 V}{\partial S^2} - rV = 0 \tag{9.1}$$

Options come in many flavors. The two most common ones are "European" and "American." A European option can only be exercised at the agreed-upon expiration date. An American option can be exercised at any time before the expiration date. This seemingly trivial difference is significant from a valuation standpoint. For example, there does not exist a closed-form mathematical solution for the value of an American put option given all the above parameters. The solution can be computed numerically, of course, but not through a formula such as the one above.

Valuation of options

In R, there are a few packages that contain closed-form solutions, as well as tree, grid, and Monte Carlo solvers for European and American options. Some of these packages are **fOptions**, **RQuantLib**, **AmericanCallOpt**, and **LSMonteCarlo**. In this chapter, we will utilize the **RQuantLib** package.[2]

According to the http://www.quantlib.org website: "QuantLib is a free/open-source library for modeling, trading, and risk management in real-life. QuantLib is written in C++ with a clean object model, and is then exported to different languages such as C#, Objective Caml, Java, Perl, Python, GNU R, Ruby, and Scheme."

After installing and loading the package, we can look at all the available functions by using the `lsf.str()` command:

```
install.packages("RQuantLib")
library(RQuantLib)

lsf.str("package:RQuantLib")
## adjust : function (calendar = "TARGET", dates = Sys.Date(),
##     bdc = 0)
## advance : function (calendar = "TARGET", dates = Sys.Date(),
##     n, timeUnit, period, bdc = 0, emr = 0)
## AmericanOption : function (type, underlying, strike, dividendYield
##     riskFreeRate, maturity, volatility, timeSteps = 150,
##     gridPoints = 149, engine = "BaroneAdesiWhaley")
## AmericanOption.default : function (type, underlying, strike,
##     dividendYield, riskFreeRate, maturity, volatility,
##     timeSteps = 150, gridPoints = 149, engine = "BaroneAdesiWhaley")
## AmericanOptionImpliedVolatility : function (type, value,
##     underlying, strike, dividendYield, riskFreeRate,
##     maturity, volatility, timeSteps = 150, gridPoints = 151)
## AmericanOptionImpliedVolatility.default : function (type, value,
##     underlying, strike, dividendYield, riskFreeRate, maturity,
##     volatility, timeSteps = 150, gridPoints = 151)
## ...
```

To value a European option, we can use the `EuropeanOption()` function. The analytical closed-form solution for a call is

$$c = SN(d_1) - Ke^{-rT}N(d_2) \tag{9.2}$$

For a put, the equation is

$$p = -Ke^{-rT}N(-d_2) - SN(-d_1) \tag{9.3}$$

The terms d_1 and d_2 are

$$d_1 = \frac{ln(S/K) + (r + \sigma^2)T}{\sigma\sqrt{T}}, d_2 = d_1 - \sigma\sqrt{T} \tag{9.4}$$

The Greeks for European calls and puts have similar closed form solutions.[3]
Let us take a look at a numerical example:

```
call_value <- EuropeanOption(type = "call", underlying = 100,
    strike = 100, dividendYield = 0, riskFreeRate = 0.03,
    maturity = 1.0, volatility = 0.30)

## Concise summary of valuation for EuropeanOption
## value      delta    gamma    vega      theta
## 13.2833    0.5987   0.0129   38.6668   -7.1976
```

```
## rho     divRho
## 46.5873 -59.8706
```

The object call_value is of class:

```
class(call_value)
## [1] "EuropeanOption" "Option"
```

The neat thing about the EuropeanOption() object is that it contains both the value of the option, as well as the Greeks. Here is some R code that will help us explore the payoff profile of a European call option with its associated Greeks, as a function of the underlying price. A similar sensitivity analysis can be run on volatility, time to expiration, interest rates, and dividends.

```
type <- "call"
underlying <- 20:180
strike <- 100
dividendYield <- 0
riskFreeRate <- 0.03
maturity <- 1.0
volatility <- 0.10

# Function to create plots of option values and Greeks.
option_values <- function(type, underlying, strike,
  dividendYield, riskFreeRate, maturity, volatility) {

  # Output list with option values and Greeks
  out <- list()
  for(i in seq_along(underlying)) {
    out[[i]] <- EuropeanOption(type = type, underlying = i,
      strike = strike, dividendYield = dividendYield,
      riskFreeRate = riskFreeRate, maturity = maturity,
      volatility = volatility)
  }

  # Set up the plot window
  par(mfrow = c(3, 2))
  names <- c("Value", "Delta", "Gamma",
    "Vega", "Theta", "Rho")

  for(i in 1:6) {
    plot(unlist(lapply(out, "[", i)) , type = "l",
      main = paste(names[i], "vs. Underlying"),
      xlab = "Underlying", ylab = names[i])
```

```
        grid()
        abline(v = strike, col = "red")
    }
    return(out)
}
```

The function invocation produces the following output:

```
option_values(type, underlying, strike, dividendYield,
    riskFreeRate, maturity, volatility)

## ...
## [[96]]
## Concise summary of valuation for EuropeanOption
## value    delta    gamma     vega    theta
## 3.3493   0.4768   0.0415   38.2336  -3.1843
## rho    divRho
## 42.4222 -45.7715

## [[97]]
## Concise summary of valuation for EuropeanOption
## value    delta    gamma     vega    theta
## 3.8468   0.5181   0.0411   38.6575  -3.3252
## rho    divRho
## 46.4098 -50.2566

## [[98]]
## Concise summary of valuation for EuropeanOption
## value    delta    gamma     vega    theta
## 4.3853   0.5588   0.0403   38.6707  -3.4449
## rho    divRho
## 50.3788 -54.7642
```

Let us see what the graphs look like when the maturity of the option is reduced.

```
option_values(type, underlying, strike, dividendYield,
    riskFreeRate, maturity = 0.1, volatility)
```

This type of analysis is very useful when dealing with portfolios of options as well. Shocks on the underlying parameters can be simulated in an efficient manner, and the sensitivity of the aggregate Greeks can be easily explored.

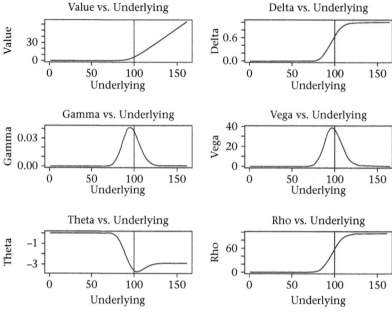

Figure 9.2 Option sensitivities.

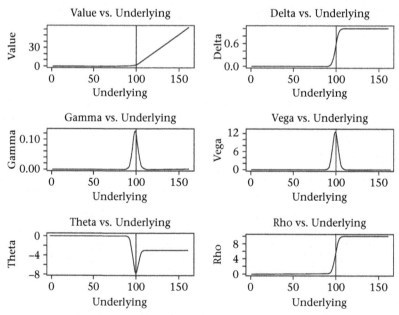

Figure 9.3 Short dated option sensitivities.

Exploring options trade data

We will now take a look at all the option trades that occurred on April 15, 2013 for the SPY option chain. This trade information is, again, courtesy of **Tick Data, Inc.** The naming convention used for each file is Symbol, Call/Put, Expiration, Strike, Date, Trade. An example file might be called something like this: SPY_C_20130420_124.00_XX_20130415_T.csv

```
# Create a vector of filenames
folder <- "path/Options/SPY_20130415_T/"
available_files <- list.files(folder)

# Explore the first few lines of the file
temp <- read.csv(file = paste0(folder, available_files[1]),
  header = FALSE, stringsAsFactors = FALSE)
```

```
## head(temp)
##              V1              V2     V3        V4 V5 V6     V7
## 1 04/15/2013 15:11:32.191 TRUE   7943215  A  L 35.94
## 2 04/15/2013 15:24:54.590 TRUE  24152315  N  L 36.21
## 3 04/15/2013 15:24:54.629 TRUE  24152415  N  L 36.21
## 4 04/15/2013 15:45:51.843 TRUE  45189165  N  L 35.60
## 5 04/15/2013 15:46:22.622 TRUE  45773488  I  Q 35.63
## 6 04/15/2013 15:46:53.716 TRUE  46313964  A  L 35.74
```

```
##      V8     V9  V10  V11    V12   V13 V14     V15 V16
## 1  2500 155.92  400    P @ 155.91     3 155.92  41
## 2  2400 156.05  300    P F 156.06    10 156.07 155
## 3   100 156.05  300    P F 156.06    10 156.07 155
## 4  5000 155.61  100    P F 155.59    75 155.61  83
## 5  2500 155.66 1900    P @ 155.65    55 155.66  21
## 6  4500 155.72  200    P F 155.71    73 155.72  24
```

Let us give these columns some better names:

```
column_names <- c("date", "time", "trade_indicator",
  "sequence_number", "option_exchange_code",
  "option_condition_code", "sale_price", "sale_size",
  "underlying_last_trade_price",
  "underling_last_trade_size",
  "stock_exchange_code", "stock_condition_code",
  "underlying_bid_price", "underlying_bid_size",
  "underlying_ask_price", "underlying_ask_size")
names(temp) <- column_names
```

A typical use case of such options trade data is to visualize the volume of contracts traded across strikes and across maturities.

```r
output <- list()
for(i in 1:length(available_files)) {
  file_name <- available_files[i]

  type <- substr(file_name, 5, 5)
  date <- substr(file_name, 7, 14)
  date <- as.Date(date, format = "%Y%m%d")
  strike <- substr(file_name, 16, 26)
  strike <- strsplit(strike, "_XX")[[1]][1]

  temp <- read.csv(file = paste0(folder, file_name),
    header = FALSE, stringsAsFactors = FALSE)
  names(temp) <- column_names

  number_of_trades <- nrow(temp)
  avg_trade_price <- round(mean(temp$sale_price,
    na.rm = TRUE), 3)

  if(number_of_trades <= 1) {
    sd_trade_price <- 0
  } else {
    sd_trade_price <- round(sd(temp$sale_price,
      na.rm = TRUE), 3)
  }

  total_volume <- sum(temp$sale_size, na.rm = TRUE)
  avg_underlying_price <- round(mean(
    temp$underlying_bid_price, na.rm = TRUE), 2)
  underlying_range <- max(temp$underlying_ask_price) -
    min(temp$underlying_bid_price)

  output[[i]] <- data.frame(symbol = 'SPY', date = date,
    type = type, strike = strike,
    trades = number_of_trades,
    volume = total_volume,
    avg_price = avg_trade_price,
    sd_price = sd_trade_price,
    avg_stock_price = avg_underlying_price,
    stock_range = underlying_range,
    stringsAsFactors = FALSE)
```

```
}

# Convert the list into a table
results <- do.call(rbind, output)

head(results)
##    symbol       date type strike trades volume
## 1     SPY 2013-04-20    C 120.00     12  33000
## 2     SPY 2013-04-20    C 124.00      1     15
## 3     SPY 2013-04-20    C 130.00      1      2
## 4     SPY 2013-04-20    C 133.00      1      1
## 5     SPY 2013-04-20    C 140.00      4     95
## 6     SPY 2013-04-20    C 142.00      1      6

## avg_price sd_price avg_stock_price stock_range
## 35.973      0.261          155.74        0.68
## 31.380      0.000          155.44        0.01
## 26.210      0.000          156.24        0.02
## 24.600      0.000          157.58        0.01
## 16.465      0.751          156.44        1.51
## 13.920      0.000          155.87        0.01
```

Now that we have our results in a workable format, let us take a look at some distributions of traded option volume versus maturity and strike. We can also partition these graphs by type (puts or calls.)

```
unique_maturities <- unique(results$date)

today <- as.Date("2013-04-15")
days_to_expiration <- as.Date(unique_maturities[1]) - today

# Extract only the relevant maturity range
single_maturity_table <- results[results$date ==
  unique_maturities[1], ]

# Look at the calls and puts separately
calls <- single_maturity_table[
  single_maturity_table$type == "C", ]
puts <- single_maturity_table[
  single_maturity_table$type == "P", ]

par(mfrow = c(2, 1))
plot(calls$strike, calls$volume,
```

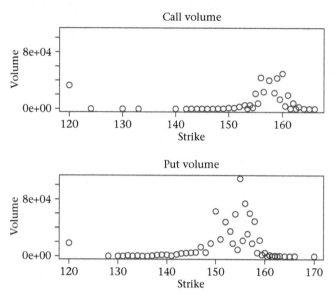

Figure 9.4 Option traded volumes.

```
    xlab = "Strike", ylab = "Volume",
    main = "Call volume", cex.main = 0.9)
  abline(v = mean(calls$avg_stock_price), lty = 2)
  grid()
  plot(puts$strike, puts$volume,
    xlab = "Strike", ylab = "Volume",
    main = "Put volume", cex.main = 0.9)
  abline(v = mean(puts$avg_stock_price), lty = 2)
  grid()
```

For the five-day maturity option, we observe that the bulk of the volume traded slightly out-of-the-money. It is interesting to also note the outlier volume at a strike price of 120.

Implied volatility

The price of an option is not the most important variable in the minds of many traders. What they really care about is the implied volatility of that option, especially, the dynamics of the implied volatility across strikes, maturities, and even other related products.

Consider the following two quotes:

1. "Implied volatility is the wrong number to insert into the wrong formula to get the right price." – Riccardo Rebonato [90].
2. "Essentially, all models are wrong, but some are useful." – George Box.

In options trading, both of these hit the nail on the head. Despite the fact that the Black-Scholes model is mediocre at capturing the true underlying price dynamics of the options it tries to model, it is nevertheless used by the vast majority of option traders around the world. Thinking in terms of implied volatilities of this incorrect, yet useful, model, has become the norm.

There is a lot of information available in options quote data. Each listed maturity is comprised of both puts and calls for multiple strike prices. Each one of these option contracts, in turn, has its own quote and trade profile recorded throughout the day.

The file format for option quotes is similar to what we saw for the option trades file. The name specifies the underlying symbol, whether it is a put or a call, the expiraton date, the strike price, and the trading day (i.e., SPY_C_20130412_145.00_XX_20130410_QT.csv).

For this next example, we will proceed as follows:

1. extract all the bid-ask prices for a single maturity,
2. compute the mid-price from the quotes and impute the implied volatilities,
3. plot the implied volatility smile throughout the day.

```
# Create a vector of filenames
folder <- "path/SPY_20130410_QT/"
available_files <- list.files(folder)

# Explore the first few lines of the file
temp <- read.csv(file = paste0(folder, available_files[1]),
  header = FALSE, stringsAsFactors = FALSE)

head(temp)
##          V1              V2       V3    V4 V5 V6    V7  V8
## 1 04/10/2013 08:30:00.189  Q 21538   Z  F  0.00   0
## 2 04/10/2013 09:30:00.710  Q 26105   Z  A 14.68   1
## 3 04/10/2013 09:30:00.727  Q 26856   Z  A 14.68   3
## 4 04/10/2013 09:30:00.730  Q 27019   Z  A 14.68   3
## 5 04/10/2013 09:30:00.892  Q 33429   N  R 16.80 118

##     V9 V10 V11 V12    V13 V14    V15 V16
##   0.00   0   P   R 157.06   4 157.07 186
##  19.68   1   P   R 157.16  33 157.17   7
##  19.68   1   P   R 157.16  33 157.17   7
##  19.68   3   P   R 157.16  33 157.17   7
##  17.59  10   P   R 157.16  33 157.17   7

column_names <- c("date", "time", "trade_indicator",
```

```
"sequence_number", "option_exchange_code",
"option_condition_code", "bid_price", "bid_size",
"ask_price", "ask_size", "stock_exchange_code",
"stock_condition_code", "underlying_bid_price",
"underlying_bid_size", "underlying_ask_price",
"underlying_ask_size")
```

We will focus on the options that expire on July 20, 2013. As a reference point, the current trading date is set to April 10, 2013. This is an option chain that expires in 101 days.

```
# Find files for July 20, 2013 expiry
files_to_use <- available_files[grep("20130720",
  available_files)]

length(files_to_use)
## [1] 142

strikes <- sapply(strsplit(files_to_use, "_"), "[", 4)
type <- sapply(strsplit(files_to_use, "_"), "[", 2)

# Extract relevant columns of data
quote_list <- list()
for(i in 1:length(files_to_use)) {
  temp <- read.csv(file = paste0(folder, files_to_use[i]),
    header = FALSE, stringsAsFactors = FALSE)
  names(temp) <- column_names

  # Extract quotes from CBOE only
  filter <- temp$trade_indicator == "Q" &
    temp$option_exchange_code == "C"

  data <- temp[filter, ]

  # Create xts object
  require(xts)
  time_index <- as.POSIXct(paste(data$date, data$time),
    format = "%m/%d/%Y %H:%M:%OS")
  data_filtered <- data[, c("bid_price", "ask_price",
    "underlying_bid_price", "underlying_ask_price")]
  data_filtered$type <- type[i]
  data_filtered$strike <- strikes[i]
  xts_prices <- xts(data_filtered, time_index)
```

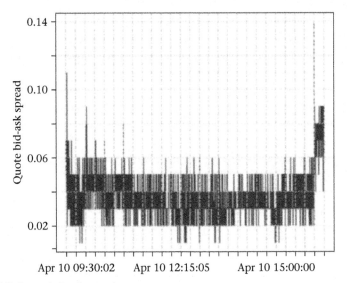

Figure 9.5 Spread of option quotes.

```
    quote_list[[i]] <- xts_prices
}
```

What does the bid-ask spread for option quotes look like throughout the trading day? We will look at the 158-strike option time series since it is an at-the-money option.

```
data <- quote_list[[49]]
spread <- as.numeric(data$ask_price) -
  as.numeric(data$bid_price)
plot(xts(spread, index(data)),
  main = "SPY | Expiry = July 20, 2013 | K = 158",
  cex.main = 0.8, ylab = "Quote bid-ask spread")
```

Next, let us take a look at a cross-section of strikes at a particular point in time.

```
time_of_interest <- "2013-04-10 10:30:00::
  2013-04-10 10:30:10"

strike_list <- list()
for(i in 1:length(quote_list)) {
  data <- quote_list[[i]][time_of_interest]
  if(nrow(data) > 0) {
    mid_quote <- (as.numeric(data$bid_price) +
      as.numeric(data$ask_price)) / 2
    mid_underlying <- (as.numeric(data$underlying_bid_price) +
```

```
      as.numeric(data$underlying_ask_price)) / 2
    strike_list[[i]] <- c(as.character(index(data[1])),
      data$type[1], data$strike[1], names(quote_list[i]),
      mid_quote[1], mid_underlying[1])
  }
}


# Aggregate the columns
df <- as.data.frame(do.call(rbind, strike_list),
  stringsAsFactors = FALSE)
names(df) <- c("time", "type", "strike",
  "mid_quote", "mid_underlying")

head(df)
##                      time type strike mid_quote mid_underlying
## 1 2013-04-10 10:30:00  C 110.00     47.98        157.905
## 2 2013-04-10 10:30:00  C 111.00    46.985        157.905
## 3 2013-04-10 10:30:00  C 112.00    45.985        157.905
## 4 2013-04-10 10:30:00  C 113.00    44.995        157.905
## 5 2013-04-10 10:30:00  C 114.00    43.995        157.905

plot(as.numeric(df$strike), as.numeric(df$mid_quote),
  main = "Option Price vs. Strike for Calls and Puts",
  ylab = "Premium",
  xlab = "Strike",
  cex.main = 0.8)
grid()
```

The graph shows the premiums for both calls and puts superimposed onto the same x-axis. For the purposes of switching over to implied volatility space, we need to filter the data so that we only keep the out-of-the-money options. At this point we are entering the realm of both art and science. Coming up with good implied volatility fits to option prices is fairly difficult. There is a lot of ongoing research into this topic, and many trading firms consider this step an important ingredient in their secret sauce for effectively trading volatility.

```
# Filter the otm options
otm_calls <- df$type == "C" & df$mid_underlying <= df$strike
otm_puts <- df$type == "P" & df$mid_underlying > df$strike
otm <- df[otm_calls | otm_puts, ]
```

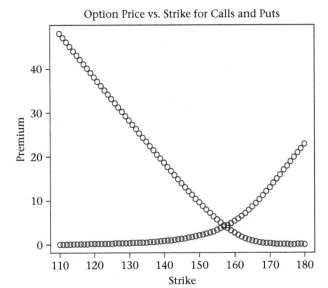

Figure 9.6 Call and put premiums.

```
# Order by strike
otm <- otm[order(otm[, "strike"]), ]
plot(otm$strike, otm$mid_quote,
  main = "OTM prices",
  xlab = "Strike",
  ylab = "Premium",
  cex.main = 0.8)
  grid()
```

Since the SPY options are American, we need to employ either a Monte Carlo approach, a tree, or a finite-difference solver in order to extract the implied volatilities from the quoted prices. The AmericanOptionImpliedVolatility() function from **RQuantlib** will be used for this purpose. The dividend yield and the risk-free interest rate are arbitrarily chosen in this example. In practice, these parameters are crucial to obtaining decent fits. If the correct forward price is not accounted for, there will be discontinuities between the put and the call implied volatilities.

```
# Compute the implied vols for otm options
otm$iv <- NA
for(i in 1:nrow(otm)) {
  type <- ifelse(otm$type[i] == "C", "call", "put")
  value <- as.numeric(otm$mid_quote[i])
  underlying <- as.numeric(otm$mid_underlying[i])
```

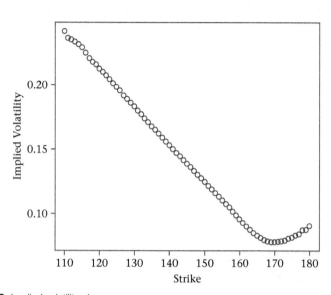

Figure 9.7 Implied volatility skew.

```
strike <- as.numeric(otm$strike[i])
dividendYield <- 0.03
riskFreeRate <- 0.02
maturity <- 101/252
volatility <- 0.15

otm$iv[i] <- AmericanOptionImpliedVolatility(type,
  value, underlying, strike,dividendYield,
  riskFreeRate, maturity, volatility)$impliedVol
}

# Generate plot
plot(otm$strike, otm$iv,
  main = "Implied Volatility skew for SPY on April 10,
  2013 10:30 am",
  xlab = "Strike",
  ylab = "Implied Volatility",
  cex.main = 0.8)
grid()
```

Summary

This chapter explores options pricing via the **RQuantlib** package. A quick review of basic options theory is provided, and the Black-Scholes formula is introduced. The sensitivities of some of the important Greeks are illustrated via custom R-code snippets and graphs. An intra-day analysis of tick data on options trades and quotes is performed by leveraging the Tick Data, Inc. high-frequency data set. Option prices are analyzed throughout a single trading day and across strike prices. The chapter ends with the calculation for the intra-day implied volatility skew at a single point in time for the SPY ETF.

This page intentionally left blank

10 | Optimization

Consider the problem of finding the best asset allocation strategy across thousands of investments so that the highest return is achieved with the smallest amount of risk. The methodology for coming up with the answer to such a question requires us to select parameters that will maximize/minimize our objective function subject to constraints. In our case, a plausible objective function might be the total return of a strategy divided by the maximum drawdown of the strategy over a predefined period. The constraints might be the total amount of capital devoted to each asset within the portfolio. Many interesting problems in finance, computer science, and the physical sciences rely on the specification and use of models. These mathematical formulations typically include one or more parameters as part of their input specifications. Optimization is a branch of mathematics that provides techniques for finding the best values for these parameters under constraints. R has a slew of packages that deal with optimization, and we will look at a few of them in this chapter.

The motivating parabola

What value of x will yield the lowest value for the function $f(x) = (1+x)^2$?

Calculus gives us a way to answer this question. We can take the first derivative of $f(x)$ with respect to x and set this to zero. The solution of the resulting equation is the answer to our question:

$$\frac{df(x)}{dx} = 2(1+x) = 0 => 2 + 2x = 0 => x = -1 \tag{10.1}$$

Whether the solution is a maximum or a minimum can be answered by looking at the second derivative. The point of this example is not to do a review of basic calculus. It is just to motivate the use of derivates and their higher dimensional analogues. Many optimization algorithms rely on the manipulation of such derivates in one way or another.

The following graph illustrates both the function $f(x)$ and its derivative $f'(x)$:

```
# Create the function
f <- function(x) {
```

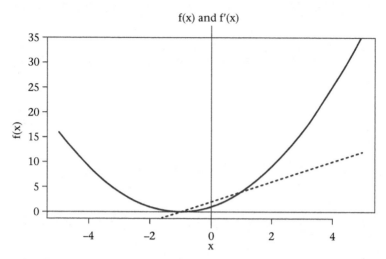

Figure 10.1 Parabolic function and its derivative.

```
    return((1 + x) ^ 2)
}
# Create the derivative
fp <- function(x) {
   return(2 * (1 + x))
}

# Plot the function and its derivative
x <- seq(-5, 5, 0.1)
plot(x, f(x), type = 'l', lwd = 2,
   main = "f(x) and f'(x)",
   cex.main = 0.8,
   cex.lab = 0.8,
   cex.axis = 0.8)
grid()
lines(x, fp(x), lty = 3, lwd = 2)
abline(h = 0)
abline(v = 0)
```

The dotted line (derivative of $f(x)$) crosses the $y = 0$ line at $x = -1$.

This method assumes that we know the functional form of the derivative. The same approach can be extended to multiple dimensions, provided we know the partial derivatives of the function.

Newton's method

Newton's method is a popular procedure for numerically computing the zeros of a function [95]. We mentioned previously that many optimization problems we care about can be solved by manipulating the first and second derivatives of a given objective function. Finding the zeros of such functions is an important part in the process of obtaining fast answers to optimization problems. Newton's method is one of many such available algorithms. It is the simplest one to comprehend, and we will briefly review it below. For more robust algorithms, we will rely on special R libraries to perform the necessary calculations.

Newton's method utilizes a Taylor series expansion of $f(x)$ around x_n and constructs a sequence x_n that converges to the stationary point x^* such that $f'(x^*) = 0$. It starts off by assuming an initial value x_0 and then refines the estimate in an iterative fashion. The algorithm for generating the next value in the sequence is:

$$x_{n+1} = x_n - f(x_n)/f'(x_n), n = 0, 1, \ldots \tag{10.2}$$

In R, we can do the following:

```
f <- function(x) {
   return(x ^ 2 - 4 * x + 1)
}
```

A plot of this function reveals two roots around -4 and 0:

```
uniroot(f, c(-8, -1))
## $root
## [1] -4.236068

## $f.root
## [1] -2.568755e-07

## $iter
## [1] 8

## $estim.prec
## [1] 6.103516e-05

uniroot(f, c(-1, 2))
## $root
## [1] 0.236044

## $f.root
## [1] -0.0001070205

## $iter
## [1] 6
```

```
## $estim.prec
## [1] 6.103516e-05
```

The function uniroot() is part of the base R installation, and returns what we are interested in. The actual values are closer to -4.236068 and 0.236044. We will use these as a control in order to compare them against our naive version of Newton's technique.

The following is based on: http://www.theresearchkitchen.com/archives/642. The author goes over a simple Newton's method implementation in R and also introduces the eval() function. We will use eval() in the second method of our implementation to evaluate derivatives in a symbolic manner.

```
# Newton's method with a first order approximation
newton <- function(f, tol = 1E-12, x0 = 1, N = 20) {
  # N = total number of iterations
  # x0 = initial guess
  # tol = abs(xn+1 - xn)
  # f = function to be evaluated for a root

  h <- 0.001
  i <- 1; x1 <- x0
  p <- numeric(N)
  while (i <= N) {
    df_dx <- (f(x0 + h) - f(x0)) / h
    x1 <- (x0 - (f(x0) / df_dx))
    p[i] <- x1
    i <- i + 1
    if (abs(x1 - x0) < tol) {
      break
    }
    x0 <- x1
  }
  return(p[1:(i-1)])
}
```

For our function $f(x) = x^2 - 4x + 1$, newton() should produce a vector of convergent answers that approach the actual root. We will have to call this function twice with different x_0 values since we have two roots to identify:

```
newton(f, x0 = -10)
## [1] -6.312270 -4.735693 -4.281609 -4.236513
## [5] -4.236068 -4.236068 -4.236068 -4.236068

newton(f, x0 = 10)
```

```
## [1] 4.2085746 1.5071738 0.4665599 0.2468819
## [5] 0.2360964 0.2360680 0.2360680 0.2360680
```

The reason the same number is repeating is due to the tolerance threshold we have specified. This is set to 1e-12. If we increase the precision of the displayed digits, we can distinguish the granularity in our answer:

```
options(digits = 14)
newton(f, x0 = 10)
## [1] 4.20857464272283 1.50717378796250 0.46655991958819
## [5] 0.24688186711921 0.23609640037269 0.23606798403444
## [8] 0.23606797750125 0.23606797749979 0.23606797749979
```

This is close enough for government work. It becomes obvious that the closer the initial guess is to the real root, the fewer iterations will be required to compute the correct value. The answer is also a function of the required tolerance. A smaller tolerance (smaller degree of precision) will speed up the calculation:

```
newton(f, x0 = 0.25)
## [1] 0.23611419684515 0.23606798830978 0.23606797750221
## [4] 0.23606797749979 0.23606797749979
```

R is also capable of performing symbolic calculations. Given a mathematical expression, the function D() can evaluate the symbolic derivative with respect to any specified variable. Here's an example of a symbolic computation:

```
# Create an expression
e <- expression(sin(x))

# Compute the derivative
D(e, "x")
## cos(x)
```

Here is one way to evaluate the function and its derivative. We have to work with expression objects in R:

```
f_expr <- expression(x ^ 2 + 4 * x - 1)
```

In order to evaluate an expression at a particular value of x, we can pass that value into the eval() function within a list:

```
eval(f_expr, list(x = 2))
[1] 11
```

We can now use the D() function to compute the symbolic derivative within our newton() function:

```r
newton_alternate <- function(f, tol = 1E-12, x0 = 1, N = 20) {
  # N = total number of iterations
  # x0 = initial guess
  # tol = abs(xn+1 - xn)
  # f = expression to be evaluated for a root

  # Compute the symbolic derivative
  df_dx = D(f, "x")

  i <- 1; x1 <- x0
  p <- numeric(N)
  while (i <= N) {
    x1 <- (x0 - eval(f, list(x = x0)) /
      eval(df_dx, list(x = x0)))
    p[i] <- x1
    i <- i + 1
    if (abs(x1 - x0) < tol) {
      break
    }
    x0 <- x1
  }
  return(p[1:(i-1)])
}

newton_alternate(f_expr, x0 = 10)
## [1] 4.20833333333333 1.50685123042506 0.46631585084907
## [4] 0.24681560399775 0.23609368309733 0.23606797764754
## [7] 0.23606797749979 0.23606797749979

newton_alternate(f_expr, x0 = -10)
## [1] -6.3125000000000 -4.7359601449275 -4.2817360731259
## [4] -4.2365249924418 -4.2360680241934 -4.2360679774998
## [7] -4.2360679774998
```

The brute-force approach

This next example looks at the determination of a best fit line through a cloud of points. A best fit line is characterized by its slope and its intercept. Given the cloud of points, we can come up with the optimal slope and intercept parameters that minimize a certain objective function. The idea of maximizing or minimizing certain functions given constraints on the input parameters is what optimization is all about. In our example, the objective function will be the sum of squared differences between the points and the best fit line that we eventually want to obtain. In order to illustrate this process, we will proceed to create an artificial scatter plot in which we know exactly the true value for both the slope and the intercept. Our goal will be to reverse engineer this process in order to determine the values for the slope and intercept through the data:

```
# Create a set of random points x
set.seed(123)
x <- rnorm(100, 0, 1)

# Make y a function of x
y <- 3.2 + 2.9 * x + rnorm(100, 0, 0.1)

plot(x, y)
```

It should be obvious that there exists a linear relationship between the x and y random variables. If we did not know any better, we could hypothesize that the true relationship is of the form $y = ax + b$. Our goal is to find the true a and b.

Here is the objective function that we will minimize:

```
objective_function <- function(y, x, a, b) {
  value <- sum((y - (a * x + b)) ^ 2)
  return(value)
}
```

The values for a and b that yield the lowest value for our objective function, are our candidates for the true a and b. A brute-force approach to solving this problem is:

```
# Create a range of a and b values and loop through all of them
a <- seq(-10, 10, 0.25)
b <- seq(-10, 10, 0.25)

output <- list()
z <- 1
for(i in 1:length(a)) {
  for(j in 1:length(b)) {
    output[[z]] <- c(objective_function(y, x, a[i], b[j]),
      a[i], b[j])
    z <- z + 1
  }
}

# Create a matrix out of the list and find the minimum value
mat <- do.call(rbind, output)
```

```
colnames(mat) <- c("obj", "a", "b")

smallest <- which(mat[, "obj"] == min(mat[, "obj"]))

mat[smallest, ]
## obj       a       b
## 2.16076 3.00000 3.25000
```

We can see that our brute-force approach got close to the true values. It did not find the exact values since the granularity of our search space was not refined enough. If we make the intervals for a and b smaller, we will increase our computational time, but get closer to the global minimum:

```
a = seq(-5, 5, 0.1)
b = seq(-5, 5, 0.1)
```

Here is the answer for this set of parameters:

```
## obj       a       b
## 0.9077592 2.9000 3.2000
```

An extensive brute-force search will eventually recover the optimal parameters for any minimization problem regardless of the number of variables and/or complexity of the search space. The only problem is whether we want to wait long enough to get the answer back. A brute-force search is only feasible for the simplest of problems we might encounter in practice. For all other problems, it just takes too long.

In most real-world applications, we are not provided with convenient closed-form expressions for objective functions, nor their derivatives. In such instances, we have to rely on other numerical optimization methods in coming up with parameter estimates that make sense.

R optimization routines

R provides canned functions that take us a long way toward solving optimization problems. The noteworthy ones are optimize(), optim(), solve.QP(), and DEoptim() [10, 11, 60]. There exist numerous third-party libraries that also tackle optimization problems from various angles.[1]

The optim() function can be used when we have a particular objective function in mind. Here are the arguments for optim():

```
args(optim)
function (par, fn, gr = NULL, ...,
  method = c("Nelder-Mead",
   "BFGS", "CG", "L-BFGS-B", "SANN", "Brent"),
  lower = -Inf,
```

```
upper = Inf,
control = list(),
hessian = FALSE)
```

The `fn` argument represents the function that we want to minimize. This function needs to take the parameter vector `par` as an input and return a scalar value. The `par` argument is a vector of initial values. The sum of squared residuals is a common objective function that is often used in practice. The `method` argument provides six separate optimization models to choose from. The "BFGS" method is considered a quasi Newton method, and is similar in spirit to what we have already covered. It uses information from the function and its gradient to solve the optimization problem. Some of the other approaches, like "CG," for example, employ conjugate gradient implementations that might be used to tackle optimization problems with many parameters.[2]

A curve-fitting exercise

This next use case might be of interest to a fixed-income trader. Assume we have a yield curve of maturities on the x-axis and interest rates on the y-axis. Our goal is to fit a smooth curve through those points. A similar approach might be employed by options traders to fit smooth curves through implied volatility profiles. We will not be concerned as to whether these curves are `arbitrage-free`.[3] This is just a simple curve-fitting exercise:

```
# Create fictitious yields
rates = c(0.025, 0.03, 0.034, 0.039, 0.04,
  0.045, 0.05, 0.06, 0.07, 0.071,
  0.07, 0.069, 0.07, 0.071, 0.072,
  0.074, 0.076, 0.082, 0.088, 0.09)
maturities = 1:20

plot(maturities, rates, xlab = "years",
  main = "Yields",
  cex.main = 0.8,
  cex.lab = 0.8,
  cex.axis = 0.8)
grid()
```

We can try to fit this plot with a simple fifth-degree polynomial.

```
poly_5 <- function(x, p) {
  f <- p[1] + p[2] * x + p[3] * x^2 +
    p[4] * x^3 + p[5] * x^4 + p[6] * x^5
  return(f)
```

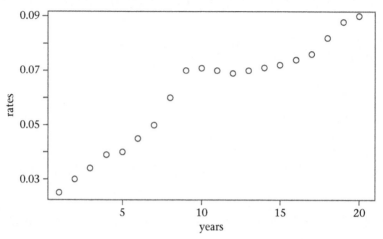

Figure 10.2 Rates and maturities graph.

```
}

obj_5 <- function(x, y, p) {
  error <- (y - poly_5(x, p)) ^ 2
  return(sum(error))
}

# Fit the parameters. Assume 0 for all initial values
out_5 = optim(obj_5, par = c(0, 0, 0, 0, 0, 0),
  x = maturities, y = rates)

out
## $par
## [1]   2.4301235956099e-02   1.3138951147963e-03
## [3]   5.5229326602931e-04   7.5685740385076e-07
## [5]  -4.2119475163787e-06   1.5330958809806e-07


## $value
## [1] 0.00017311660458207


## $counts
## function gradient
##      501       NA


## $convergence
## [1] 1
```

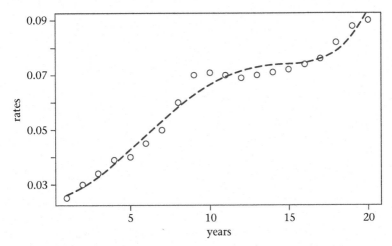

Figure 10.3 Rates graph with polynomial fit.

```
## $message
## NULL
```

We can now extract the coefficients and superimpose the polynomial onto the plot:

```
lines(poly_5(maturities, out_5$par), lwd = 1.5, lty = 2)
```

It seems like we obtained a decent fit to the data, but we feel like we can do better. The polynomial is not flexible enough to accommodate the hump in the middle of the graph. We can try a higher-order polynomial and see what that gets us:

```
poly_7 <- function(x, p) {
  f <- p[1] + p[2] * x + p[3] * x^2 +
    p[4] * x^3 + p[5] * x^4 +
    p[6] * x^5 + p[6] * x^6 +
    p[7] * x^7
  return(f)
}

obj_7 <- function(x, y, p) {
  error <- (y - poly_7(x, p)) ^ 2
  return(sum(error))
}

# Fit the parameters. Assume 0 for all initial values
out_7 <- optim(obj_7, par = c(0, 0, 0, 0, 0, 0, 0, 0),
  x = maturities, y = rates)

lines(poly_7(maturities, out_7$par), lwd = 1.5, lty = 3)
```

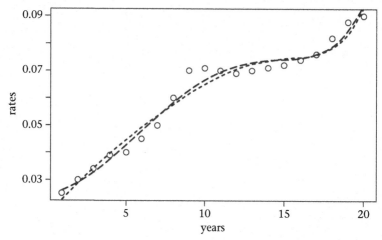

Figure 10.4 Rates graph with 2 polynomial fits.

This new fit is not much better than what we had before. We can make the fit almost exact by increasing the power of the polynomial, but that would be a mistake since it would most likely lead to overfitting.[4]

An alternative approach, is to realize that around the ten-year mark, some kind of regime shift appears to be occurring given our data plot. We can hopefully reduce the overfitting problem by splicing two lower-order polynomials together and by making sure that the resulting curve is continuous. This approach is more of an art than a science, and it relies on the fact that the practitioner is able to inject a personal bias into the curve-fitting exercise. For example, due to various macro economic reasons, the trader might feel justified in believing that the shorter-maturity yields behave differently than the middle-to longer-maturity ones.

```
# Specify two polynomials to be used for fitting purposes
poly_5 <- function(x, a) {
  f <- a[1] + a[2] * x + a[3] * x ^ 2 +
    a[4] * x ^ 3 + a[5] * x ^ 4 +
    a[6] * x ^ 5
  return(f)
}

poly_3 <- function(x, offset, intercept, b) {
  f <- intercept + b[1] * (x - offset) +
    b[2] * (x - offset) ^ 2 +
    b[3] * (x - offset) ^ 3
  return(f)
}
```

When the maturity is equal to nine, we need to make sure that the two polynomials have the same value. We can accomplish this by using an offset value for the x-axis for the third-order polynomial. When x is equal to this offset, all the terms will drop to zero except for the intercept. This intercept should be constrained to be equal to the value of the fifth-order polynomial. This is how we will tie the polynomials together in a smooth manner:

```
obj_3_5 <- function(x, y, offset, p) {

  # All points are at infinity initially
  fit <- rep(Inf, length(x))
  ind_5 <- x <= offset
  ind_3 <- x > offset

  fit[ind_5] <- poly_5(x[ind_5], p[1:6])
  fit[ind_3] <- poly_3(x[ind_3], offset,
    poly_5(offset, p[1:6]), p[7:9])

  error <- (y - fit) ^ 2
  return(sum(error))
}


# Fit the parameters.  Assume 0 for all initial values
offset <- 9
out_3_5 <- optim(obj_3_5, par = rep(0, 9),
  x = maturities, y = rates, offset = offset)

plot(maturities, rates, xlab = "years",
  main = "Yields",
  cex.main = 0.8,
  cex.lab = 0.8,
  cex.axis = 0.8)
grid()
lines(poly_5(maturities[maturities <= offset],
  out_3_5$par[1:6]), lwd = 2)
lines(c(rep(NA, offset),
  poly_3(maturities[maturities > offset], offset,
  poly_5(offset, out_3_5$par[1:6]),
  out_3_5$par[7:9])), lwd = 2)
abline(v = offset)
```

The above method for fitting two polynomials to data is somewhat contrived, and there are indeed better ways to accomplish the same goal. The use of smoothing

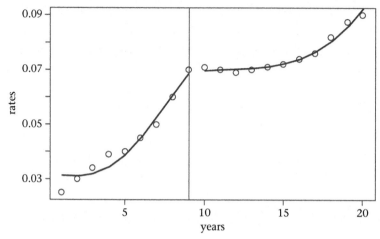

Figure 10.5 Rates graph with piecewise polynomial fits.

`splines` is one approach. Yet another popular approach is the application of a locally weighted regression method to the data. The `loess()` function is perfectly suited for such a task:

```
# Fit loess to the data
obj <- loess(rates ~ maturities, span = 0.5)

# Plot the data and the fit
plot(maturities, rates, main = "Rates", cex.main = 0.8)
lines(predict(obj), lty = 2)
```

The **span** argument controls the degree of smoothing applied to the local fit.

The purpose of the exercise was to illustrate the use of the `optim()` function and to show that the objective function can become arbitrarily complex. This insight will allow us to solve a variety of practical, finance-related, optimization problems.

Portfolio optimization

Optimization techniques can certainly be applied to the problem of creating an investment portfolio with desirable risk-reward metrics given monetary constraints. The following optimization example is based on the work of Guy Yolin [39]. His presentation can be found here:
http://www.rinfinance.com/RinFinance2009/presentations/yollin_slides.pdf.

We are often interested in identifying portfolios of stocks with optimal risk-reward characteristics. The often-cited example in the literature is that of attaining the minimum-variance portfolio. This portfolio is obtained by evaluating the

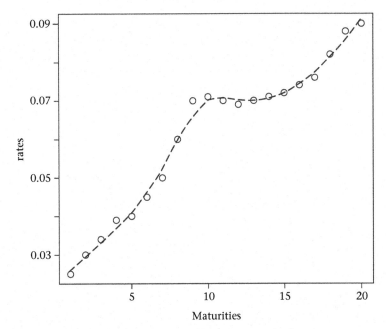

Figure 10.6 Rates graph with `loess` fits.

following quadratic program:

$$Obj = c^T x + \frac{1}{2} x^T Q x$$
$$s.t\ Ax \geq b \qquad\qquad (10.3)$$
$$x \geq 0$$

In effect, we need to minimize the total portfolio risk subject to a constraint on the overall portfolio return. We can also place restrictions on the weights of each stock within the portfolio. It turns out that these quadratic problems can be solved in a very efficient manner. The **quadprog** package in R contains a general quadratic program solver called `solve.QP()`.

More interesting and practical examples deal with minimizing objective functions that are not well behaved and that do not have elegant mathematical solutions. In such cases, we must rely on more sophisticated optimization implementations. The **DEoptim** package provides such an algorithm. According to Yolin, "DE is a very simple and yet very powerful population based stochastic function minimizer that is ideal for global optimization of multidimensional multimodal functions (i.e., really hard problems). It was developed in mid-1990 by Berkeley researchers Ken Price and Rainer Storm [62]." We will not cover the inner workings of the DE algorithm in this section. Those details can be found here: http://www1.icsi.berkeley.edu/storn/code.html.

The example in which we are interested is the following: Given a list of potential stocks, find the optimal weight in each security such that the maximum drawdown of the portfolio is minimized. One requirement we need to allow for is that the sum of all the weights be equal to 100 percent. We can also add the requirement that any weight less than 2 percent be set to zero.

This is a rather complicated objective function. Luckily, we can code it up in only a few lines of R code:

```
install.packages("DEoptim")
require(DEoptim)

# Drawdown function
compute_drawdown <- function(x, returns_default = TRUE,
  geometric = TRUE) {

# x = Vector of raw pnl or returns
# If returns_default = FALSE, the geometric
# argument is ignored and the pnl is used.
# Output = the maximum drawdown

if(returns_default) {
  # Cumulative return calculation
  if(geometric) {
    cumulative_return <- cumprod(1 + x)
  } else {
    cumulative_return <- 1 + cumsum(x)
  }
  max_cumulative_return <- cummax(c(1, cumulative_return))[-1]
  drawdown <- -(cumulative_return / max_cumulative_return - 1)
} else {
  # PnL vector is used
  cumulative_pnl <- c(0, cumsum(x))
  drawdown <- cummax(cumulative_pnl) - cumulative_pnl
  drawdown <- drawdown[-1]
}

# Drawdown vector for either pnl or returns
return(drawdown)
}

obj_max_drawdown <- function(w, r_matrix, small_weight) {
  # w is the weight of every stock
  # r_matrix is the returns matrix of all stocks
```

```
# Portfolio return
portfolio_return <- r_matrix %*% w

# Max drawdown
drawdown_penalty <- max(compute_drawdown(portfolio_return))

# Create penalty component for sum of weights
weight_penalty <- 100 * (1 - sum(w)) ^ 2

# Create a penalty component for negative weights
negative_penalty <- -sum(w[w < 0])

# Create penalty component for small weights
small_weight_penalty <- 100 * sum(w[w < small_weight])

# Objective function to minimize
obj <- drawdown_penalty + weight_penalty +
  negative_penalty + small_weight_penalty

return(obj)
}

# Calculate a returns matrix for multiple stocks
symbol_names <- c("AXP", "BA", "CAT", "CVX",
  "DD", "DIS", "GE", "HD", "IBM",
  "INTC", "KO", "MMM", "MRK",
  "PG", "T", "UTX", "VZ")

# Load these prices into memory
price_matrix <- NULL
for(name in symbol_names) {
  # Extract the adjusted close price vector
  price_matrix <- cbind(price_matrix, get(name)[, 6])
}
colnames(price_matrix) <- symbol_names

# Compute returns
returns_matrix <- apply(price_matrix, 2, function(x)
diff(log(x)))

# Specify a small weight below which the allocation should
 be 0%
small_weight_value <- 0.02
```

```
# Specify lower and upper bounds for the weights
lower <- rep(0, ncol(returns_matrix))
upper <- rep(1, ncol(returns_matrix))

optim_result <- DEoptim(obj_max_drawdown, lower, upper,
  control = list(NP = 400, itermax = 300, F = 0.25, CR = 0.75),
  returns_matrix, small_weight_value)
```

Here are the results that display in the console after the optimization has ended. This display can be disabled by setting trace = FALSE within the control vector.

```
. . .
Iteration: 299 bestvalit: 0.515606 bestmemit:
      0.020494       0.021594       0.020232
      0.044563       0.020729       0.172967
      0.021248       0.105254       0.084343
      0.032526       0.067988       0.034999
      0.020617       0.196651       0.042869
      0.033833       0.056965

Iteration: 300 bestvalit: 0.515606 bestmemit:
      0.020494       0.021594       0.020232
      0.044563       0.020729       0.172967
      0.021248       0.105254       0.084343
      0.032526       0.067988       0.034999
      0.020617       0.196651       0.042869
      0.033833       0.056965
```

The output of the DEoptim() function is a list of lists. The optim list contains the parameters of interest. The nested bestmem element of the list contains the best weights.

```
weights <- optim_result$optim$bestmem
```

It is interesting to see that all the nonzero weights are higher than 2 percent. This is due to the contribution of the small-weight penalty term we added to our objective function. We can also verify that the sum of the weights equals 1.

```
sum(weights)
0.9978
```

At this point we can scale the weights to be exactly equal to one.

```
weights <- weights / sum(weights)
```

So let us take a look at the portfolio cumulative return with the recommended set of weights versus an equally weighted portfolio. Our hope is to validate the **DEoptim** result by checking that the maximum drawdown is indeed smaller for the recommended portfolio.

```
# Equally weighted portfolio
equal_weights <- rep(1 / 17, 17)
equal_portfolio <- returns_matrix %*% equal_weights
equal_portfolio_cumprod <- cumprod(1 + equal_portfolio)

# Optimal max drawdown portfolio
optimized_portfolio <- returns_matrix %*% weights
drawdown_portfolio_cumprod <- cumprod(1 + optimized_portfolio)

main_title <- "Equal vs. Optimized Weights"
plot(drawdown_portfolio_cumprod, type = 'l', xaxt = 'n',
  main = main_title, xlab = "", ylab = "cumprod(1 + r)")
lines(equal_portfolio_cumprod, lty = 3)
grid(col = 'black')

# Set x-axis labels
label_location <- seq(1, length(drawdown_portfolio_cumprod),
  by = 90)
labels <- rownames(returns_matrix)[label_location]
axis(side = 1, at = label_location, labels = labels,
  las = 2, cex.axis= 0.8)
```

Here are the values for the maximum drawdown for both portfolios:

```
# Equal weighted
max(compute_drawdown(equal_portfolio))
[1] 0.597

# Optimized for the smallest max drawdown
max(compute_drawdown(optimized_portfolio))
[1] 0.515
```

The optimized portfolio exhibits a better cumulative geometric-return profile. This result is expected since we ran the analysis on the in-sample data set. In order to determine whether the optimized weights are indeed better, we have to run the same study on an out-of-sample set and, potentially, reserve a third batch of data for robustness and validation testing.

It is also important to note that the Differential Evolution algorithm will give different results every time it is run. This is due to the inherent stochastic nature

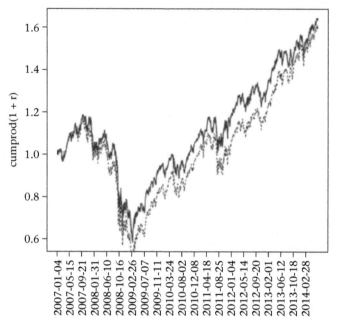

Figure 10.7 Equal and optimized weights.

of the algorithm itself. The output results of any optimization algorithm should be taken with a grain of salt, and extensive due diligence is required on the part of the portfolio creator to ensure that the selected weights are not only sensible and stable but also truly provide the expected performance.

The mathematical theory on optimization is vast. For those interested in further exploring these ideas in R, I recommend the following excellent starting point: http://zoonek.free.fr/blosxom/R/2012-06-01_Optimization.html.

Summary

This chapter is all about leveraging R's optimization tool set for solving problems that deal with minimizing or maximizing custom objective functions subject to constraints. A motivating example is presented, and Newton's method, along with a brute-force approach is used to solve it. The optim() function is applied to a curve-fitting exercise, and the chapter concludes with an in-depth portfolio optimization example that utilizes the **DEoptim** (Differential Evolution) package.

11 | Speed, Testing, and Reporting

This last chapter could have easily been labeled as the "Miscellaneous" chapter. It includes a discussion on three important topics of which R programmers need to be aware. The first topic addresses the methods that can be used to speed up native R code and to allow interoperability between R and C++. The second topic revolves around the idea of test-driven development and how R users can write unit tests in order to improve their code quality and reliability. The chapter ends with a discussion on research reproducibility and reporting within R. Over the last few years, R has made great strides in all of these arenas. Performance improvements in the core language are constantly being made,[1] and packages such as **Rcpp**, **Rcpp11** and **RInside** have also contributed greatly to the cause [20, 21]. The **testthat** package is used to demonstrate the methodology for creating unit tests [41]. A streamlined and elegant reporting workflow has been made possible by the recent work of the RStudio team and packages such as **sweave** and **knitr** [145, 146]. The generation of a sample .pdf report via **knitr** is presented at the end of the chapter.

Runtime execution improvements

Even though R provides fairly efficient implementations for most of the popular algorithms, for some applications, they are just not fast enough. Generally speaking, algorithmic efficiency and speed of execution are two things that every programmer eventually needs to address at some point in their career. Getting the correct functionality, though, out of his or her code, should be the primary concern of any developer. Optimization comes later on in the process and only if it is warranted. It is perfectly fine to work with slow code if the answer is only going to be computed once and the results are not time sensitive in nature. Donald Knuth said it best: "We should forget about small efficiencies, say about 97 percent of the time: premature optimization is the root of all evil [23]."

Ideally, all the programs we write from now on are accurate, maintainable, and efficient. This holy-grail state is something we can eventually attain, but not from the start. As a general rule, a programmer should first focus on obtaining the correct result, and only then focus on making the run time as fast as possible. Code maintainability and efficiency tend to be contradictory goals at times. The business requirements will dictate which is more important.

In R, there are a few ways to address the speed-of-execution issue. The first way is to write better R code. Better is a relative term, and what seems fast in one language, might not necessarily be so in R. The typical example is the use of `for` loops. The following code written in R will take a long time to run:

```
sum_with_loop_in_r <- function(max_value) {
  sum <- 0
  for(i in 1:max_value) {
    sum <- sum + i
  }
  return(sum)
}
```

This next version uses vectorization, and is significantly faster:

```
sum_with_vectorization_in_r = function(max_value) {
  numbers <- as.double(1:max_value)
  return(sum(numbers))
}
```

Benchmarking R code

We can use the **microbenchmark** library to test the relative time difference of both implementations.

```
library(microbenchmark)
microbenchmark(loop = sum_with_loop_in_r(1e5),
  vectorized = sum_with_vectorization_in_r(1e5))

## Unit: microseconds
## expr           min        lq         median
## loop           57615.323 59424.740  60992.7720
## vectorized     260.602   273.673    286.5495


## uq            max         neval
## 89608.441     96694.469   100
## 294.236       414.349     100
```

The vectorized version is around 213 faster than the for loop!

Most of the R code we write is interpreted code. The **compiler** package allows us to compile certain functions within R, thus making them faster to execute during runtime. More information on this package can be found here: http://homepage.stat.uiowa.edu/luke/R/compiler/compiler.pdf. The compiler utility has been available since R version 2.13.0.

```
compiled_sum_with_loop_in_r <- cmpfun(sum_with_loop_in_r)

microbenchmark(loop = sum_with_loop_in_r(1e5),
  compiled = compiled_sum_with_loop_in_r(1e5),
  vectorized = sum_with_vectorization_in_r(1e5))
```

```
## Unit: microseconds
## expr         min         lq          median
## loop         56746.652   58343.8945  60602.445
## compiled     4688.146    4758.6770   4892.246
## vectorized   249.457     273.8635    284.050


## uq          max         neval
## 86599.9875  96736.750   100
## 5498.9710   46484.009   100
## 292.3135    473.927     100
```

The compiled implementation is faster than the for loop, but not as fast as the vectorized version. The cmpfun() is by no means a magic bullet. Applying it to functions that have already been precompiled or functions that have internal implementations written in a compiled language will likely not produce any speed advantage.

The Rcpp solution

For comparison purposes, the following C++ function executes much faster:

```
long add_cpp(long max_value) {
  long sum = 0;
  for(long i = 1; i <= max_value; ++i) {
  sum = sum + i;
  }
  return sum;
}
```

The R-framework allows one to code up fast implementations in Fortran, C, or C++. These implementations can subsequently be called from within R. The "Writing R Extensions" document, which can be referenced here: http://cran.r-project.org/doc/manuals/R-exts.html, provides all the necessary details in order to get started down this path. This approach, however, is not straightforward. The process of writing R extensions in Fortran and C is somewhat involved, and we will not cover the details here.

Instead, we will utilize the **Rcpp** library, which is written and maintained by Dirk Eddelbuettel and Romain Francois. Relevant information on **Rcpp** can be found here: http://dirk.eddelbuettel.com/code/rcpp.html. Francois has recently released the **Rcpp11** version of this package. Details and other links can be found here: http://blog.r-enthusiasts.com/. Hadley Wickham also provides a nice tutorial here: http://adv-r.had.co.nz/Rcpp.html.

Suffice it to say that **Rcpp** allows one to write C++ code in a clean and concise manner. Connecting that code to R also becomes a breeze. Users need not concern themselves with any of the internal C API workings in order to get things working.

Most R functions that come with the base installation are already written in a complied language like Fortran, C, or C++. The function names can be typed into the R console. If nothing but R code appears, then the function is written in R. If something like the following appears: .C, .Call, .Fortran, .External, .Internal, or .Primitive, then the function is written in a compiled language.

Example of a function that calls .Internal()

```
lapply
## function (X, FUN, ...)
## {
##   FUN <- match.fun(FUN)
##   if (!is.vector(X) || is.object(X))
##       X <- as.list(X)
##       .Internal(lapply(X, FUN))
## }
```

The code for lapply() illustrates how it is entirely possible to combine R syntax with calls to internal compiled implementations written in another language. And now for the fun part. Here is how to create a C++ compiled function that can be leveraged within R.

Setup Steps:

1. Ensure that a working C++ compiler is installed on your machine. More information on setting this up can be found here:
   http://dirk.eddelbuettel.com/code/rcpp/Rcpp-FAQ.pdf and here:
   https://www.rstudio.com/ide/docs/packages/prerequisites.
   Windows users need the **Rtools**[2] package installed on their machines in order to utilize command-line tools and the MinGW compiler.
2. Install and load the **Rcpp** package and its dependencies

At this point, we are ready to write C++ code for use within R. We will make use of the two functions cppFunction() and sourceCpp(). The function cppFunction() allows one to write inline C++ code, whereas the sourceCpp() function can reference an external .cpp file.

```
library(Rcpp)

# Create a C++ function
cppFunction('
  long add_cpp(long max_value) {
    long sum = 0;
    for(long i = 1; i <= max_value; ++i) {
     sum = sum + i;
    }
    return sum;
  }'
)
```

This is what the function signature looks like:

```
add_cpp
## function (max_value)
## .Primitive(".Call")(<pointer: 0x10f52fbb0>, max_value)
```

Now that the function has been compiled, it can be used like any other R function.

```
add_cpp(1e5)
## [1] 5000050000
```

The **microbenchmark** test highlights the execution efficiency of the C++ implementation.

```
microbenchmark(loop = sum_with_loop_in_r(1e5),
  compiled = compiled_sum_with_loop_in_r(1e5),
  vectorized = sum_with_vectorization_in_r(1e5),
  compiled_cpp = add_cpp(1e5))
```

```
## Unit: microseconds
## expr             min         lq          median
## loop             73049.461   76640.5945  79635.8810
## compiled         7359.040    7487.9655   7795.9125
## vectorized       804.773     932.9285    1031.9695
## compiled_cpp     79.573      88.2615     98.9385

## uq              max          neval
## 80676.6600      94618.174    100
## 12101.8610      135353.743   100
## 1373.8565       2148.409     100
## 105.2440        135.781      100
```

The C++ implementation is at least 800 times faster than the native R loop. This is exciting news for those of us interested in harnessing the power of a compiled language within the R-environment. This performance metric hints at the fact that speed should not really be a concern for the average R user. Any "mission critical" functionality that requires speed of execution can now be written in C++.

Writing C++ functions inline with the R code provides a perfectly workable and efficient solution. However, it becomes cleaner if we split up the C++ code into its own separate file. The sourceCpp() allows us to pull in that external .cpp file.

The .cpp file could be something like this:

```
#include <Rcpp.h>
using namespace Rcpp;

// [[Rcpp::export]]
long add_2_cpp(long max_value) {
  long sum = 0;
  for(long i = 1; i <= max_value; ++i) {
    sum = sum + i;
  }
  return sum;
}
```

The sourceCpp() function will first compile the function, create an R equivalent function with the same name, and then place the function inside the local R environment. (http://adv-r.had.co.nz/Rcpp.html)

```
sourceCpp('path/add_2_file.cpp')
```

```
add_2_cpp(100)
## [1] 5050
```

Calling R from C++ with RInside

Sometimes we need a way to directly call R functionality from within a C++ program. **RInside** is a package which "provides an abstraction layer around the R embedding API and makes it easier to access an R instance inside your application. Moreover, thanks to the classes provided by **Rcpp**, data interchange between R and C++ becomes very straightforward [18]."

In his book, Eddelbuettel provides helpful examples on how to compile and run R code wrapped around C++ semantics. Here is one such example:

```
#include <RInside.h>

int main(int argc, char *argv[]) {
```

```
// create an embedded R instance
RInside R(argc, argv);

// assign a char* (string) to "txt"
R["txt"] = "Hello, world!\n";

// eval the init string, ignoring any returns
R.parseEvalQ("cat(txt)");

exit(0);
}
```

Writing unit tests with testthat

Testing is something that many developers shy away from. It is often considered a boring and tedious task, and even something of a novelty. This could not be further from the truth. Ever since I adopted a test-driven approach in my coding workflow, I have seen my productivity increase and the number of bugs introduced into my code decrease. Test driven development[3] is more of a mindset than a formal set of requirements. The basic idea is the following:

1. Conceptually, separate the functionality of a required program into many small modular components. The idea is to have each component (function) do one thing and do it well.
2. Write a test for each of the functions. Initially, make the tests fail.
3. Run all the tests. You should see failing tests.
4. Start writing the code that will implement the functionality.
5. Run the tests again. This time, they should pass.
6. Keep refactoring the code and always make sure that the tests pass.

The two most popular testing packages in R are: **RUnit** and **testthat**. The latter is another wonderful contribution by Hadley Wickham, and more information on its motivation and use can be found here: http://adv-r.had.co.nz/Testing.html.

This next example will implement **testthat** into our workflow. We will consider the task of computing the log returns given a vector of prices. According to our recipe above, we will first write the skeleton of our function and make the test fail:

```
# Define function
convert_to_returns <- function(prices) {
  return(9)
}
```

Here is the initial test that fails. The `context()` function helps group together related functionality. The `test_that()` function bundles together all the expected behavior. The test itself starts with the `expect_` keyword:

```
require(testthat)

# Group related functionality together with context()
context("Price to log-return conversion")

# Define the expectations using expect_that()
test_that("convert_to_returns produces the correct values", {

  # For these inputs
  input_prices <- c(100, 101, 102, 103, 99)

  # Expect these outputs
  expected_returns <- c(0.009950331,
    0.009852296, 0.009756175, -0.039609138)

  # Verify the expectation of equality
  expect_equal(expected_returns,
    convert_to_returns(input_prices))
})
```

When we run this test, we get the following output:

```
## Error: Test failed: 'convert_to_returns produces
## the correct values'
## Not expected: expected_returns not equal to
## convert_to_returns(input_prices)
## Numeric: lengths (1, 4) differ.
```

Time to work on our implementation. We will add one piece of functionality and make sure that our test now passes:

```
# Define function
convert_to_returns <- function(prices) {
  return(diff(log(prices)))
}
```

When the test is run, no error is produced. At this point, we can augment the function to check for prices of length less than two and issue an appropriate error message when this condition is encountered. But first, we need the test to fail.

```
# Verify the error message
input_prices <- c(100)
msg <- "Not enough price entries."

expect_message(msg, convert_to_returns(input_prices))
## Error: expected_message no messages shown
```

Now we rewrite the function to account for the corner case:

```
# Function with corner case check
convert_to_returns <- function(prices) {
  if(length(prices) < 2) {
    message("Not enough price entries.")
  }
  return(diff(log(prices)))
}
```

It turns out we can test for multiple scenarios and expectations. A full list of tests is given here: http://adv-r.had.co.nz/Testing.html. One way to run the tests is to create a separate source file and then execute the following command:

```
test_file("example_test_file.r")
```

Using knitr for documentation

Up to this point, we have focused our efforts on writing R scripts that process, analyze, and visualize data. By doing so, I have subtly hinted at the adoption of a specific workflow throughout this text. A workflow is a systematic way of executing tasks that allows a quant or developer to better manage their research, to easier reproduce their results and to reliably disseminate their findings to the public or other interested parties. It might consist of the following steps:

1. Formulate a hypothesis about a particular trading strategy or market micro-structure event.
2. Gather the necessary data needed to test that hypothesis.
3. Transform, process, and filter the data.
4. Write code that performs calculations on the filtered data.
5. Visualize the results and generate summary statistics.

The last step in the process is the efficient and accurate reproducibility of the important findings. External observers need to be able to replicate claims of others in a timely and accurate manner. This is, after all, how science advances. How can we help better facilitate this process?

Practically speaking, the observer would need to have access to the original data along with the code that generated the graphs, tables and results of the analysis. The way it currently works in most of academia and industry, is that the code, data and documentation is loosely coupled to the final published output. It is very difficult to obtain any or sometimes all of these elements from the vast majority of scientific publications out there.

To see why this loose coupling of data, code, and documentation might be troubling, imagine a researcher who needs to present dozens of tables and charts as part of a research proposal. The likelihood of correctly labeling those elements, and in general, keeping track of them, diminishes greatly as the complexity of the problem increases. What happens when the researcher has to juggle multiple research projects? Then the problem of managing all these resources becomes even harder. Another problem occurs when the underlying data itself changes. The analysis would have to be repeated, which would naturally lead to the production of different graphs, tables, and results.

One solution that addresses most of these issues is to intertwine the data with the code and then to embed the code within the properly formatted documentation. We can do this now with the **knitr** package. Yihui Xie (author of **knitr**) set out to provide a convenient way to weave together R code with LaTeX and Markdown syntax. LaTeX and Markdown are popular scripting meta-languages that create great-looking .pdf and .html documents. The beauty of **knitr** is that it can embed running R scripts within the LaTeX or Markdown code.

The following steps allow us to combine all the needed elements into a workable solution:

1. Create a .rnw file that will contain the R code and the LaTeX or Markdown syntax.
2. Compile the .rnw file, using `pdfLatex`, into a .tex and .pdf document.

RStudio (http://www.rstudio.org) will be used to accomplish both of these steps. The same tasks can, of course, be accomplished via command line arguments within the R console. The RStudio route simply makes it easier to execute the workflow. RStudio is a full Integrated Development Environment (IDE) for the R language and can be downloaded for free from here: http://www.rstudio.com/ide/download/. Depending on the operating system in use, the appropriate version of the LaTeX compiler also needs to be installed. The LaTeX complier for Windows (MikeTeX) can be downloaded from http://miktex.org/download. Mac users can opt for the MacTeX distribution at http://www.tug.org/mactex/. Here are the steps required for the configuration:

1. Open RStudio and install the **knitr** package by typing the following into the console: `install.packages("knitr"); require(knitr)`
2. Click on Tools-> Options -> Sweave and make sure to select **knitr** and pdfLaTeX.
3. In RStudio, click on File -> New -> R Sweave.

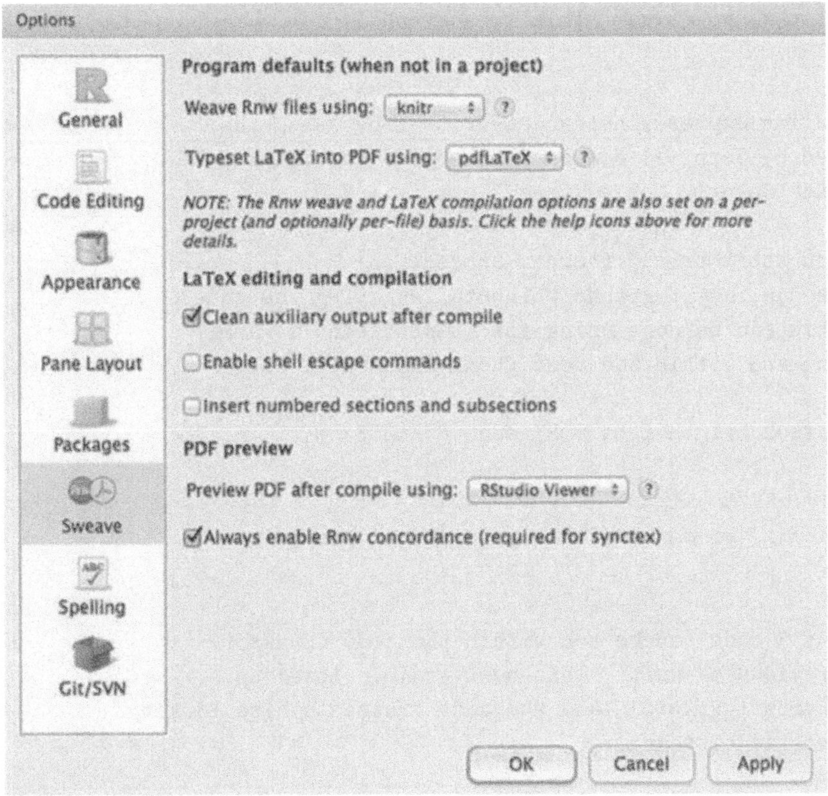

Figure 11.1 Setting up **knitr** and **pdflatex**.

4. Once the .rnw document is finalized, compile it into a .pdf document by clicking on the compile PDF button.

The following Github repo includes multiple examples on how to use **knitr.** https://github.com/yihui/knitr-examples/. We will pick one and modify it to illustrate some of the basic capabilities of the package.

```
\documentclass{article}
\usepackage[T1]{fontenc}

\begin{document}

This is an example LaTeX document with some embedded
R code woven in for convenience.

<<foo, fig.height = 4>>=
x = 1:10
y = x ^ 2
```

```
plot(x, y, main = "This is a graph")
@
```

Inline expressions can be written by using the
\verb|\Sexpr{}| convention, e.g. $\pi=\Sexpr{pi}$
and \Sexpr{2.3492e7} and \Sexpr{x / 2.0}.

\subsection*{A different subsection}
We can insert graphs without displaying the code.
This can be done using the \texttt{echo = FALSE}
command within the code chunk argument list.

```
<<foo2, fig.height = 3, echo = FALSE>>=
x = 1:10
y = x ^ 3
plot(x, y, main = "This is a second graph")
@
```

Any R code can be run within the code chunks
provided by knitr. This next example loads up
\texttt{ggplot2}, and the code creates a nice looking
density histogram.

```
<<foo3, fig.height = 6, tidy = FALSE >>=
require(ggplot2)
my_data = data.frame(returns = c(0.03, 0.04, 0.05,
  0.032, 0.01, 0.23, 0.4, 0.05, 0.066, 0.5),
  stock = c("SPY", "CVX", "CVX", "SPY",
  "XOM", "XOM", "CVX", "SPY", "SPY", "XOM"))

ggplot(my_data, aes(x = returns, fill = stock)) +
  geom_density(alpha = 0.2)
@
\end{document}
```

Figures 11.2 and 11.3 illustrate the sample .pdf output when the .rnw file is compiled
via pdfLatex

This is and example LaTex document with some embedded R code weaved in for convenience.

```
x = 1:10
y = x^2
plot(x, y, main = "This is a graph")
```

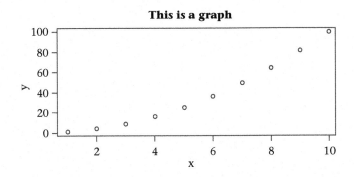

Inline expressio can be written by using the \Sexpr() convention, e.g. = 3.1416, and 2.3492 × 10^7 and 0.5, 1, 1.5, 2, 3, 3.5, 4, 4.5, 5.

A different subsection

We can insert graphs without displaying the code. This can be done using the echo=FALSE command within the code chunk argument list.

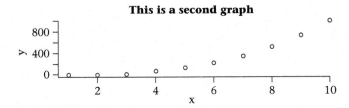

Any R code can be run within the code chunks provided by knitr. This next example loads up ggplot2 and the code creats a nice looking density histogram.

1

Figure 11.2 Sample pdf document output.

Summary

This chapter discusses four concepts with which all serious R programmers need to familiarize themselves, namely, speed of runtime execution, interoperability of R and C++ code, testability of code through unit testing, and reproducibility of research via the combination of code and LaTeX or Markdown syntax. Runtime efficiency is something that is accomplished by writing "better" R code and by

```
require (ggplot2)
```

Loading required package: ggplot2

```
my_data = data.frame (returns = c(0.03, 0.04, 0.05, 0.032, 0.01,
                                  0.23, 0.4, 0.05, 0.066, 0.5),
                      stock = c ("SPY", "CVX", "CVX", "SPY", "XOM",
                                 "XOM", "CVX", "SPY", "SPY", "XOM"))
```

```
ggplot (my_data, aes (x=returns, fill=stock)) +
    geom_density (alpha = 0.2)
```

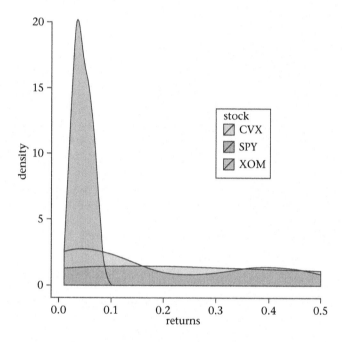

2

Figure 11.3 A pdf with a **ggplot2** plot.

leveraging packages such as **Rcpp** and **Rcpp11**. The interoperability aspect is briefly mentioned, and the use of the **RInside** package is recommended for implementing this. R can also be called directly from within C++ through the **RInside** package. Timing comparisons between different implementations are made with the **microbenchmark** package, and it is shown that for certain types of problems, the C++ approach can offer significant speed advantages. Testability of code is demonstrated via the use of **testthat**. A .pdf document that includes both R code and LaTeX syntax is generated by using a combination of the **knitr** package and the RStudio framework.

Notes

Chapter 1

1. One the best available online resources for brushing up on basic math skills is Khan Academy. The following courses are recommended:

   - Linear Algebra = https://www.khanacademy.org/math/linear-algebra.
   - Differential Calculus = https://www.khanacademy.org/math/differential-calculus.
   - Integral Calculus = https://www.khanacademy.org/math/integral-calculus.
   - Probability and Statistics = https://www.khanacademy.org/math/probability.

2. The Python language is a popular scripting language with a wide variety of data-processing and analytical capabilities, as well as, huge support from academia and industry. The following links provide excellent introductory resources:

   - https://wiki.python.org/moin/BeginnersGuide/NonProgrammers.
   - http://www.youtube.com/show/python101.

   The user WiseOwlTutorials on YouTube has a nice series of introductory videos on Excel/VBA and SQL. Both technologies are ubiquitous in the financial world, and it is worthwhile spending the time to learn how to use them. The link to the YouTube playlists is

   - http://www.youtube.com/user/WiseOwlTutorials/playlists.

3. In ancient Greece, the agora was a central place of assembly, typically at the center of a city, where citizens would gather to listen to speeches by politicians, cast votes, and trade goods. The modern Greek words for "I purchase", *agorazo* and "I publicly speak," *agorevo* are derivates of agora [68, 113].

4. The financial regulation landscape, at least in the United States, is a fairly complicated one, to say the least. For the stock and options exchanges, US Securities and Exchange Commission (SEC) reigns supreme. The SEC was created in 1934 by the Securities Exchange Act. Its introduction followed one of the most tumultuous periods in US Financial history. According to www.sec.gov, the SEC's mission is to protect investors, maintain fair, orderly, and efficient markets and facilitate capital formation [139]. The futures and some options markets are regulated by the US Commodity Futures Trading Commission (CFTC.) The CFTC

was created in 1974 by the Commodity Futures Trading Commission Act [118]. Its main purpose was to replace the US Department of Agriculture's Commodity Exchange Authority. Even though the SEC and the CFTC are different entities, they do collaborate with each other. More information on the CFTC can be found at www.cftc.gov.

5. Broadly speaking, there are three types of actions a trader can take when interacting with an electronic exchange. The first one is to submit market orders to the exchange. A market order, in effect, tells the exchange that immediacy of execution is the most important thing to the trader. Price does not matter as much. The second action is to submit limit orders to the exchange. Here, price matters. Price is more important than the immediacy of execution. The third action is that of modifying or canceling orders on the exchange. Limit orders effectively populate the orderbook with orders and provide a steady supply of liquidity to those who wish to execute market orders.

6. Trading Technologies, Inc. actually owns patents on the concept of a vertically displayed orderbook, specifically, U.S. Patent Nos. 6,766,304 and 6,772,132, which were issued in 2004.

Chapter 2

1. A programming paradigm is a mathematically derived set of concepts that lends itself to the efficient and elegant solution of a specific problem. For example, problems that can be decomposed into an abstraction of hierarchical interacting objects can best be expressed via the object-oriented programming style [85, 137]. Functional programming is well suited for problems that involve the manipulation, transformation, and processing of data. Functional programming is based on the λ-calculus first formulated by Alonzo Church in 1936. Functions are considered as the basic building blocks in this programming paradigm. The main idea is to have functions that produce results based only on the inputs to the function. These functions are not allowed to mutate data external to the function.

2. A programming language is considered to be Turing Complete if it can be used to simulate any single-taped Turing machine. A single-taped Turing machine is a mechanical construct that can be used to emulate any computing machine utilizing limited memory. A great explanation of such a Turing machine is given here:

http://en.wikipedia.org/wiki/Turing_machine.

From a practical aspect, Turing completeness is another way of stating that a programming language is capable of computing almost anything that is computable given enough resources.

3. Compilation of a program is the transformation of human readable code into machine-level code. Compiled code is fast. The drawback with code compilation

is the amount of time it takes to compile the code. An alternative mode of operation is for the computer to interpret the human readable code into something more manageable. This interpreted method allows for faster interaction between the developer and the code. The drawback is that it is slower.

4. Julia is a relatively new programming language that is showing a lot of promise in the scientific programming space. Its powerful LLVM-based just-in-time compiler makes it extremely fast (comparable to C) for most numerical applications. More details can be found here: http://julialang.org/.

5. Reference semantics imply that variables do not store objects by value. Rather, they store the address of an object's location in memory. This allows for more efficient code since larger objects do not have to be copied every time they are passed around

6. The Big-O notation in computer science describes the limiting behavior of functions when their arguments approach infinity. The following entry lists the mathematical properties of $O()$: http://en.wikipedia.org/wiki/Big_O_notation. From a practical standpoint, $O(1)$ means that the execution time will be the same no matter the size of the input. $O(n)$ implies that the time increases linearly with size n.

7. CRAN task views provide a comprehensive list of packages that are related by topic. The following link mentions the more important graphing related ones: http://cran.r-project.org/web/views/Graphics.html.

8. In R, the order of precedence for argument matching is first by name, then by prefix matching, and finally by position: http://adv-r.had.co.nz/Functions.html.

9. Abstraction is one of those ideas in computer science that is not mathematically well defined. It can refer to the decrease in repetitious code by abstracting away all the details of an implementation and by coding up the general idea as a module that can be reused by other functions.

10. Good R resources can be found here:

   - List of contributed documents on CRAN: http://cran.r-project.org/other-docs.html
   - An Introduction to R: http://cran.r-project.org/doc/manuals/R-intro.pdf
   - The R Inferno: http://www.burns-stat.com/pages/Tutor/R_inferno.pdf
   - Advanced R: http://adv-r.had.co.nz/

11. A good explanation on regular expressions is given here: http://en.wikipedia.org/wiki/Regular_expression. In a nutshell, these constructs are sequences of characters that create a search pattern for textual information. Regular expression programs then translate these patterns into nondeterministic finite automata.

12. The three most popular correlation estimators are Pearson's product-moment coefficient, Spearman's rank correlation coefficient, and the Kendall tau rank correlation coefficient [138].

Chapter 3

1. Yahoo Finance: http://finance.yahoo.com/ provides free daily data on multiple securities and indexes. The data can be downloaded into R via the **quantmod** package [99].
2. The Hadley Wickham book on Advanced R Programming has a nice section on package creation here: http://adv-r.had.co.nz/Philosophy.html.
3. Jeffrey Ryan is a Chicago quant/developer. He has created or co-created some of the most popular finance related R packages. These include: **quantmod, xts, mmap** and **greeks** [49, 99].
4. The `library()` and `require()` both load packages into memory. The first package will throw an error if the package has not been installed, whereas the second method will only produce a warning. The `require()` call also generates a boolean FALSE if the package does not exist
5. The CRAN task-view on web technologies contains some of the most popular packages that facilitate the retrieval and parsing of data from the Web: http://cran.r-project.org/web/views/WebTechnologies.html.
6. NoSQL is an acronym that stands for Not Only SQL. These databases are not relational in type and typically employ a key value, and a graphical or a document storage paradigm. Some popular NoSQL databases include:

   - MongoDB
   - Redis
   - Neo4j
   - Cassandra

7. The Wikipedia entry on SQL lists it as a "special-purpose programming language designed for managing data held in relational database management systems (RDBMS)." It has been around since the early seventies and is based on Edgar Codd's relational model, which he described in a paper titled "A Relational Model of Data for Large Shared Data Banks." The language itself was developed at IBM by Donald D. Chamberlin and Raymond F. Boyce. They originally called it SEQUEL (Structured English Query Language).
8. The following link shows how to install MariaDB, create a data directory, and then instantiate a database: https://github.com/hadley/dplyr/blob/master/vignettes/notes/mysql-setup.Rmd. According to the mariadb.org website, "MariaDB is an enhanced, drop-in replacement for MySQL."
9. This is another wonderful tabular structure that provides extremely efficient lookups and data manipulation operations. This recent presentation by Matt Dowle explains the workings of this package in greater detail: http://www.rinfinance.com/agenda/2014/workshop/MatthewDowle.pdf.

10. POSIX stands for "Portable Operating System Interface." It is a family of standards specified by IEEE for designing operating systems. POSIXct is a representation that represents the signed number of seconds since the beginning of 1970.

11. Polymorphism is an object-oriented programming concept and refers to the ability of different objects to invoke the same function with different behavior. A cat object, when invoking the speak() function will get a different result than the dog object invoking the same function.

12. Some of the popular date-time packages are:

    - **lubridate**
    - **chron**
    - **timeData**

13. A description of these concepts can be found here:
    http://vita.had.co.nz/papers/layered-grammar.pdf.

Chapter 4

1. Statistics computed from biased samples can have the effect of consistently over or under estimating the true population parameter [30]. For some examples of this effect, visit:
   http://en.wikipedia.org/wiki/Sampling_bias.

2. In statistics, the degree of freedom is the number of available values that can change in the computation of a statistic. The classic example is that of the sample variance estimator in which only N-1 values can vary since 1 value is taken up in estimating the mean.

3. Jensen's inequality is a mathematical expression stating that a secant line of a convex function lies above the graph of the convex function [125]. It is often used to prove that the expectation of a convex function is greater than the function of the expectation:

$$E(f(x)) \geq f(E(x)) \tag{4.25}$$

4. The dW_t term is referred to as a Wiener process or a Brownian motion process. This is the main building block of many stochastic time series representations:
   http://en.wikipedia.org/wiki/Wiener_process.

5. A few popular variance estimators include:

    - Andersen et al. RV estimator,
    - Barndorff-Nielsen and Shephard Cov estimator,
    - Zhang's nonsynchronous volatility measure.

Chapter 5

1. Statistical inference is the theory, methods, and practice of determining population parameter properties based off of sample statistic behavior.
2. When talking about a probability distribution, the zeroth moment is the total probability (i.e., one), the first moment is the mean, the second moment is the variance, and the third moment is the skewness:
   http://en.wikipedia.org/wiki/Moment_(mathematics).
3. Cointegration is a statistical property of time series. When two or more nonstationary time series can be combined in a linear way such that the resulting time series is stationary, then we say that the those time series are cointegrated. The term was coined in a seminal 1987 paper by Robert Engle. The tests used for detecting cointegration are: the Engle-Granger two-step method, the Johansen test, and the Phillips-Ouliaris cointegration test.
   http://en.wikipedia.org/wiki/Cointegration.
4. A p-value is the probability of observing an event given that the null hypothesis is true. If our goal is to reject the null-hypothesis, then a small p-value gives us confidence in doing so.
5. A helpful tutorial on robust statistics can be found here:
   http://www.rci.rutgers.edu/~dtyler/ShortCourse.pdf.
6. The rank correlation is a measure of the linear dependence between the rankings of random variables. Ranking requires some preprocessing of the data in order to properly assign the labels *first*, *second*, *third*, etc. to each observation of the data set. The ranking correlation is also fairly robust to outliers [138].
7. References to the Fisher approximate unbiased estimator and the Olkin-Pratt estimator can be found here:
   http://www.uv.es/revispsi/articulos1.03/9.ZUMBO.pdf.

Chapter 6

1. The pair trading idea was supposedly pioneered by Gerry Bamberger, and later led by Nunzio Tartaglia's quantitative group at Morgan Stanley in the 1980s.
2. The Fama-French three-factor model is an example of a factor model that attempts to decompose returns into a small caps component, a price-to-book ratio component, and a value vs. growth stock component.
3. A good introduction on cointegration can be found here:
   http://faculty.washington.edu/ezivot/econ584/notes/cointegration.pdf.
4. Total least squares, or orthogonal regression, is a type of errors-in-variables regression in which errors on both dependent and independent variables are taken into account. See http://en.wikipedia.org/wiki/Total_least_squares for more details.

5. According to Wikipedia, "Principal component analysis is a statistical procedure that uses an orthogonal transformation to convert a set of observations of possibly correlated variables into a set of values of linearly uncorrelated variables called principal components [133]." In finance, this technique is used often to model the behavior of the yield curve or the dynamics of the implied volatility surface.

6. There have been a total of three Basel Accords thus far. Basel II regulations were first published in June 2004 [114]. The recent Basel III accords have superseded the previous proceedings. Effectively, these accords establish a voluntary regulatory structure on bank capital adequacy, stress testing, and liquidity risk.

Chapter 7

1. Interactive Brokers has some of the lowest fees in the industry for retail investors. Their homepage can be found here: https://www.interactivebrokers.com.

2. A very good introduction to the workings of **quantstrat** is the presentation by Jan Humme and Brian Peterson:
http://www.rinfinance.com/agenda/2013/workshop/Humme+Peterson.pdf.

3. Andreas Clenow is a successful entrepreneur, hedge fund trader, quant analyst, and author of *Following the Trend: Diversified Managed Futures Trading*. A link to the trend following approach referenced in this book is:
http://www.followingthetrend.com/2014/03/improving-the-free-trend-following-trading-rules/.

4. Laurence Connors has authored and co-authored: *How Markets Really Work*, *Short Term Trading Strategies That Work*, and the *High Probability ETF Trading*". His opinions have been featured in the Wall Street Journal, Bloomberg, and on Dow Jones.

5. The **PerformanceAnalytics** package is a workhorse of quantitative finance. It is highly recommended that you include the functionality offered by this package into your workflow. A great resource is the following:
http://braverock.com/brian/R/PerformanceAnalytics/html/PerformanceAnalytics package.html.

Chapter 8

1. Microstructure refers to the granular market price dynamics in stocks, bonds, options, futures, and other financial instruments. Various correlation and volatility measures that outperform their classical counterparts can be derived by studying the underlying market microstructure. Such analysis is typically conducted by analyzing tick-data on the entire orderbook.

2. This figure is based on the sample files of SPY intra-day data provided by Tick Data, Inc.
3. One of the main criticisms against high-frequency trading is that the algorithms retract their limit orders at the worst possible time, that is, when most institutional investors and retail clients need the liquidity the most. High-frequency algorithms are able to detect market changes faster than other participants and are therefore faster to move out of the way. The argument is that the liquidity that such firms provide is simply an illusion.
4. Some third-party tick-databases are:

   - **OneTick** from OneMarketData:
     http://www.onetick.com,
   - **kdb** from Kx Systems:
     http://kx.com,
   - **SciDB** from:
     http://www.scidb.org/.

5. The bid-ask bounce is the description given to trades that occur either on the bid or the ask. For some liquid products, multiple trades can occur on the inside market without the price moving at all. This effect gives the impression that there is movement, when in effect, there is none. Calculations for intra-day volatility that rely on such prices will exaggerate the estimate.
6. An autoregressive model attempts to relate the output variable of a time-series as a function of its previous input variables. The general form looks something like this:

$$X_t = \alpha + \sum_{i=1}^{p} \beta_i X_{t-i} + \epsilon_t \tag{8.2}$$

7. A tutorial on using the **highfrequency** package can be found here:
   http://cran.r-project.org/web/packages/highfrequency/vignettes/highfrequency.pdf.

Chapter 9

1. This is also known as the Black-Scholes-Merton model. Merton made extensive contributions to the mathematical theory of options pricing, and he coined the term: "Black-Scholes options pricing model".
   http://en.wikipedia.org/wiki/Black-Scholes_model.
2. Dirk Eddelbuettel has created an R wrapper around QuantLib [2]. Examples, installation instructions, and more information can be found here:
   http://dirk.eddelbuettel.com/code/rquantlib.html.

3. The formulas for the sensitivities of the option price to: underlying, volatility, dividends, interest rates, and strike can be found here:
http://en.wikipedia.org/wiki/Black-Scholes_model.

Chapter 10

1. R is jam-packed with optimization routines that implement some of the latest research in the field. The following CRAN task-view lists some of the available packages:
http://cran.r-project.org/web/views/Optimization.html.
2. Gradient descent methods utilize the gradient (derivative) of a function and take steps proportional to the negative of this derivative at the points of interest. These techniques are fast but require the computation of a gradient or partial gradient.
http://en.wikipedia.org/wiki/Gradient_descent.
3. Arbitrage-free pricing implies that the relationship between instruments of various maturities (for fixed-income instruments) and strikes (for options) needs to be defined in such as way as to not allow the creation of a riskless profit opportunity. In other words, it should be unlikely to create a portfolio with a zero or negative cash outlay that has the potential of yielding a positive return in the future.
4. Overfitting is a nasty condition in which a fitted model produces output that can be completely erroneous or have no predictive power whatsoever. It is very hard to detect overfitting, especially in very high dimensional models. Great care has to be exercised when fitting models to data. Techniques such as regularization and shrinkage are just some of the things that can be applied to limiting this problem.

Chapter 11

1. Luke Tierney gives a nice presentation on the R-engine performance:
http://www.rinfinance.com/agenda/2014/talk/LukeTierney.pdf.
2. The **Rtools** package was originally created by Brian Ripley. It is currently being maintained by Duncan Murdoch. The relevant installation files and release notes can be referenced from:
http://cran.r-project.org/bin/windows/Rtools/.
3. An explanatory overview of TDD can be found here:
http://www.agiledata.org/essays/tdd.html.

This page intentionally left blank

References

[1] Clenow A.F. *Following the trend: diversified managed futures trading*. Wiley Trading. Wiley, New York, 2012.

[2] Ferdinando Ametrano and Luigi Ballabio. Quantlib - a free/open-source library for quantitative finance, 2003.

[3] Clenow Andreas. Twelve months momentum trading rules - part 2. http://www.followingthetrend.com/2014/03/improving-the-free-trend-following-trading-rules/, March 2014.

[4] Pfaff B. *Analysis of Integrated and Cointegrated Time Series with R*. Springer, New York, second edition, 2008. ISBN 0-387-27960-1.

[5] Johnson Barry. *Algorithmic Trading and DMA: An introduction to direct access trading strategies*. 4Myeloma Press, February 2010.

[6] Ripley Brian D. *Spatial statistics*. Wiley-Interscience, Hoboken, NJ, 2004.

[7] Bacon Carl R. *Practical portfolio performance: measurement and attribution*. Wiley finance. Wiley, Chichester, England, 2nd edition, 2008.

[8] Bartholomew Daniel. *Getting started with MariaDB*. Packt Publishing, Birmingham, UK, 2013.

[9] Ardia David, Ospina Arango Juan, and Gomez Norman Giraldo. Jump-diffusion calibration using Differential Evolution. *Wilmott Magazine*, 55:76–79, 2011.

[10] Ardia David, Mullen Katharine M., Peterson Brian G., and Joshua Ulrich. *DEoptim: Differential Evolution in R*, 2013. version 2.2-2.

[11] Ardia David, Boudt Kris, Carl Peter, Mullen Katharine M., and Peterson Brian G. Differential Evolution with DEoptim: An application to non-convex portfolio optimization. *The R Journal*, 3(1):27–34, 2011.

[12] Smith David. Fast and easy data munging, with dplyr. http://blog.revolutionanalytics.com/2014/01/fast-and-easy-data-munging-with-dplyr.html.

[13] Belsley David A. and Kontoghiorghes Erricos John. *Handbook of computational econometrics*. Wiley, 2009.

[14] James David A. and DebRoy Saikat. Package rmysql. `http://cran.r-project.org/web/packages/RMySQL/RMySQL.pdf`, July 2014.

[15] Tyler David E. A short course on robust statistics. `http://www.rci.rutgers.edu/~dtyler/ShortCourse.pdf`, July 2014.

[16] Kwiatkowski Denis and Philips Peter C. B. Testing the null hypothesis of stationarity against the alternative of a unit root. *Journal of Econometrics*, 54:159–178, 1991.

[17] Derryberry DeWayne R. *Basic data analysis for time series with R*. Wiley, 2014.

[18] Eddelbuettel Dirk. *Seamless R and C++ integration with RCPP*. Springer, New York, 2013.

[19] Eddelbuettel Dirk. Rcpp overview. `http://dirk.eddelbuettel.com/code/rcpp.html`, July 2014.

[20] Eddelbuettel Dirk and Francois Romain. Rcpp: Seamless R and C++ integration. *Journal of Statistical Software*, 40(8):1–18, 2011.

[21] Eddelbuettel Dirk and Francois Romain. *RInside: C++ classes to embed R in C++ applications*, 2014. R package version 0.2.11.

[22] Chance Don. A brief history of derivatives. `http://husky1.stmarys.ca/~gye/derivativeshistory.pdf`, July 2014.

[23] Knuth Donald E. Structured programming with go to statements. *ACM Comput. Surv.*, 6(4):261–301, December 1974.

[24] Zimmerman Donald W., Zumbo Bruno D., and Williams Richard H. Bias in estimation and hypothesis testing of correlation. *Psicologica*, 24:133–158, 2003.

[25] Zivot Eric and Wang Jiahui. *Modeling financial time series with S-plus*. Springer, New York, NY, 2nd edition, 2006.

[26] Chan Ernie. How useful is order flow and vpin? `http://epchan.blogspot.com/2013/10/how-useful-is-order-flow-and-vpin.html`, October 2013.

[27] Black Fischer and Scholes Myron S. The Pricing of Options and Corporate Liabilities. *Journal of Political Economy, University of Chicago Press*, 81(3):637–54, May-June 1973.

[28] James Gareth, Witten Daniela, Hastie Trevor, and Tibshirani Robert. *An Introduction to Statistical Learning: with Applications in R*. Springer Texts in Statistics. Springer New York, 2014.

[29] A.K.I.I. Gary, J.U. Schluetter, and H. Brumfield. Click based trading with intuitive grid display of market depth, August 3, 2004. US Patent 6,772,132.

[30] Henry Gary T. *Practical Sampling*. SAGE Publications, Inc., 1990.

[31] Box George E. P. and Draper Norman Richard. *Empirical model-building and response surfaces*. Wiley, New York, 1987.

[32] Mirai Solutions GmbH. Xlconnect 0.2-0. http://www.r-bloggers.com/xlconnect -0-2-0/, July 2012.

[33] Mirai Solutions GmbH. Package xlconnect. `http://cran.r-project.org/web/packages/XLConnect/XLConnect.pdf`, July 2014.

[34] CME Group. Leading products q1 2014. `http://www.cmegroup.com/education/files/cme-group-leading-products-2014-q1.pdf`.

[35] CME Group. Growth of cme globex platform: A retrospective. *CME Group*, page 2, 2012.

[36] CME Group. Daily exchange volume and open interest. *CME Group*, 2014.

[37] Zaner Group. A study in platform volume. *CME Group*, page 2, 2010.

[38] Lebanon Guy. Bias, variance, and mse of estimators. `http://www.cc.gatech.edu/~lebanon/notes/estimators1.pdf`.

[39] Yollin Guy. R tools for portfolio optimization. `http://www.rinfinance.com/RinFinance2009/presentations/yollin_slides.pdf`, April 2009.

[40] Wickham Hadley. *ggplot2: elegant graphics for data analysis*. Springer New York, 2009.

[41] Wickham Hadley. testhat: Get started with testing. *The R Journal*, 3/1, June 2011.

[42] Wickham Hadley. Advanced r. `http://adv-r.had.co.nz/`, July 2014.

[43] Wickham Hadley. Tidy data. *The Journal of Statistical Software*, Submitted.

[44] Wickham Hadley and Francois Romain. Introduction to dplyr. `http://cran.rstudio.com/web/packages/dplyr/vignettes/introduction.html`.

[45] Wickham Hadley and Francois Romain. *dplyr: dplyr: a grammar of data manipulation*, 2014. R package version 0.2.

[46] Allaire J. Rstudio and inc. (2014), rmarkdown: R markdown document conversion, r package. `github.com/rstudio/rmarkdown`, 2014.

[47] Maindonald J. H. and Braun John. *Data analysis and graphics using R: an example-based approach*, volume 10 of *Cambridge series in statistical and probabilistic mathematics*. Cambridge University Press, 3rd edition, 2010.

[48] Humme Jan and Peterson Brian G. Using quantstrat to evaluate intraday trading strategies. `http://www.rinfinance.com/agenda/2013/workshop/Humme+Peterson.pdf`, 2013.

[49] Ryan Jeffrey A. and Ulrich Joshua M. *xts: eXtensible Time Series*, 2013. R package version 0.9-7.

[50] Knight J.L. and Satchell S. *Forecasting Volatility in the Financial Markets*. Butterworth-Heinemann Finance. Butterworth-Heinemann, 2002.

[51] Weisenthal Joe. The story of the first-ever options trade in recorded history. http://www.businessinsider.com/the-story-of-the-first-ever-options-trade-in-recorded-history-2012-3, March 2012.

[52] Fox John and Weisberg Sanford. *An R companion to applied regression*. SAGE Publications, Thousand Oaks, CA, 2nd edition, 2011.

[53] Miyamoto John. Demo 02-1: Using r to think about bayesian inference. `https://faculty.washington.edu/jmiyamot/p548/demo02-1.p548.w14.pdf`, July 2014.

[54] Mount John. Frequentist inference only seems easy. `http://www.win-vector.com/blog/2014/07/frequenstist-inference-only-seems-easy/`, July 2014.

[55] O'Connor John J. and Robertson Edmund F. The mactutor history of mathematics archive. `http://www-history.mcs.st-and.ac.uk/`.

[56] Kruschke John K. *Doing bayesian data analysis: a tutorial with R and BUGS*. Academic Press, Burlington, MA, 2011.

[57] Cornelissen Jonathan, Boudt Kris, and Payseur Scott. *highfrequency: highfrequency*, 2013. R package version 0.2.

[58] Ulrich Joshua. How can i view the source code for a function? http://stackoverflow.com/questions/19226816/how-can-i-view-the-source-code-for-a-function, October 2013.

[59] Ulrich Joshua. *TTR: Technical Trading Rules*, 2013. R package version 0.22-0.

[60] Mullen Katharine, Ardia David, Gil David, Windover Donald, and Cline James. DEoptim: An R package for global optimization by differential evolution. *Journal of Statistical Software*, 40(6):1–26, 2011.

[61] Price Kenneth and Storn Rainer. Differential evolution (de) for continuous function optimization. `http://www1.icsi.berkeley.edu/~storn/code.html`, July 2014.

[62] Price Kenneth V., Storn Rainer M., and Lampinen Jouni A. *Differential Evolution - A Practical Approach to Global Optimization*. Natural Computing. Springer-Verlag, January 2006. ISBN 540209506.

[63] Andrey N. Kolmogorov. *Foundations of the Theory of Probability*. Chelsea Pub Co., 2 edition, June 1960.

[64] Boudt Kris, Cornelissen Jonathan, and Payseur Scott. Highfrequency: Toolkit for the analysis of highfrequency financial data in r. `http://cran.r-project.org/web/packages/highfrequency/vignettes/highfrequency.pdf`, July 2014.

[65] Connors L.A. and Alvarez C. *Short Term Trading Strategies that Work: A Quantified Guide to Trading Stocks and ETFs*. Tradingmarkets Publishing Group, 2009.

[66] Torgo Luis. *Data mining with R: learning with case studies*. Chapman and Hall/CRC data mining and knowledge discovery series. Chapman and Hall/CRC, Boca Raton, FL, 2011.

[67] Tierney Luke. A byte code compiler for r. `http://homepage.stat.uiowa.edu/~luke/R/compiler/compiler.pdf`, March 2012.

[68] Lang Mabel L. *Life, death, and litigation in the Athenian Agora*, volume no. 23. American School of Classical Studies at Athens, Princeton, NJ, 1994.

[69] Blais Marcel and Protter Philip. Signing trades and an evaluation of the leeready algorithm. *Annals of Finance*, 8(1):1–13, 2012.

[70] Bogard Matt. Regression via gradient descent in r. `http://econometricsense.blogspot.gr/2011/11/regression-via-gradient-descent-in-r.html`, July 2014.

[71] Golder Matt and Golder Sona. Lecture 8: Estimation. `https://files.nyu.edu/mrg217/public/lecture8_handouts.pdf`, July 2014.

[72] Dowle Matthew. Introduction to the data.table package in r. `http://cran.r-project.org/web/packages/data.table/vignettes/datatable-intro.pdf`, February 2014.

[73] Kuhn Max and Johnson Kjell. *Applied predictive modeling*. Springer, New York, 2013.

[74] Way Michael J. *Advances in machine learning and data mining for astronomy*. Chapman and Hall/CRC data mining and knowledge discovery series. Chapman and Hall/CRC, 2012.

[75] Naguez Naceur and Prigent Jean-Luc. Kappa performance measures with johnson distributions. *International Journal of Business*, 16(3):210, 2011.

[76] Sommacal Nicola Sturaro. Read excel file from r. `http://www.milanor.net/blog/?p=779`, July 2013.

[77] Ross Noam. Faster! higher! stronger! - a guide to speeding up r code for busy people. `http://www.noamross.net/blog/2013/4/25/faster-talk.html`, April 2013.

[78] Matloff Norman S. *The art of R programming: tour of statistical software design*. No Starch Press, San Francisco, 2011.

[79] Valavanes Panos and Delevorrias Angelos. *Great moments in Greek archaeology*. J. Paul Getty Museum, Los Angeles, CA, 2007.

[80] Teetor Paul. *25 recipes for getting started with R*. O'Reilly Media, Beijing, 1st ed edition, 2011.

[81] Teetor Paul. *R cookbook*. O'Reilly, Beijing, 1st edition, 2011.

[82] Cowpertwait Paul S. P. and Metcalfe Andrew V. *Introductory time series with R*. Use R! Springer, Dordrecht, 2009.

[83] Carl Peter and Peterson Brian G. *PerformanceAnalytics: Econometric tools for performance and risk analysis*, 2013.

[84] Diggle Peter and Chetwynd Amanda. *Statistics and scientific method: an introduction for students and researchers*. Oxford University Press, 2011.

[85] Roy Peter V. Programming paradigms for dummies: What every programming paradigms for dummies: What every programmer should know. `http://www.info.ucl.ac.be/~pvr/VanRoyChapter.pdf`.

[86] Spector Phil. *Data manipulation with R*. Springer, New York, 2008.

[87] Qusma. Equity curve straightness measures. `http://qusma.com/2013/09/23/equity-curve-straightness-measures/`, September 2013.

[88] R Core Team. *R: A Language and Environment for Statistical Computing*. R Foundation for Statistical Computing, Vienna, Austria, 2014.

[89] Subba Rao, T., Subba Rao, S., and Radhakrishna Rao C. *Time series analysis: methods and applications*, volume v. 30 of *Handbook of statistics*. North Holland, Amsterdam, 1st edition, 2012.

[90] Rebonato Riccardo. *Volatility and correlation: the perfect hedger and the fox*. J. Wiley, Chichester, West Sussex, England, 2nd edition, 2004.

[91] Becker Richard A. and Chambers John M. *S: An interactive environment for data analysis and graphics*. Wadsworth Advanced Book Program, Belmont, CA, 1984.

[92] Bookstaber Richard M. *A demon of our own design: markets, hedge funds, and the perils of financial innovation*. J. Wiley, Hoboken, NJ, 2007.

[93] Becker Rick. A brief history of s. *ATT Bell Laboratories*, 11, 1994.

[94] Peng Roger D. Interacting with data using the filehash package. *The Newsletter of the R Project*, 6/4, 2006.

[95] Winston Rory. Newton's method in r. http://www.theresearchkitchen.com/archives/642, July 2014.

[96] Ihaka Ross and Gentleman Robert. R: A language for data analysis and graphics. *Journal of Computational and Graphical Statistics*, 5(3):299–314, 1996.

[97] Tsay Ruey S. *Analysis of financial time series*. Wiley series in probability and statistics. Wiley, Cambridge, MA, 3rd edition, 2010.

[98] Higginbottom Ryan. Introduction to scientific typesetting. lesson 12: Verbatim text and drawing in latex. http://www2.washjeff.edu/users/rhigginbottom/latex/resources/lecture12.pdf, January 2012.

[99] Jeffrey A. Ryan. *quantmod: Quantitative Financial Modeling Framework*, 2013. R package version 0.4-0.

[100] Meyers Scott. *Effective STL: 50 specific ways to improve your use of the standard template library*. Addison-Wesley, Boston, 2001.

[101] Meyers Scott. *Effective C++: 55 specific ways to improve your programs and designs*. Addison-Wesley, Upper Saddle River, NJ, 3rd edition, 2005.

[102] Ao Sio-Iong, Rieger Burghard B., and Amouzegar Mahyar A. *Advances in machine learning and data analysis*, volume 48 of *Lecture notes in electrical engineering*. Springer Science+Business Media, Dordrecht, 2010.

[103] Prata Stephen. *C++ primer plus*. Addison-Wesley, Upper Saddle River, NJ, 6th ed edition, 2012.

[104] R Core Team. R language definition. http://cran.r-project.org/doc/manuals/r-devel/R-lang.pdf.

[105] Stan Development Team. Rstan: the r interface to stan, version 2.3. http://mc-stan.org/rstan.html, 2014.

[106] Stan Development Team. Stan; a c++ library for probability and sampling, version 2.3. http://mc-stan.org, 2014.

[107] Andersen Torben G. *Handbook of financial time series*. Springer, Berlin, 2009.

[108] Hastie Trevor, Tibshirani Robert, and Friedman Jerome. H. *The elements of statistical learning: data mining, inference, and prediction*. Springer series in statistics. Springer, New York, 2nd edition, 2009.

[109] Durden Tyler. Here is how high frequency trading hurts everyone. http://www.zerohedge.com/news/2014-02-20/here-how-high-frequency-trading-hurts-everyone, February 2014.

[110] Zoonekynd Vincent. Optimization. http://zoonek.free.fr/blosxom/R/2012-06-01_Optimization.html, July 2014.

[111] Venables W. N. and Ripley Brian D. *Modern applied statistics with S*. Springer, New York, 4th edition, 2002.

[112] Brainerd Walter S. and Landweber Lawrence H. *Theory of computation*. Wiley, New York, 1974.

[113] Wikipedia. Agora—Wikipedia, the free encyclopedia. http://en.wikipedia.org/wiki/Agora, July 2014.

[114] Wikipedia. Basel committee on banking supervision—Wikipedia, the free encyclopedia. wikipedia.org/wiki/Basel_Committee_on_Banking_Supervision, July 2014.

[115] Wikipedia. Bayes theorem—Wikipedia, the free encyclopedia. http://en.wikipedia.org/wiki/Bayes'_theorem, July 2014.

[116] Wikipedia. Black scholes model—Wikipedia, the free encyclopedia. http://en.wikipedia.org/wiki/Black-Scholes_model, July 2014.

[117] Wikipedia. Central limit theorem—Wikipedia, the free encyclopedia. `http://en.wikipedia.org/wiki/Central_limit_theorem`, July 2014.

[118] Wikipedia. Cftc—Wikipedia, the free encyclopedia. `http://en.wikipedia.org/wiki/Commodity_Futures_Trading_Commission`, August 2014.

[119] Wikipedia. Checking whether a coin is fair—Wikipedia, the free encyclopedia. `http://en.wikipedia.org/wiki/Checking_whether_a_coin_is_fair`, July 2014.

[120] Wikipedia. Chicago board of trade—Wikipedia, the free encyclopedia. `http://en.wikipedia.org/wiki/Chicago_Board_of_Trade`, July 2014.

[121] Wikipedia. Fama-french three-factor model—Wikipedia, the free encyclopedia. `http://en.wikipedia.org/wiki/Fama%E2%80%93French_three-factor_model`, July 2014.

[122] Wikipedia. Frequentist probability—Wikipedia, the free encyclopedia. `http://en.wikipedia.org/wiki/Frequentist_probability`, July 2014.

[123] Wikipedia. Gaussmarkov theorem—wikipedia, the free encyclopedia, 2014. [Online; accessed 13-September-2014].

[124] Wikipedia. Hello world programs—Wikipedia, the free encyclopedia. `http://en.wikipedia.org/wiki/List_of_Hello_world_program_examples`, July 2014.

[125] Wikipedia. Jensen's inequality—wikipedia, the free encyclopedia, 2014. [Online; accessed 13-September-2014].

[126] Wikipedia. Law of large numbers—Wikipedia, the free encyclopedia. `http://en.wikipedia.org/wiki/Law_of_large_numbers`, July 2014.

[127] Wikipedia. Markdown—Wikipedia, the free encyclopedia. `http://en.wikipedia.org/wiki/Markdown`, July 2014.

[128] Wikipedia. Omega ratio—Wikipedia, the free encyclopedia. `http://en.wikipedia.org/wiki/Omega_ratio`, July 2014.

[129] Wikipedia. Operational risk—Wikipedia, the free encyclopedia. `wikipedia.org/wiki/Operational_risk`, July 2014.

[130] Wikipedia. Option (finance)—Wikipedia, the free encyclopedia. `http://en.wikipedia.org/wiki/Option_(finance)`, July 2014.

[131] Wikipedia. Pairs trade—Wikipedia, the free encyclopedia. `http://en.wikipedia.org/wiki/Pairs_trade`, July 2014.

[132] Wikipedia. Posix—wikipedia, the free encyclopedia, 2014. [Online; accessed 13-September-2014].

[133] Wikipedia. Principal component analysis—wikipedia, the free encyclopedia, 2014. [Online; accessed 14-September-2014].

[134] Wikipedia. Probability axioms—Wikipedia, the free encyclopedia. `http://en.wikipedia.org/wiki/Probability_axioms`, July 2014.

[135] Wikipedia. Probability interpretations—wikipedia, the free encyclopedia, 2014. [Online; accessed 13-September-2014].

[136] Wikipedia. Program / optimization—Wikipedia, the free encyclopedia. `http://en.wikipedia.org/wiki/Program/optimization`, July 2014.

[137] Wikipedia. Programming paradigm—Wikipedia, the free encyclopedia. `http://en.wikipedia.org/wiki/Programming_paradigm`, July 2014.

[138] Wikipedia. Rank correlation—Wikipedia, the free encyclopedia. `en.m.wikipedia.org/wiki/Rank_correlation`, July 2014.

[139] Wikipedia. Sec—Wikipedia, the free encyclopedia. `http://en.wikipedia.org/wiki/Securities_and_Exchange_Commission`, August 2014.

[140] Wikipedia. Sharpe ratio—Wikipedia, the free encyclopedia. `wikipedia.org/wiki/Sharpe_ratio`, July 2014.

[141] Wikipedia. Test driven development—Wikipedia, the free encyclopedia. `http://en.wikipedia.org/wiki/Test-driven_development`, July 2014.

[142] Wikipedia. Ulcer index—Wikipedia, the free encyclopedia. `wikipedia.org/wiki/Ulcer_index`, July 2014.

[143] Wikipedia. Unbiased estimation of standard deviation—Wikipedia, the free encyclopedia. `http://en.wikipedia.org/wiki/Unbiased_estimation_of_standard_deviation`, July 2014.

[144] Wikipedia. Vpin—Wikipedia, the free encyclopedia. `http://en.wikipedia.org/wiki/VPIN`, July 2014.

[145] Xie Yihui. *Dynamic Documents with R and knitr*. Chapman and Hall/CRC, Boca Raton, Florida, 2013. ISBN 978-1482203530.

[146] Xie Yihui. *knitr: A general-purpose package for dynamic report generation in R*, 2014. R package version 1.6.

[147] Xie Yihui. knitr reference card. `http://cran.at.r-project.org/web/packages/knitr/vignettes/knitr-refcard.pdf`, May 2014.

[148] Ross Zev. Four reasons why you should check out the r package dplyr. http://zevross.com/blog/2014/03/26/four-reasons-why-you-should-check-out-the-r-package-dplyr-3/.

This page intentionally left blank

Index

This page intentionally left blank

This page intentionally left blank

Printed by Printforce, the Netherlands